"While other recent books on current-day prophetic evangelicalism have focused on individuals, *Return to Justice* surveys the
historical institutional foundations of today's prophetic movement. With sharp discernment and clarity, Rah and VanderPol
offer the church an invaluable gift—perspective. They show us
the decades-long journey  uence of evangelical
institutions in modern times. By
looking back cclesial compass for
future genera stice laid out before
us all."

— Lisa Sharon Harper, chief church engagement officer,
Sojourners

"As the social concern among evangelicals grows, it behooves them
not only to look at present needs and plan for the future, but also
to revisit the stories of pioneers and trailblazers. *Return to Justice*
provides a well-documented historical orientation for an engaged
twenty-first-century evangelicalism. In this fascinating narrative
we find inspiration, constructive lessons, and pointed challenges
for embodying compassion and doing justice. Rah and VanderPol
teach us that looking back offers needed perspective for moving
forward."

—M. Daniel Carroll R. (Rodas), Wheaton College

"This is an outstanding primer on the resurgence of evangelical
biblical justice activism over the past several decades. Its six historical snapshots of this surge, when viewed together, offer just the
right kind of historical background to the present-day interest of
Gen-X and Millennial evangelicals, especially, in ministry to the
poor, marginalized, and oppressed. I pray that it will inspire even
more evangelicals to walk the way of Jesus and spend themselves
for those in need."

—Douglas A. Sweeney, Trinity Evangelical Divinity School

"Justice has always been an essential part of the proclamation of
the gospel. The early followers of Jesus stood out in their communities because they were the ones rescuing discarded female
infants from the dung heap. They not only preached the gospel,
they were the gospel. Rah and VanderPol have demonstrated that

a lived gospel has also been essential to the evangelical movement. If you care about the gospel of Jesus, then you should drink deeply from *Return to Justice*. It is the gospel."

—**Frank A. James III**, Biblical Theological Seminary/
Philadelphia

"The story of evangelicalism in the United States, and specifically the exciting story of how many in the modern evangelical movement have increasingly embraced justice concerns in the post–World War II era, is inspiring—but also complex and underappreciated. In *Return to Justice*, Rah and VanderPol have done a masterful job, telling six compelling stories, with scholarly rigor and highly accessible prose, of evangelicals rediscovering their nineteenth-century justice heritage. Calling the church to return to its true vocation and embrace biblical justice has been the central motivating force of my own life and vocation. So I cannot recommend this book strongly enough. *Return to Justice* should be read by anyone who wants to understand evangelicals and Christianity on a much deeper level than the shallow political definitions in the media."

—**Jim Wallis**, *New York Times* bestselling author of *America's Original Sin: Racism, White Privilege, and the Bridge to a New America*; president of Sojourners; editor-in-chief of *Sojourners* magazine

"In the lifetime I have spent within the circle called evangelicalism the single-most noteworthy development is not the much-discussed shift toward activism among the political Right in the Reagan years, but rather the much deeper stream flowing now with dramatic force into social justice activism on the part of many evangelicals. The resurgence of concern for justice emerges from deep wells in the evangelical tradition, and the story needs to be told—and in fact has now been told in *Return to Justice*. While this story reveals some unexamined assumptions or activisms, the commitment to justice in all its forms—some central and some sadly neglected—is inherent to the deep evangelical tradition. Many who write the history of the twentieth century have ignored these deep wells but they are now visible for all to see."

—**Scot McKnight**, Northern Seminary

RETURN

TO

JUSTICE

SIX MOVEMENTS THAT REIGNITED OUR CONTEMPORARY EVANGELICAL CONSCIENCE

SOONG-CHAN RAH AND GARY VANDERPOL

BrazosPress

a division of Baker Publishing Group
Grand Rapids, Michigan

Published by Brazos Press
a division of Baker Publishing Group
P.O. Box 6287, Grand Rapids, MI 49516-6287
www.brazospress.com

Printed in the United States of America

Library of Congress Cataloging-in-Publication Data
Names: Rah, Soong-Chan, author.
Title: Return to justice : six movements that reignited our contemporary evangelical conscience / Soong-Chan Rah and Gary VanderPol.
Description: Grand Rapids : Brazos Press, 2016. | Includes bibliographical references and index.
Identifiers: LCCN 2016006111 | ISBN 9781587433764 (pbk. : alk. paper)
Subjects: LCSH: Social justice—Religious aspects—Christianity—History. | Evangelicalism—History.
Classification: LCC BR115.J8 R3145 2016 | DDC 261.8—dc23
LC record available at http://lccn.loc.gov/2016006111

16 17 18 19 20 21 22   7 6 5 4 3 2 1

Dedicated to our mutual church community
at Cambridge Community Fellowship Church.

To my son, Elijah.
May these examples inspire you to see
the work of God in your own life.
—SCR

To my mother,
who has always known just how to listen.
—GVP

Contents

Acknowledgments

Thanks to my writing partner and friend Gary VanderPol for making this a thoroughly enjoyable collaboration. I am grateful for our partnership and friendship in the gospel.

Some of the names featured in this book have also been dear friends and respected colleagues of mine. I am thankful for not only their friendship but also their willingness to invite me into their communities and to help shape me as a follower of Jesus. With tremendous gratitude to Jim Wallis, Mary Nelson, Barbara Williams-Skinner, John Perkins, Wayne Gordon, Noel Castellanos, Jo Anne Lyons, Rich Stearns, Jim Bere, Joan Mussa, Ron Sider, Bill Pannell, Ruth Bentley, Wes Granberg-Michaelson, Ron Potter, Carl Ellis, Russ Knight, and Peter Sjoblom.

Thanks to my friends and colleagues at North Park Theological Seminary, North Park University, and the Evangelical Covenant Church. These communities intersect my work, my vocation, my calling, and my ministry, and I am grateful for those who have been an integral part of these learning communities: Gary Walter, David Parkyn, Dave Kersten, Michael Emerson, Joe Jones, Stephen Chester, Terry Lindsay, Dan White Hodge, Mary Trujillo,

Elizabeth Pierre, Dick Lucco, Debbie Blue, Cecilia Williams, John Teter, and Jerome Nelson.

My teaching assistants during the process were of immense help. Tim Rhee reviewed much of the content for this book, while Brandon Wrencher's work on the *Christian Community Development Association Theological Journal* freed me to focus my efforts on this work. I have also been blessed with past students who have deeply shaped my present work: Valerie Landfair, Dominique Gilliard, Vince Bantu, Diana Bantu, Evelmyn Ivens, Kevin Brown, Prajakta David, and Nilowona Nowlin.

I am indebted to my academic mentors in the field of American Religious Studies. Doug Sweeney, Grant Wacker, Kate Bowler, Mark Chaves, Valerie Cooper, and A. G. Miller are top-notch scholars who have helped shaped the content of this book but also my growing love for American church history. In my theological studies, Willie Jennings, Emmanuel Katongole, J. Kameron Carter, Eldin Villafane, Humberto Alfaro, Ellen Davis, Sam Wells, Amy Laura Hall, Terry LeBlanc, Ray Aldred, Doug Hall, and Judy Hall have been essential in shaping the trajectory of my theological inquiry. In recent years, the friendship among Evangelicals for Justice has been instrumental in the formation of my ongoing passion to see God's work for justice among evangelicals: Lisa Sharon Harper, Andrea Smith, Mae Cannon, Sandra VanOpstal, Liz VerHage, Paul Metzger, Randy Woodley, and Jimmy McGee as well as the friendships forged through the Christian Community Development Association and Sojourners communities: Mark Charles, Kathy Khang, Peggy Flanagan, Adam Taylor, Ernest and Camryn Smith, Chanequa Walker-Barnes, Bethany Harris, Danny Carroll, Leroy Barber, Ken Wytsma, Michael McBride, Gabriel Salguero, and many others who have helped shape my personal passion for God's social justice.

I want to extend much gratitude toward our extended family, my father-in-law in Korea, my brother-in-law in California, my sisters and their families in Maryland, and my mom for their support and encouragement.

Every time I finish a writing project, I am reminded how much my family shapes my writing efforts. I often write with my children, Annah and Elijah, in mind. I pray that my words would encourage and inspire you to live into God's calling for your lives. My hope for you comes from my understanding of God's work and faithfulness. My wife Sue serves as an example of God's faithfulness toward me. I thank God every day for a partner in life and a family that encourages and strengthens me to serve Him.

Soong-Chan Rah

As a scholar-pastor, I have tried to bring together the best of the academy and the church, which means I have embodied neither as well as I would like. But the work of integration has been one of the chief joys of my life. I hope that mentors and friends from my academic, activist, and pastoral communities will recognize their influence in this book.

First and foremost, thanks to my co-author and friend Soong-Chan Rah, who I hold as a model of genuinely prophetic ministry. It has been a privilege to work with you in yet one more arena of service.

My doctoral advisors Dana Robert and David Hempton patiently and insightfully guided me through (too many!) years of academic research for this book. Their critical but deeply respectful grasp of the global evangelical story has profoundly impacted the way I see my tradition. I am grateful for their investment in me. My time at Boston University was also shaped by a stimulating learning community whose equal I have not yet found. I want to thank Eric Baldwin, Brian Clark, Ben Hartley, Yeonseung Lee, and Glen Messer for faithfully imagining together the way in which knowledge of evangelicalism's past might shape its future.

My colleagues at Denver Seminary—especially Daniel Carroll Rodas, Bob Cutillo, Jeff Johnson, Michelle Warren, and president Mark Young—provided a collegial, encouraging atmosphere conducive to the integration of scholarship and activism. Thanks so much for your support.

I am grateful also for friends and mentors who have helped me dream beyond the limitations of rigid academic and ecclesial boundaries, especially Vince Bantu, Nic and Maurine Bekaert, Cameron Wu-Cardona, Warren Chiang, Marthinus Daneel, Jim and Ruth Padilla DeBorst, Roger and Claire Dewey, Josh Harper, Albert Olson Hong, Larry Kim, Mako Nagasawa, Jimmy Quach, Colin Chan Redemer, Dan Schmitz, and Melissa Yeh.

I want to recognize the sisters and brothers who have walked with me on my own personal return to justice at New Hope Covenant Church in Oakland, California; Cambridge Community Fellowship Church in Cambridge, Massachusetts; Comunidad Emaús in San José, Costa Rica; and my Spiritual Direction Men's Group (SpiDer Men). You have helped me to live what I am writing about: thank you. To my current community, Church Without Walls in Berkeley, California—I count it a privilege to create through our life together a new chapter in the story I have tried to recount in these pages.

Finally, I am grateful to my wife Jodi, who has always inspired me on my justice journey—often because I'm just trying to keep up with her! Thank you for growing with me this far. And thanks to our kids, Isaiah and Camila, who have patiently endured being dragged around the world with us as we pursue the next step God has for us. I pray that you will have an ever-greater measure of the Spirit behind the trailblazers in this book.

Gary VanderPol

Introduction

In 1947, budding theologian Carl F. H. Henry wrote a short book titled *The Uneasy Conscience of Modern Fundamentalism*. In it he surveys the American fundamentalist movement's engagement with the most important social issues of the day. Henry does not so much attack the fundamentalists for their social ethic as for their lack of one. Within their ranks, he finds little or no contribution to politics, economics, race and labor relations, intellectual life, or the arts. He paints a picture of fundamentalists with their backs turned to the world as they devotedly dissect the minutiae of obscure prophecy, taking pride in their total disconnect from a society destined to perdition.

Such a characterization might not seem an unusual interpretation of fundamentalism for a theologian trained at liberal institutions like Boston University and Harvard, as Henry was. But what makes *Uneasy Conscience* stand out is that Henry was himself a fundamentalist, intent on provoking his compatriots to apply the insights of conservative biblical theology to their contemporary context. Skeptical that fundamentalism's old guard could rise from its slumber, he placed his hope in a younger generation who called themselves evangelicals—a group he hoped could reinvigorate the social consciousness of conservative American Protestantism.

Sixty years later, after the dawn of the twenty-first century, the largest privately funded global relief and development organization in the world is evangelical, and hundreds of smaller organizations funnel more than $2 billion overseas to meet the needs of the poor. For more than a decade one of the most famous evangelical mega-church pastors in America has been attempting the complete socioeconomic restructuring of a small African nation. Evangelicals are zealously campaigning against child slavery and sex trafficking, bringing their voices to formerly complacent churches and also to the broader public through social media and traditional television and newspaper outlets. Furthermore, thousands of neighborhood renewal ministries have enlisted millions of American evangelicals in Christian community development of various kinds. In just two generations, evangelicals have "moved from almost complete silence on the subject of justice to a remarkable verbosity."[1]

These two snapshots illustrate major changes in the worldview and identity of evangelicalism, one of American's largest religious movements. This book seeks to tell the story of how these changes came about in the span of a single lifetime, from 1947 to the present. The "movie trailer" version of our narrative goes something like this: between the two World Wars, conservative Protestants in the United States were consumed by their defense of the "supernatural" elements of the faith; they energetically built independent churches, schools, radio broadcasts, and parachurch organizations as bulwarks against secular society and the "liberal" churches. In this setting, prophetic engagement with poverty, racism, or injustice was viewed suspiciously—as either a distraction from evangelism or a sellout to liberals. But in the waning years of World War II, where our book begins, a new movement of American conservative Protestants emerged. They distinguished themselves from their fundamentalist forebears by taking a less militant, more engaged stance toward cultural and intellectual life, yet they retained a high view of Scripture and traditional doctrinal orthodoxy. Many of these "evangelicals" continued to de-emphasize most justice issues, preferring to channel their growing social concern toward opposing communism, secularization, abortion, and (more recently) gay marriage.

However, while initially less in the public eye than other contenders against these controversial issues, American evangelicals gradually increased their efforts on behalf of justice. Shocked by the gruesome realities of global poverty, they founded a number of increasingly prominent relief and development organizations as early as the 1950s. In the late 1960s and early 1970s these efforts expanded rapidly, with missions conferences, popular periodicals, intentional Christian communities, mass-market books, and even television telethons promoting concern about poverty, sometimes in radical terms. As racial issues gained prominence, a vocal minority of African-Americans and others from the Global South broke into the previously all-white club of evangelical leadership. By the turn of the twenty-first century, most evangelicals, at least rhetorically, embraced some form of commitment to justice as a nonnegotiable part of God's mission.

We think this is an important story that has not been given enough attention. Much analysis of contemporary evangelicalism has tried to interpret its political proclivities for a broader audience in an effort to understand the new conservative force in American politics. Thus, the contentious concerns of the religious right often dominate the narrative, overwhelming the justice issues that increasingly unite evangelicals far more than politics. We hope that this retelling brings needed balance to the public perception of twentieth-century evangelicalism. Because of space limitations, we in no way offer this book as a comprehensive analysis of the evangelical rediscovery of biblical justice. Our goal is simply to introduce the reader to a small but vital selection of key figures and seminal organizations that propelled the movement forward. It is our hope that many readers will go on to study more deeply the activists, theologians, pastors, and organizers in this book, perhaps after meeting them here for the first time. Nevertheless, we believe that those from any faith tradition (or none at all) who seek a critical, nuanced introduction to post–World War II evangelical activism will find just that in the pages that follow.

The heart of our motivation for writing this book lies in the future, not the past. We write as actors in an unfolding script. In our roles as pastors, professors, and activists, we have learned much from the previous two generations of evangelical leaders. In fact, it would not be too much to say that our lives have been shaped by them. Our desire is not only that those who read this book will encounter solid historical analysis but also that the people and events of the past will help to form the next generation. We have observed that many times zealous believers with the best intentions rush in to fight the world's worst injustices; unfortunately, they often wind up harming as much as helping. What is often lacking is simply the patience (and sometimes the humility) to listen first. In essence, this book is an opportunity to hear the voices of those who have gone before us so that we can adopt their strengths and avoid their struggles.

So, for readers who share our hunger and thirst for God's justice, we offer three ways in which these stories can have an explosive impact on your own practice of justice ministry.

Inspiration. While this study was generated by years of primary-source research on our topic, we unabashedly believe that the story the research tells is inspiring. For those who share the evangelical faith of the characters in the following chapters, these are not just names and dates to be dutifully chronicled; they are mentors whose lives call us to deeper commitment. Even those who are deceased are part of the "cloud of witnesses" (Heb. 12:1) that forms the broader horizon of our Christian community. Those of us who long to be mentored by godly, experienced saints can find some of what we're looking for right here.

Today, when "justice" is marketed on church websites, when organizations that fight sex trafficking have millions of Facebook "likes," and when thousands of teens with matching T-shirts condense "missions" into an annual week of spiritual tourism, it is highly valuable to encounter the men and women who reignited the justice aspects of God's mission at a time when justice was not only unpopular but suspect. Because talking about race or poverty or the environment in the 1950s, '60s, and '70s was often seen as political—and thus inappropriate for the pulpit—those who pushed forward were usually strong on the virtue of courage; they frequently did justice despite the active resistance of their fellow churchgoers. There was no bandwagon to jump on; they built the bandwagon.

Critique. Nevertheless, we are not offering a collection of carefully polished stained-glass saints. Critical history allows access to people and movements as they were embedded in their socioeconomic and political contexts. With hindsight, we are more likely to see the blind spots of which they were unaware and thus hopefully avoid them ourselves. Evangelicals have come a long way in their pursuit of justice, but we also have a long way to go. Careful attention to a study such as this one will help identify areas of inadequacy, paternalism, ignorance, and good intentions gone astray.

For example, one theme that recurs throughout the narrative is the evangelical penchant for choosing justice issues that do not implicate their own lifestyles or pocketbooks. It is much harder to advocate for a cause that calls for personal repentance than one that only requires fighting a common enemy. This book is a call not only to admiringly emulate leaders of the past but also to critically reform the work that they have courageously begun.

Perspective. Understanding the origins of this movement is essential, particularly if we want to shape where it is going. This dynamic is especially important for evangelicals, who frequently have little sense of being part of a tradition that forms them. Many commentators point out that because evangelicalism desires to go directly "back to the Bible" for its theology and practice, it underestimates tradition's power to unconsciously shape attitudes, behaviors, and values.

Perhaps an analogy would be helpful here: consider how our families of origin have powerfully influenced our fundamental orientations toward marriage, conflict resolution, financial management, and commitment to personal relationships. Yet it is not until we go to counseling or otherwise reflect critically on the roots of such deeply rooted patterns that we become aware of how much our own family history impacts us today. In the same way, reading a book like this can be a kind of "therapy," enabling those who identify as evangelicals to understand how the very distinctive culture handed down by previous generations predisposes us to certain patterns of thought and practice. By becoming conscious of how tradition has shaped us, it is possible to discover the freedom to embrace evangelicalism's positive aspects and turn away from that which has become counterproductive. Only through careful attention to the past can we determine the best way forward.

The value of historical perspective is even greater because the cultural patterns handed down by the evangelical tradition are not monolithic but essentially contested. Even within the focused area of justice activism, each generation evolved in many different directions, both among peers and in respect to its elders. As we show in the pages ahead, evangelicals have argued for many different visions of justice: compassion for individuals, transformational development, racial reconciliation, and penitent protest against oppression. Sometimes these approaches have been seen as synergistic; at other times, one approach was seen as trumping the rest. And in order to legitimize their efforts, some activists fought just as energetically against other evangelicals as they did against injustice itself. Thus, untangling the different strands gives us the power to cling to those we find most compelling. Awareness of competing approaches allows us to find our place within the tradition.

This text offers six historical snapshots of how evangelicals have engaged in the ministry of biblical justice. In part 1, we examine the power of story and how a personal connection to a story results in domestic efforts at community development and ministries of compassion to combat global poverty. In part 2, we reveal efforts to exhibit biblical justice in the public realm by addressing social injustices. Advocacy for those on the margins moved evangelicals to engage in a ministry of social and political transformation. Part 3 discusses the challenge for evangelicals to engage in the broader range of experiences and stories now found in the reality of increasing diversity. With each section, we offer pastoral insights that arise from the historical narrative.

Who Are Evangelicals?

So far we have been referring to "evangelicals" and "evangelicalism" as if the referents for those words are obvious. However, defining these terms is notoriously controversial, and academics have spilled much ink in their attempts to clarify. For the purposes of this introduction, we will not delve too deeply into scholarly minutiae that may interest only church historians. However, before we move on to our stories, it is important to establish some degree of clarity concerning what "evangelical" means and who "evangelicals" are, as many of our readers are themselves in the process of shaping the future of the evangelical tradition.

Unlike the Roman Catholic Church or the Boston Red Sox, evangelicalism has never been a clearly bounded organization with membership, leadership, and bureaucratic structure. Instead, it is more like a movement or a spirituality that has ebbed and flowed through many different Protestant churches and denominations since the Reformation. Respected historian Mark Noll says it well: "Evangelicalism has always been made up of shifting movements, temporary alliances, and the lengthened shadows of individuals."[2]

Despite the movement's amorphous nature, general agreement can be found concerning the defining characteristics of evangelicalism. Historian David Bebbington persuasively proposes that evangelicals place a strong emphasis on (1) conversionism—the spiritual transformation of the heart through personal encounter with Jesus; (2) cruciocentrism—the belief that Christ's atoning work on the cross is central for conversion; (3) activism—energetic participation in God's redeeming mission to the world; and (4) biblicism—the Bible alone is the source of spiritual truth.[3] Of course Christians of many kinds share these values, and evangelicals themselves have vigorously disagreed about the precise meaning of Bebbington's four tenets. But historically speaking, the fusion of these elements has produced a vital movement and, over time, a self-conscious tradition.

The evangelical family tree includes such European highlights as sixteenth-century Lutherans and Calvinists stressing *sola scriptura* (the Bible alone), seventeenth-century Pietists and Puritans emphasizing the religion of the heart, and eighteenth-century Moravians and Methodists driven to spread scriptural holiness to the ends of the earth. As the evangelical movement spilled over into America in the 1800s, Jacksonian democratic ideals, frontier entrepreneurial spirit, and massive tent meetings combined not only to produce scores of new "Bible-only" denominations but also to supersize European transplants like the Baptists and Methodists.

By the second decade of the nineteenth century, evangelicals had won over a majority of Americans from all social classes. Throughout the nineteenth century, American evangelicals energetically evangelized their new nation in the hope that revival would aid in the coming of God's righteous kingdom on earth. For evangelicals at this time, their God-given mission demanded a potent blend of preaching and prophetic social action. Despite our familiar stereotypes of socially conservative Christianity, nineteenth-century evangelicals were frequently on the cutting edge of causes like abolition, women's rights, poverty relief, urban reform, and advocacy for immigrants. Leaders like Charles Finney, the most famous evangelist of the antebellum era, routinely invited his hearers to *both* believe in Jesus *and* join the abolitionist cause as he toured the country preaching revival. Evangelicals founded scores of organizations (sometimes collectively called the "benevolent empire") that sought not only to provide charity for the poor but also to fundamentally reform the social structures that produced poverty in the first place. This is an extremely important point for readers of this book because it illustrates that the recent interest in justice among evangelicals is not a novelty but a rediscovery of something deep in our evangelical heritage.

In the final third of the nineteenth century, however, this holistic tradition of social engagement began to slowly erode. Shaken by the trauma of the Civil War, evangelicals began to lose their fervor for political activism (except for the prohibition of alcohol). By the turn of the twentieth century, American Protestantism was being ripped into two contending factions. On one side were the liberals, who embraced the new science of Darwinism and questioned the literal veracity of biblical miracles. Many liberals who identified with the Social Gospel movement energetically carried out justice activism as the centerpiece of their mission but de-emphasized evangelistic proclamation. In reaction, evangelicals vehemently rejected evolution and preached even stricter views of biblical inerrancy. Most tellingly for readers of this book, evangelicals also decisively distanced themselves from most forms of social action. The intense focus of those who emphasized the social gospel by challenging unjust social structures was deeply threatening to turn-of-the-century evangelicals, who came to believe that missions should be limited to personal evangelism and charity for deserving individuals. In other words, evangelicals redoubled their commitment to the gospel but "articulated only one major goal of mission: the salvation of individual souls."[4] Therefore, "as the attacks on liberalism heated up, the position that one could have both revivalism and social action became increasingly cumbersome to defend."[5]

After 1910 evangelicals adopted the term "fundamentalists" in order to better distinguish themselves from liberals. Fundamentalists fought for control of their denominations but lost battle after battle. Their most humiliating defeat came during the 1925 Scopes Trial, as the media subjected fundamentalist beliefs to national ridicule. By that time fundamentalists had so distanced themselves from all social concern that they had "forgotten the degree to which their predecessors—and even they themselves—had earlier espoused rather progressive social concerns."[6] Scholars call this rejection of social concern the Great Reversal because of its striking contrast with nineteenth-century activism. The central theme of the stories presented in this book is the way post–World War II evangelicals challenged the legacy of the Great Reversal they inherited from their fundamentalist forebears.

Besides the Great Reversal, fundamentalists set the table for twentieth-century evangelical activists by creating a dense network of parachurch agencies, such as seminaries, Bible schools, radio programs, missions agencies, and periodicals. Because they had lost control of their denominational institutions, fundamentalists busied themselves with setting up alternative structures in which conservatives could remain faithful to "the faith that was once for all entrusted to God's holy people" (Jude 1:3). When the next generation of evangelicals recovered the biblical concern for justice that fundamentalism had left behind, they ironically followed the same pattern of creating special purpose groups to do so. Thus, it is no surprise that all of the stories we have chosen for this book are not of denominations or church congregations but of parachurch agencies founded explicitly to reverse the Great Reversal.

Evangelicals with a Capital *E*

By the time of the Second World War, a new generation of conservative Protestants was emerging. One segment of younger leaders had begun to worry that the quarrelsome, belligerent tone of fundamentalist rhetoric actually impeded unity among conservatives and dampened the possibility of revival within the nation. Thus, in 1943 the National Association of Evangelicals (NAE) was born. The word "evangelical" was deliberately chosen to represent conservative Protestantism, better suited than "fundamentalism," which carried considerable contentious baggage. Instigated by J. Elwin Wright, a leader of an eclectic collection of revivalists called the New England Fellowship, and Harold Ockenga, the influential pastor at Boston's Park Street Church, the NAE attempted to unite conservative Protestants for the sake of promoting national revival. Members of the NAE called themselves "Evangelicals" in order to signify a new phase in American conservative Protestantism and to hearken back to eighteenth- and nineteenth-century Anglo-American Protestants who called themselves "evangelical." (From this point forward, the NAE-spawned movement described above will be indicated with an uppercase E [*Evangelical*], whereas lowercase e [*evangelical*] denotes the broader historical movement that has persisted since the Reformation to this day.)

Besides the NAE, Evangelicals went on to create a related cluster of institutions, including (but not limited to) the periodical *Christianity Today*, Fuller Theological Seminary, the Billy Graham Evangelistic Association, Youth for Christ, and Campus Crusade for Christ. The movement's leaders preached in each other's churches, served on each other's advisory boards, wrote articles for each other's periodicals, and attended the same conferences. Although they held no formal authority, the best-known leaders (a group sometimes lightheartedly referred to as "Billy Graham and his friends") energetically attempted to define a movement that encompassed all true Bible-believing Americans. For their followers (who were occasionally described as "card-carrying" Evangelicals), loyalty to the Evangelical movement was often more important than denominational affiliation.

Yet the NAE suffered the fate of many organizational attempts at unity within the fissiparous history of evangelicalism: it merely added another faction to the dizzying array of conservative Protestantism. It is true that the NAE united conservatives across regional frontiers and forged "a tighter national network among previously isolated centers of evangelical activity scattered around the country. . . . It re-established a link between north and south, largely absent since the Civil War."[7] But the NAE also provoked a harsh reaction from fundamentalists who interpreted its irenic tone as being soft on liberalism; its founding reignited the debate between fundamentalists who demanded strict separation from all liberal denominations and those who were content to coexist while working for a return to orthodoxy. Indeed, the counterattack from separatists kept even such conservative cornerstones as Wheaton College and the Southern Baptist Convention from joining the NAE during its early years. Therefore, "the NAE was treated more as an ordinary parachurch group rather than a normative call to Christian unity."[8]

Even more important for the purposes of this book, many believers who were "evangelical" in the theological sense were excluded from or did not join NAE-affiliated groups. Offshoots of Methodism such as Holiness churches and many Pentecostal groups were especially uncomfortable with the Reformed tone set by the best-known Evangelical leaders. African-Americans, whose churches have been one of the driving forces of evangelicalism since the early nineteenth century, were shut out by the white, male leaders of Evangelicalism's founding generation. It is one of the great ironies of Evangelicalism (and one of the central themes of this book) that the return to biblical justice was led in large part by ethnic minorities and peace churches such as the Mennonites, who were on the margins of the space created by mainstream, Calvinist-leaning, white-dominated Evangelical leadership.

Evangelicalism's break with fundamentalism also must not be overplayed. Despite its self-conscious desire to differentiate itself from the excesses of fundamentalism, the nascent post–World War II Evangelical movement could be seen as a wing of fundamentalism until at least the late 1950s, when Evangelical leaders began to distinguish themselves much more sharply and polemically. Nevertheless, as historian Joel Carpenter summarizes, the NAE "unleashed an idea, a new collective identity, and a dynamic force for religious initiatives. 'Evangelicalism' had been born."[9]

Perhaps the most telling feature of the slow divorce between Evangelicals and fundamentalists was the Evangelical rejection of the fundamentalist disengagement from the surrounding culture—that is, their reversing of the Great Reversal. Henry's *Uneasy Conscience of Modern Fundamentalism*, cited in the opening paragraph of this introduction, is certainly the best-known call to return to social engagement and deserves its symbolic place as the starting point for the reopening of the door for Evangelical concern for justice. Nevertheless, *Uneasy Conscience* is somewhat vague on specifics. Even when Henry spoke in concrete terms, he was mainly concerned with secularism, whether it was taking root through "godless" universities and mainstream media in the United States or "godless" communism abroad. Many other early Evangelical leaders were motivated to reengage with society by the same fears of creeping secularization.

In fact, most historians have portrayed Evangelicalism's early social engagement as focused on issues that would not now be termed "social justice." For example, intellectual respectability was the consuming preoccupation for many key leaders. They felt that unless Evangelicals produced quality scholarship that was recognized by "the world" as excellent, they would never win a hearing among the influential sectors of society. Thus, the driving force behind evangelicalism's newfound social engagement was a small band of highly-educated scholars and sympathetic pastors whose founding of Fuller Seminary in 1947 was "a truly epochal event, the beginning of a new age for Evangelicalism."[10] This longing for intellectual respectability was so evident that it was lampooned by some fundamentalists, one of whom defined Evangelical leaders as "people who say to liberals, 'I'll call you a Christian if you'll call me a scholar.'"[11]

Cultivation of intellectual life was clearly an important expression of the reemergence of Evangelical social concern. However, it needs to be supplemented by influences from the burgeoning justice initiatives chronicled in the pages that follow. The stories in the pages that follow show that nascent Evangelical social concern had an additional source found not in the apologetics of Fuller professors but in direct encounters with injustice, oppression, and raw human suffering in the Global South and the inner cities of the United States.

PART 1

Justice Is Personal and Relational

1

The Power of Personal Story

John Perkins and the Christian Community Development Association

The first summer after planting our church in an inner-city neighborhood in Cambridge, Massachusetts, we conducted a Vacation Bible School for the children of the community. Cambridge Community Fellowship Church (CCFC) was composed mostly of college students and young singles in their twenties who had been attracted to the church, in part, because of its urban ministry and social action vision. These young men and women were energized by the chance to work with urban children and youth, many of whom came from low-income housing near the church. That summer as I (Soong-Chan) observed Ivy League students and alumni demonstrate the gospel with the beginnings of a social engagement in the urban context, I realized that for many of our church members, this type of Christian involvement proved foreign to their church background.

In subsequent years, CCFC would continue evangelistic outreach to the children and youth of the low-income community in Cambridge as well as serve indigent senior citizens in a convalescence home near the church. The church partnered with a Latino church to offer tutoring and computer courses in a predominantly Latino neighborhood in Boston and also with African-American churches and the Boston TenPoint Coalition to address the issue of gang-related youth violence.

One of the ministries of the Boston TenPoint Coalition intervened in the national gangs' attempt to infiltrate Boston schools. Teamed with local police and armed with my clerical collar, I rode in the back of a police car to visit youth who had appeared on the school police blotter. We engaged the youth in the classic bad cop, good pastor routine. The police officer threatened the full force of the law, including the possibility of federal prosecution for gang activity. My role as the good pastor was to assure the youth that the community loved him and that the church would be there for him. Our shared goal was to keep the young man from joining the national gangs that were attempting to infiltrate our city. Law and grace worked together for justice.

When I look back on my experiences in urban ministry, I realize that neither my theologically conservative immigrant church upbringing nor my Evangelical seminary education had prepared me for this kind of civic engagement. I had no theological lens to understand this act of pastoral care. The seemingly singular focus on personal evangelism among many Evangelicals prevented me from seeing how riding around in a police car could actually be an integral part of the work of the church. Like many late-twentieth-century Evangelicals, I had embraced a dysfunctional and inadequate theology that revealed the impact of a twentieth-century American church history that divorced evangelism from works of social justice.

In contrast, CCFC attempted to embody the principles of the Christian Community Development Association (CCDA), a national ministry founded by and rooted in the teachings of John Perkins. As the founding pastor of CCFC, I had been influenced by the teachings of John Perkins through his books and through attendance at CCDA national conferences. John Perkins provides an Evangelical role model of a Christian leader passionately committed to personal evangelism with a deep concern for the lost. At the same time, Perkins has ministered to the poor and to the disenfranchised and has spoken about the radical biblical values of relocation, reconciliation, and redistribution. John Perkins revolutionized the way Evangelicals consider the role of the church in the context of a broken world. My own spiritual and ministry journey was shaped by the transformative power of his challenging words, which were amplified by the power of his story. John Perkins has lived a life that integrates personal evangelism and social concern in a way that challenged the status quo of late-twentieth-century Evangelicalism.

From Jerusalem to Babylon[1]

As discussed above, twentieth-century Evangelicalism witnessed a conspicuous and unfortunate divorce between acts of social justice and efforts of personal evangelism. This Great Reversal was a contrast to the integration of the two streams throughout the nineteenth century. In the twentieth century, American Evangelicals demonstrated suspicion about the world. Since the world was destined for destruction, only worthy individuals in the world, not the world itself, needed saving. An optimistic view of society would be replaced by a negative approach to the world. This approach to ministry is most evident in American Evangelical engagement with the urban context.

American Christians have held a complicated relationship with the city. Often, the view of the city reflects their view of society as a whole: an optimistic view of the larger society translates into optimism about the city. The first wave of European colonialists carried an optimistic view of the New World and its cities. The blank slate of the Americas allowed for the self-perception that an exceptional people would build an exceptional society.[2] The *tabula rasa* of the New World would be filled with the best of the Western world.[3] Colonial American Christians anticipated that the cities of the New World would become cities set on a hill, New Jerusalems and Zions.[4]

This optimistic view of the American city would shift over the course of the nineteenth and twentieth centuries. Industrialization, urbanization, and migration impacted the city in ways that the founders of these cities could not predict. The time period following the end of the Civil War and well into the latter half of the twentieth century witnessed drastic changes in the demographics of US cities. African-Americans participated in the Great Migration, relocating from former slave states in the South to cities in the North and on the East Coast. The cities also witnessed the influx of non-Protestant and non-Western European immigrants, resulting in notable growth.

However, the influx of these "unwanted elements" in the cities meant that white Protestants now perceived cities as dangerous places. As Robert Orsi states, "City neighborhoods appeared as caves of rum and Romanism, mysterious and forbidding, a threat to democracy, Protestantism, and virtue alike."[5] Cities were no longer perceived as cities set on a hill or as New Jerusalems, but instead as Babylons, the center of sin and evil. Randall Balmer notes that "Evangelicals suddenly felt their hegemonic hold over American society slipping away. . . . The teeming, squalid ghettoes, . . . festering with labor unrest, no longer resembled the precincts of Zion that postmillennial evangelicals had envisioned earlier in the century."[6]

Meanwhile, suburban communities offered an attractive alternative for former residents of the city.[7] White Americans (including white American Christians) would embrace the narrative that the city was a broken place while the newly formed suburbs were the new places of hope and possibility. The hope for a city set on a hill was replaced with a suburb set on a hill. The culmination of this shifting perspective came to be known as "white flight." As a result, the twentieth century witnessed the departure of whites and white churches from the city in significant numbers.[8] The suburbs became the new outposts for white Christians fearful of the changes in the city.

The perspective of the city as a sinful place is found in the numerous books on the city that emerged during the height of white flight. No longer were US cities considered to be cities "built on a hill" (Matt. 5:14). Instead they were portrayed as *The Secular City* or *The Unheavenly City*. These *Sick Cities* were *Babylon by Choice*, which had gone *From New Creation to Urban Crisis*, and where now *Home Is a Dirty Street*. This state of affairs compelled Christians to question *The Meaning of the City* and to ask, *Is There Hope for the City?*[9] With the narrative of decline dominating the Christian imagination of the city, participants in white flight could easily justify their actions. White Christians could flee the city as a spiritual act, citing the desire to be a stranger to the evil of the world, to separate themselves from the evil workings of Babylon, and to flee to the comfort and safety of suburban life. The suburbs would be the new destination for those seeking to build a New Jerusalem in America. The pivot toward the suburbs resulted in the rise of quick and easy answers to successful church ministry. With the challenges of the city behind them, these suburban churches would look for effective ways to build up the church. Church growth books and church resources became readily available.

In the latter half of the twentieth century, churches in the suburbs carried out these principles of success and growth. New, state-of-the-art church buildings would attract new members to suburban congregations.[10] Suburban church attendance swelled, but this did not lead to more conversions.[11] Instead, suburban church growth was merely indicative of the population shift of the white community.

Harvie Conn summarizes studies conducted by Dennison Nash and Peter Berger: "The impressive increases in church membership statistics in suburbia were only a reflection of the increased number of families with school-aged children in the country, the postwar 'baby boom' that had helped to produce the suburban migration itself."[12] The much-trumpeted growth of suburban churches had little to do with new and innovative evangelism and church growth techniques and more to do with the timing of a population shift in American society.

As the population of white Christians shifted to the suburbs, numerous seminaries and denominations taught and advocated for church growth ministry practices that supported the suburbanization of Evangelicalism. Church growth methodology enticed pastors of fledgling churches as formulas for successful ministry, and the homogeneous unit principle (HUP) operated as one of the key magic formulas employed to grow suburban churches. The HUP asserted that churches would grow faster if they focused on reaching their kind of people. By removing the barriers of racial, cultural, and socioeconomic diversity, churches would experience their desired levels of growth in the suburban enclaves. The HUP gave ecclesial justification for de facto segregation, which was already exacerbated by white flight.

Whether intentional or not, the HUP applied by suburban churches affirmed the wisdom of white flight, allowing the suburban churches to capture the migration of whites to the suburbs and leading to numerical growth. In turn, the growth of the suburban church gave (false) credence to, and perpetuated, the Church Growth movement principles, which offered methods of growth that were supposedly applicable to all churches everywhere.

The narrative of the city as fallen Babylon and the suburbs as the New Jerusalem continues to this day. Suburban churches in the latter half of the twentieth century believed that they were the locus of American Evangelical life. This belief in themselves as the New Jerusalem was clearly demonstrated by the numerical growth of Evangelical churches and the building of new, beautiful, and impressive church buildings.

In recent years, as suburban white Evangelicals have returned to the city to contribute to urban gentrification, the city is still perceived as Babylon, in need of help from those who had built New Jerusalems in the suburbs. Urban ministry books again reflect this narrative with titles such as *The Urban Mission*, *The Urban Challenge*, *Redeeming the City*, *City Reaching*, and *The Urban Face of Mission*.[13] Cities that were once envisioned as beacons set on a hill, sending out missionaries to the world, were now Babylons in desperate need of missionaries—who would most likely come from the Jerusalem outposts of the American suburbs. The cities needed *The Church That Takes on Trouble* and suburban transplants as *They Dare to Love the Ghetto*, serving as *Apostles to the City*, each as *The Change Agent* who will be *Taking Our Cities for God*.[14]

These transplanted suburbanites envisioned themselves as bringing the heavenly city of Jerusalem from the suburbs to the city. While one could argue that this return to the city reflects a better narrative than the cultural disengagement that led to white flight, it isn't much better. Both narratives reveal a deeply rooted assumption of the supremacy of an Evangelical theology rooted in Western cultural forms of church. Both narratives assume desperate cities are mission fields. While the white flight narrative allowed Evangelicals to flee the city, which in its decline had become the New Babylon, the narrative of the Jerusalem suburbs encouraged Evangelicals to return as saviors of the city.

Both narratives assume the inferiority of the city and those who have remained there. The poor and the marginalized are objects of scorn and pity. One must either flee from this reality or seek ways to be a missionary within it. Both narratives elevate white

Evangelicals in the suburbs; they have made the right choices and are the exemplary Christians. Fleeing the city was a spiritual act of purity, and returning to the city was a spiritual act of Evangelical activism.

John Perkins's Story

John Perkins offers an alternative narrative both to the story of withdrawal from the places of suffering and to the narrative of the white savior sent to the city to save the poor blacks. Through his personal story, Perkins reveals the folly of twentieth-century Evangelicalism, which had forsaken the poor and the marginalized in order to build Christian empires among the privileged. Perkins also represents a different narrative of the poor black man who, with limited education, could impact and transform the broader Evangelical narrative. His ability to speak a prophetic challenge to mainstream Evangelical Christianity arises from his own evangelical conversion story, a story of spiritual triumph that called apathetic Evangelicals to an activist faith.

Perkins's story is familiar to many. A quick survey of those who have met John Perkins reveals how a one-time meeting, hearing John's story and his real presence and engagement, irrevocably changed them. An important aspect of John Perkins's impact is his ability to communicate a powerful story of evangelical conviction. Ron Sider notes that "John is a great storyteller. Anyone who has listened to him speak knows how he weaves his own personal story into a call to empower the marginalized and overcome racism. That his own story is so powerful and compelling certainly helps. But he tells it in a way that wins hearts and minds—even donors to a great ministry."[15]

One of John Perkins's key theological contributions is the power of his story lived out in the face of great trials and tribulations. While other Evangelical leaders may possess a great testimony, few rival the embodied story of Jesus's redemptive power in John Perkins. Among twentieth-century Evangelical leaders, few have done more with less and few have overcome as many obstacles. His story takes the classic American success story and infuses it with an Evangelical spirituality that affirms the power of the gospel while simultaneously challenging existing paradigms of active Christian faith.

John Perkins was born to a family of sharecroppers, bootleggers, and gamblers. Historian A. G. Miller notes that "much of Mississippi black culture in which John Perkins grew up was a world in which blacks were redefining their worldview against the prevailing white and Christian values. The blues reflected the black counterculture within which Perkins identified himself (gamblers, bootleggers, and lawbreakers)—those folk who were not afraid of southern white people and struggled to control their own destiny."[16] Miller recognizes that despite the reality of poverty and marginalization, Perkins's cultural context reveals a high degree of yearning for self-determination, even if that desire surfaced in ways that skirted the law. While understanding the dominant southern white culture in which he lived, Perkins engaged that culture with a deep-seated desire to assert human agency.

The murder of his brother by the local police was another assault on Perkins's understanding of power and powerlessness. Watching his older brother shot down as he stood up to the police revealed a cultural reality that attempted to instill fear and deprive African-Americans of self-determination. Perkins experienced the conflict felt by many blacks in the Deep South—the constant barrage against self-determination and identity. That sense of agency (established in his early upbringing) led Perkins toward an interaction with the dominant culture that defied typical categorization.

In order to embrace Christian faith, however, Perkins needed to leave not only the cultural trappings of the South but also the unhealthy expression of Christian identity that was conflated with white supremacy. A. G. Miller notes, "Perkins's openness to the exploration of faith came in stages after he left the South, joined the army, and eventually settled in the Los Angeles area after his discharge from the military. Perkins's conversion to Christianity was not an immediate process. He had to leave the South and its extreme environment, racial hatred, prejudice, and oppression in order to find enough mental and physical space to explore more social and spiritual matters."[17] Perkins needed distance from the strictures of the South and southern Christianity to experience a conversion that affirmed his human agency and worth.[18]

Perkins's description of his own conversion demonstrates a deeply evangelical experience and the roots of an Evangelical identity. John Perkins began to attend church after he saw "something beautiful develop" in his son, who was attending the Bethlehem Church of Christ Holiness.[19] Perkins's conversion occurred as a result of an encounter with Scripture. He became fascinated with the writings of Paul. As Perkins says, "I began to enjoy the Bible because of what I was learning about the Apostle Paul, how he endured so much for religion. . . . When I learned that the Apostle Paul was the writer of most of the New Testament books of the Bible, I began to study the Bible myself for the first time."[20] Even before his conversion, he had become a biblicist.

Perkins's conversion also required a Christocentric experience. As he writes in his first book, *Let Justice Roll Down*:

> For the first time I understood that my sin was not necessarily and altogether against myself and against my neighbor. My sin was against a holy God who loved me, who had already paid for my sins. I was sinning in the face of His love. I didn't want to sin anymore. I wanted to give my life to Christ, so He could take care of my sin. I sensed the beginning of a whole new life, a new structure of life, a life that could fill that emptiness I had even on payday. God for a black man? Yes, God for a black man! This black man! Me! That morning I said yes to Jesus Christ.[21]

In this passage, Perkins unabashedly proclaims his Christocentric understanding of the gospel that led him to new birth. At the same time, he reveals how this experience emerges from his identity as a black man. Christ as savior transcends the barrier of race for Perkins. As a result, Perkins's foundational message stresses that a person is in need of God because of sins committed against God and that Christ is the only answer for sin.

Perkins's conversion experience takes on greater significance because he had weighed and rejected other options. He confesses that he explored Christian Science, Father Divine, and Science of the Mind. He even admits, "If I hadn't become a Christian, I would have become a Black Muslim. Their strict devotion and discipline have always appealed to me."[22] As an adult, Perkins made a cognitive and rational decision to become a Christian. He had read the key biblical texts that pointed him toward Jesus, and he had rejected the non-Christian options. He had moved from being the child of bootleggers and gamblers to someone who explored other faiths to an evangelist who spoke plainly about his personally experienced salvation. Perkins embodied a conversionist faith.

Upon his conversion, his activist zeal found expression in his evangelistic efforts. "I began to share this inward peace with people in the area where I lived. In about six months' time I was sharing my life and my testimony in many churches—white and black. . . . And I was teaching children's Bible classes four or five nights a week."[23] Evangelism, with a particular focus on child evangelism, marked the immediate period after his conversion, and evangelical activism eventually compelled Perkins to seek a return to Mississippi under the auspices of continuing to pursue his evangelistic zeal in his home state. Perkins's move from California to Mississippi provided an alternative narrative to the phenomenon of white flight. Instead of staying in a growing ministry with potential for financial stability, he returned to Mississippi to minister to the poor and the marginalized. His actions gave weight to his later teachings on relocation as an expression of Christ's incarnation in the community.

When Perkins returned to Mississippi in 1960, he continued to focus on child evangelism. His initial efforts at evangelism stemmed from the fundamentalist roots of his conversion experience: he would change the world by changing individual lives. However, Perkins quickly identified the significant inequity between black kids and white kids in the school system. As a result, Perkins recognized that more was needed than a simple Bible study group for children. According to Perkins, the impact of the gospel needed to extend beyond the simple articulation of the faith. "I knew that if the Bible I was teaching could ever really do something here, it would have to be a visible truth."[24]

While Perkins eventually moved beyond a personal evangelism approach to ministry, he did not abandon the value of personal evangelism altogether. He advocated for the value of holistic evangelism. His approach was not simply to rescue the poor children of Mississippi and move them to the suburbs; instead, it required a whole gospel for the whole person. The context of his ministry—working with the poor—resulted in a different narrative and trajectory for those he was trying to reach with the gospel. The fundamentalist-evangelical narrative of saving individual souls from the evil world proved insufficient for Perkins's ministry context.

Perkins's story of reaching his community with a holistic gospel reached another level of sociocultural engagement in 1970. Living in Mississippi in the 1960s meant that Perkins could not avoid the civil rights movement. Perkins attended civil rights rallies, where he affirmed the validity of the issues being raised. But Perkins expressed concern that "evangelicals had surrendered their leadership in the movement by default to those with either a bankrupt theology or no theology at all. . . . The evangelical church—whose basic theology is the same as mine—had not gone on to preach the *whole* gospel."[25] Perkins articulated his concern about the civil rights movement but also placed blame on Evangelical passivity. He confirmed that he shared the basic fundamental gospel conviction but that Bible-believing Christians had failed to live up to the whole gospel message.

Perkins and his church community, Voice of Calvary, became involved in voter registration. His children would become the first black students at a previously all-white public high school. Perkins even appealed to conservative white donors in California. His activity troubled the white establishment in the area. Perkins writes that "cars began appearing at night. White men—armed, waiting. Watching for hours at a time, but edging closer and closer. Waiting for any incident to excuse a confrontation."[26]

On the evening of February 7, 1970, after a demonstration in Mendenhall, Mississippi, a group of students were arrested as they were returning to Tougaloo College near Jackson. John Perkins, accompanied by Reverend Curry Brown and Joe Paul Buckley, rushed to post bail for those who had been arrested. At the courthouse and jail, they were met by a dozen Mississippi Highway Patrol officers and placed under arrest. Perkins later testified in court that "when I got in the jail Sheriff Jonathan Edwards came over to me right away and said, this is the smart nigger, and this is a new ballgame. . . . He began to beat me, and from that time on they continued beating me, I was just beat to the floor and just punched and just really beaten."[27]

Despite the brutality of the beating, Perkins strengthened his evangelical narrative by extending forgiveness. "I began to see with horror how hate could destroy me. . . . I could try and fight back, as many of my brothers had done. But if I did, how would I be different from the whites who hate? And where would hating get me?" Perkins describes how God's Spirit worked on his life to blot out that hate with the image of Christ on the cross. Because Jesus had experienced suffering himself, he understood John Perkins's suffering. "The Spirit of God kept working on me and in me until I could say with Jesus, 'I forgive them, too.'"[28]

Perkins's story was not only a story about evangelical conversion, an evangelist's zeal, and caring for the least of these. His story also engaged the reality of racial and social injustice. His beating at the hands of the police pointed toward the need for civil rights and for social justice in the face of a great injustice. Unlike Martin Luther King Jr. or Malcom X, John Perkins expressed a story that Evangelicals could call their own. Perkins not only introduced his story to Evangelical Christianity but also sparked a movement that helped reimagine Evangelicalism beyond the boundaries of an apocalyptic fundamentalism that could remain disengaged with the world around it.

Translating the Story to a Movement

Perkins's narrative not only inspired individuals but also sparked a movement. As told in his public teaching and through his books, his story drew together a number of like-minded individuals. Perkins became the galvanizing force for the formation of the Christian Community Development Association. The CCDA website explains how John Perkins provided the foundational content for the ministry:

> The roots of the Christian Community Development Association (CCDA) stretch back to 1960 when CCDA Founder, John Perkins (along with his wife, Vera Mae) relocated their family to the struggling community of Mendenhall, Mississippi to work with the people there. The Perkinses devoted thirty-five years to living out the principles of Christian Community Development in Mississippi and California, leaving behind ministries and churches that are now headed by indigenous Christian leaders.[29]

Perkins's model of ministry served as one of the exemplar ministries in the CCDA. John Perkins issued the call to gather like-minded individuals "who were bonded by one significant commitment, expressing the love of Jesus in America's poor communities."[30]

On February 23, 1989, fifty-three people attended the first CCDA meeting at a hotel near Chicago O'Hare International Airport. The first group of attendees were drawn together by their interest in communicating the gospel and serving the poor, oppressed, and needy—through which the group found a common vision and direction. John Perkins emerged as the spiritual and inspirational leader of the group, serving as the chairman of the board. A then-unknown Chicago pastor, Wayne "Coach" Gordon, was appointed president when the first president, Lem Tucker, passed away after the first meeting.

Wayne Gordon is the founding pastor of Lawndale Community Church on the west side of Chicago. From a small Iowa town, Gordon followed an unlikely path to the inner city of Chicago. He felt called to work in the inner city while still a teenager in Iowa, then attended Wheaton College, a Christian college in an affluent Christian community about an hour outside Chicago. While at Wheaton, he spent a summer working in Chicago's inner city. Upon graduation he became a teacher and a coach at Farragut High School on the west side of Chicago. He and his wife, Anne, moved into the predominantly African-American neighborhood of Lawndale, which at the time was the fifteenth poorest neighborhood in the United States.

In 1978 Gordon—along with his wife, some high school students, and their parents—established Lawndale Community Church. He eventually attended Trinity Evangelical Divinity School and finished his seminary education at Northern Baptist Seminary after becoming the full-time pastor of Lawndale Community Church. Like Voice of Calvary in Mississippi, Lawndale became an exemplary church for the CCDA. Various types of outreach ministries developed out of the church, including sports programs, educational programs, a medical clinic, a community development center, housing programs and development, and a health and fitness center. With its urban location in the middle of the country, Lawndale Community Church became the natural incubator for

the CCDA.[31] It could be said that John Perkins served as the prophetic interlocutor and Coach Gordon served as the Evangelical
model of how a nonurban, white Evangelical could successfully
serve in the urban context. Gordon's story ran parallel to Perkins's
story in the overarching narrative of the CCDA.

The initial small group that gathered in February 1989 convened
a conference at Lawndale later that year that attracted about two
hundred attendees. In subsequent years, the CCDA national conference has met in different cities throughout the United States
and attracted several thousand to the annual meetings. Even more
important than the number of attendees, however, was that the
CCDA became a recognizable brand among Evangelicals as a
place of inspiration and teaching for ministry to the poor and
the marginalized.

John Perkins's three Rs of Christian community development
(CCD) form the core of CCDA teaching.[32] First, the concept of
relocation asserts that "the most effective messenger of the gospel
to the poor will also live among the poor that God has called the
person to." Relocation calls those who engaged in CCD to have
a personal stake in the neighborhood. "Relocation transforms
'you, them, and theirs' to 'we, us, and ours.'" Relocation offers
the opposite of white flight.

Second, the concept of *reconciliation* challenges the church to
move beyond the vertical components of salvation to incorporate
the horizontal aspects of salvation. The CCDA is clear in advocating for the need for reconciliation with God but also asks, "Can a
gospel that reconciles people to God without reconciling people
to people be the true gospel of Jesus Christ? A person's love for
Christ should break down every racial, ethnic and economic barrier." The CCDA connects the felt-need concept to the work of
reconciliation. The building of trust that moves toward reconciliation requires the privileged to listen to the needs and desires of
the poor and to seek to help meet those needs. This concept can be
interpreted and misinterpreted on multiple levels but at its heart

is a desire to build trust to work toward reconciled relationships. This concept offers another challenge to white flight and calls for Evangelical engagement on one of the more sensitive issues, the need for racial reconciliation (see chap. 5 for more on this topic).

The third core concept is *redistribution*. In recent years, the word "redistribution" has become strongly associated with communism, particularly in the context of the hyperpolarized world of partisan politics, and has been used as a code word to smear economic and political liberals. That the CCDA spoke of redistribution on the heels of the Reagan administration is a testament to the ability of John Perkins and the CCDA to effectively use language and story to communicate difficult and increasingly controversial concepts. The CCDA website describes redistribution in the following way: "When men and women in the body of Christ are visibly present and living among the poor (relocation), and when people are intentionally loving their neighbor and their neighbor's family the way a person loves him or herself and family (reconciliation), the result is redistribution, or a just distribution of resources." Redistribution is seen as a natural by-product of the building of relationships across various boundaries. The CCDA uses the language of justice in order to assert the need for redistribution. Given the political realities of the twenty-first century, the fact that the CCDA continues to use redistribution as one of its core principles demonstrates the level of trust garnered by the CCDA movement.

The three Rs of CCD were eventually supplemented by five additional categories—leadership development, listening to the community, church-based, wholistic, and empowerment—to comprise the eight key components. With the introduction of the new categories, the CCDA was able to offer more practical applications to move Christian communities toward the three Rs. By employing language such as *listening to the community, wholistic ministry,* and *empowerment*—which were expressions not typically used by Evangelical churches in the latter half of the twentieth century— the CCDA was able to challenge assumptions about the superiority of the Evangelical suburban narrative and elevate the conversation on how justice integrates with evangelism. In so doing, the CCDA provided a biblical, theological, and ecclesial framework to spur Evangelicalism beyond the models of ministry that had been propagated for most of the twentieth century.

Community development was an unfamiliar topic in the early stages of Evangelical history. Because the strength of John Perkins and the CCDA is rooted in the ability to communicate a compelling story, they were able to challenge Evangelical presuppositions about the place of the church in the world. The ecclesial heritage of Evangelicalism would need to incorporate the story of John Perkins. As a result, previously ignored aspects of the Evangelical experience—such as domestic ministry to the poor, community development, racial reconciliation, and even civil rights and redistribution of resources—moved into the mainstream of Evangelicalism.

Peter Slade identifies Perkins's impact as a quiet revolution in the culture wars. "More than forty years after Martin Luther King Jr.'s death, Perkins's unique life story enables a new generation of evangelicals to relocate themselves as participants in the continuing civil rights movement without rejecting their evangelical heritage. In the latest act of this theological drama, we find a theology of the social gospel alive and well in the most surprising of places— as a grassroots movement within the mainstream of American evangelicalism."[33] The tide of the Great Reversal had turned.

The Power of Story[34]

For American Evangelicals, stories play a prominent role in evangelism, discipleship, and spiritual formation. From an early age, American Christians are taught to appreciate the stories of biblical heroes, to be moved by the stories of exceptional missionaries, and to be enraptured by the humorous yet poignant stories of our best

preachers. Not only do we hear the stories of others but also we are challenged to share our own stories.

In my evangelism courses at an evangelical seminary, I teach the power of story. I encourage my students to listen to good storytellers, often found on NPR programs like *The Moth* and *Serial*. I give my students templates on how to make their testimony clear and engaging. I teach my students the standard evangelical truth that sharing a personal testimony provides one of the best ways to communicate the gospel message. When in doubt, share your story.

John Perkins's transformative story of suffering and struggle has been particularly impactful and significant in my own life, as it has for others. The power of his story for me stems from how my own story finds affirmation in his.

As a Korean immigrant I gained an early familiarity with stories of suffering. Embedded within Korean culture is the shared lived experience of *han*, a term for the collective suffering among Korean people. While *han* plays a prominent role in Korean culture, Korean immigrants to the United States may seek to avoid expressions of *han*. Instead, many Korean immigrant churches, as an expression of assimilation, may cling to the triumphalist narrative of American Christianity. The faith of Korean immigrant churches, therefore, may reflect a cultural captivity to Western and American expressions of Evangelical faith.

My personal story may be both a typical and an atypical product of the Korean immigrant church. The Korean immigrant church developed a personal spirituality uniquely formed for Korean immigrants. My passion for personal piety arises from years of worship services, Sunday school classes, Friday night youth group meetings, Saturday fellowship gatherings, early morning prayer meetings, summer youth retreats, winter youth retreats, summer revival meetings, fall revival meetings, and spring revival meetings. My experience in the immigrant church gave me a healthy respect for the importance of individual salvation. It was essential that I came to Christ on *my* own and received Christ as *my* personal

Savior (sometimes repeatedly, just to be sure). My personal spiritual journey reflects the common evangelical narrative of personal redemption. My journey as an Evangelical meant that I would learn the skills necessary to share my personal testimony of personal and triumphant redemption.

The triumphant conclusion of my personal testimony betrayed a less exceptional backstory. In contrast to most of my friends at church, I came from a single-parent home. My family did not fit the norm of a successful immigrant family. We lived in a rough neighborhood in a small roach-infested apartment in the inner city. We received food stamps and the school free lunch in order to get us through some rough financial patches. Despite my numerous degrees in higher education, I am still saddled with the shame of having received help from the government.

While a student at a conservative Evangelical seminary, I sat silently in a class on biblical social action as my upper-middle-class, white classmates (and future pastors and leaders of the Evangelical church) popped off about "welfare queens" and "freeloaders." They would not have believed that one of their classmates had once been the recipient of food stamps. But I have grown more bold in sharing the shameful side of my testimony. I came to recognize the power of stories in the immigrant church—particularly the stories of suffering. I am quick to share my story because I know that my story can inspire others to repentance and action.

American Evangelicalism has no shortage of triumphalist narratives. Stories of successful mega-church pastors and hipster church planters fill the bookshelves of American Evangelicals. The power of John Perkins's impact lies in his ability to embrace his humble roots and to direct his narrative toward an engagement with the suffering *other* rather than simply elevating the popularity of the storyteller. In other words, John Perkins raises the level of compassion for domestic poverty. Personal stories have high currency in American Evangelicalism. John Perkins offers the power of a personal story combined with a life that expresses Christian justice and compassion. Perkins's willingness to speak of his pain and struggle emboldens me to share the stories of my pain and struggle. Perkins's ability to rise above the struggle and speak a strong prophetic word encourages me to rise above and speak the truth no matter what the obstacles.

For much of the twentieth century, American Evangelicalism had a dysfunctional relationship with the surrounding culture, whether in the form of antagonism toward the world or an over-acquiescence to it. Perkins's narrative and ministry context necessitated his voice being raised against the injustices of society, but his connection with fundamentalist and evangelical Christianity also gave him a deep passion and appreciation for the work of personal evangelism.

In the early years of his ministry, John Perkins conducted Bible study outreaches that would have warmed the hearts of even the most fundamental of fundamentalists. Perkins's early formation Christianity was steeped in the personal evangelism emphasis of fundamentalism and Evangelicalism. These roots, however, did not prevent him from engaging the social and structural evils of his time. He was not only an advocate and practitioner of personal evangelism, but also one of the most significant and articulate voices of social, cultural engagement in the church in the twentieth century.

Perkins's ministry context and his personal experience as an African-American allowed him to raise issues that were not broached by Christians from the white majority culture. Perkins spoke on the need for racial reconciliation even after he lived through a physical attack by racists. Perkins's theological expression, therefore, arose out of the context of the African-American community but had a broader impact on majority-culture Evangelicalism. In this dual context (growing up as a black man in the South while connected to the larger context of majority-culture Christianity), Perkins could speak prophetically out of a real-life experience while understanding the language of majority-culture Christianity.

The narrative of John Perkins and the CCDA presages the possibility and the hope of a more fully formed ecclesiology for twenty-first-century Evangelicals. The twentieth century divorce of social justice from evangelism could not be sustained. John Perkins served as the theological corrective necessary for the full gospel to rise up. John Perkins and the CCDA continue to contribute to the next generation of Evangelicals who more fully integrate racial and social justice with the story of personal evangelism. Perkins brought this message out of his own life experience and cultural context and continues to provide inspiration for succeeding generations.

2

The Power of a Personal Connection

Child Sponsorship and Global Poverty

In 1947 huge crowds came to hear a thirty-two-year-old Californian preach at mass evangelistic rallies throughout China. Although Bob Pierce had no knowledge of Chinese language or culture, his message of American old-time religion was warmly received, reportedly reaching tens of thousands and even converting twenty members of General Chiang Kai-shek's personal bodyguard.[1] But despite these impressive results, Pierce's trip to Asia would be most remembered for his brief encounter with a single little girl.

In Xiamen, Dutch Reformed missionary Tena Hoelkeboer invited Pierce to preach to four hundred girls at her school. When one of her students, White Jade, informed her father that she had converted to Christianity, he beat her and threw her out of the house. Hoelkeboer was distressed at the prospect of taking on yet another orphan and demanded of Pierce, "What are you going to do about it?" Deeply moved, Pierce emptied his wallet of the five dollars it contained and promised to send the same amount every month. When he returned to the United States to report on his evangelistic exploits, Pierce told the story of White Jade in churches across the United States. In 1950 he founded World Vision in order to sponsor more needy Asian children like her.

By the turn of the century, World Vision had become the largest privately funded relief and development NGO (nongovernmental organization) in the world, and White Jade's story continued to be used both in advertising and in recounting World Vision's history. Even at the time of this writing, White Jade remains central in defining World Vision's identity and approach for its employees and donors.[2]

Because of its deep rhetorical resonance and staying power, Pierce's encounter with White Jade and Hoelkeboer might possibly be the single point at which North American Evangelical Christians began to reprioritize compassion for the poor. This chapter tells the story of World Vision's crucial role in reversing the Great Reversal that had stunted Bible-believing missions for at least a generation. But before we can move forward, we must first consider the context that brought Bob Pierce to China in the summer of 1947.

The Evangelical Missions Surge

After the Second World War, mainline Protestant missions began to decline, and nondenominational "faith" missions linked to the fundamentalist movement moved to the fore. In addition, Evangelicals founded a wave of new missions agencies that helped to cement conservative dominance of Western Protestant missions efforts. Evangelicals' firsthand experience of the war contributed to this flurry of activity. Many men (and they were always men) who founded new agencies had been impacted by the needs they witnessed overseas as soldiers and, as a result, went to Bible school on the GI Bill. In many situations, the new agencies founded by these men were even able to buy American war matériel such as planes and jeeps for their newly sanctified purpose.[3] Fresh experience of war also influenced rhetoric, as leaders frequently used bellicose images to recruit "troops" for the missions surge. In addition, post–World War II geopolitical realities intensified zeal for missions. As communism spread and nationalism spawned more new nations resistant to missionary incursion, Evangelicals sensed that they must preach the gospel while they still had the chance. Throughout the United States, fresh missionary recruits responded to pleas calling for volunteers to go to far-flung destinations like "the Orient, a suspicious land that is fast closing its doors to the white man."[4]

The new Evangelical missions sector was not, at first glance, a likely candidate for the rediscovery of Evangelical social engagement. True to their fundamentalist roots, the vast majority of Evangelical missions devoted themselves overwhelmingly to proclamation evangelism. However, a few new Evangelical agencies went beyond their immediate predecessors by focusing on the needs of the poor. Three of these agencies became long-standing leaders in international ministries of compassion: World Relief, the Everett Swanson Evangelistic Association (later known as Compassion International), and World Vision. World Relief was founded first. In 1944, the NAE (National Association of Evangelicals) launched the War Relief Commission, a subsidiary dedicated to providing food and clothing aid to European civilians displaced by World War II. Along with a host of American civic groups and organizations, Evangelicals organized similar wartime efforts. After the war, the NAE sustained its work, renaming the War Relief Commission "World Relief" in 1950. Through the 1950s and early 1960s, its activity expanded modestly.[5]

By 1960 World Relief continued to devote its efforts to supporting war widows and orphans as well as to distributing food and
tracts.[6] In the early 1960s it extended its work to Taiwan, Vietnam,
and Egypt. Because World Relief was funded mostly through the
NAE, it did not take up extensive public advertising for fundraising
and therefore made a lesser impact on the American Evangelical
public at that time.

Compassion International's story strikingly parallels that of
World Vision. Compassion traces its roots to 1952 when a Swedish-
American traveling evangelist named Everett Swanson found his
way to Korea, where, according to his figures, thirty thousand
South Korean troops responded to his message of salvation. On
one early morning walk Swanson noticed sanitation workers gently
kicking small piles of rags that lay here and there on the sidewalk.
To his horror, Swanson soon realized that the piles of rags were
homeless children, and the sanitation workers were gathering the
bodies of those who had died overnight. When a missionary colleague asked him, "What do you intend to do about it?" Swanson
took the challenge as a divine calling. Two years later Swanson
initiated a sponsorship program that enabled Americans to provide
shelter, care, and Bible lessons to Korean orphans. As he promoted
the program during his evangelistic travels, the number of orphan
sponsors grew steadily. The tally jumped more quickly when, in
1959, Swanson began to publicize his work in national magazines
like *Reader's Digest*; by the following year ten thousand orphans
had been sponsored. In 1960 Swanson also undertook "Operation
Long Underwear," which provided six thousand children with
warm winter clothes. Inspired by Matthew 15:32,[7] the organization
was renamed Compassion, Inc. in 1963. Two years later, Swanson
passed away.[8] The fact that Swanson, a successful evangelist but
not a nationally recognized leader, could garner such a significant response by himself was indicative of stateside Evangelical
willingness to become involved with ministries of compassion if
given the opportunity.

The Rise of World Vision

Amidst all this energy and spiritual entrepreneurship, World Vision made a larger impact than all the rest put together. World Vision's origins were intimately linked with another prominent Evangelical parachurch organization. Youth for Christ sought to bring revival to young people through thousands of high-profile rallies across the United States in the 1940s and early 1950s. Its early leadership was a seedbed for many patriarchs of later twentieth-century Evangelicalism, including Bob Pierce. When Pierce first joined Youth for Christ in 1943, he had just dropped out of a small Nazarene college,[9] turned his back on ministry for a time, and struggled to make ends meet as pastor of a small Baptist church.[10] But as an itinerant evangelist in the Pacific Northwest, Pierce became a popular speaker and later a vice president of Youth for Christ. During that time he formed connections with people who later became key leaders and supporters of World Vision. Billy Graham, who also got his start through Youth for Christ, was World Vision's chairman of the board of trustees for several years in the 1950s.[11]

After Pierce met White Jade in China, he began to focus his ministry overseas, making frequent trips to Asia as Youth for Christ's missionary ambassador-at-large. In the spring of 1950, after conducting a major evangelistic campaign in Korea,[12] Pierce was convinced that the coming war would create massive suffering throughout the entire population. He sensed the Holy Spirit impelling him to create his own organization in order to respond full time to the physical and spiritual needs he had encountered.[13] In the fall of 1950, supported by a seed grant from Youth for Christ, Pierce founded World Vision, which was named after Youth for Christ's "World Vision Rallies." Pierce maintained his presence in Korea after the war broke out by procuring a war correspondent's credentials so that he could preach to soldiers. After seeing the excruciating wartime suffering wreaked on Seoul, he famously wrote on the flyleaf of his Bible, "Break my heart with the things that break the heart of God," a phrase that remains a World Vision watchword to this day. Pierce's early experiences in Asia formed a pattern that would shape World Vision under his watch.

Organizational theorists speak of a "charismatic founder" period in which an organization is almost completely shaped by the personality and character of its founder. That was certainly true of World Vision. While Bob Pierce was president (1950–66), the organization's ethos was indelibly marked by his boundless energy, spontaneous generosity, and personal shortcomings. Functionally, the organization marched to the beat of Pierce's restless travels in Asia. Following the same pattern he established during his early Youth for Christ forays, Pierce's ministry was a constant cycle of evangelistic rallies and visits to missionaries and national leaders. Moved by needs wherever he found them, he returned to the United States to raise funds for those he had promised to support. Pierce clearly viewed himself as a bridge between the American Evangelical public and the individual needs he encountered in Korea (and later in Taiwan, the Philippines, India, and Hong Kong). In his appeal letters and magazine articles Pierce frequently spoke of World Vision as "a missionary go-between,"[14] calling himself "your errand boy for Christ in Asia."[15] In a sense, he considered himself to be the essential link between the two and seemed to expect this arrangement to go on forever. He invited American Evangelicals into a personal relationship with the needy, which was mediated through himself, at least symbolically.

Pierce always remained an evangelist at heart, and he continued to preach frequently throughout his presidency at World Vision. For example, in 1959 World Vision organized and sponsored a widely publicized crusade in Osaka, Japan. Almost one hundred thousand people attended, and Pierce claimed more than 7,500 conversions. However, the main thrust of World Vision's work was not focused on new outreach or rallies but in supporting missions efforts already in progress. This is clearly reflected in Pierce's original vision statement, which serves as a prism revealing how early

World Vision worked. He defined his fledgling agency as follows: "World Vision is a missionary service organization meeting emergency needs in crisis areas of the world through existing evangelical agencies."[16] As a "missionary service organization," World Vision operated definitively within the advancing post–World War II Evangelical missions surge described above. From its inception, the cover of World Vision's eponymous magazine read, "Published in the interest of World Evangelism," and throughout its pages the words "missions" and "missionary" appeared frequently.[17] World Vision's admiration of the direction of existing Evangelical missions is also illustrated by the fact that, during a time when many new organizations were sprouting, World Vision positioned itself as an agency advancing the cause of missions "through existing evangelical agencies." Pierce was adamant about not introducing another competing organization with a new angle; he was in full support of the work already in progress.

Bob Pierce's Heroines

Thus far, World Vision has been portrayed as a significant but relatively unexceptional participant in the Evangelical missions advance. But what distinguished the organization was Pierce's strong emphasis on the social aspects of the ministries he supported. The heart of World Vision's work was not in planned events (such as crusades) but in "emergency needs in crisis areas," as Pierce put it in his vision statement. The majority of World Vision's funding and discourse was invested in "Christian social welfare and emergency aid," as stated in the organization's basic objectives.[18] World Vision aimed to respond to acute situations rather than, for example, planning sustained intervention to fight chronically recurring poverty. Influenced by the context of the Korean War and perhaps the example of the Marshall Plan, World Vision saw its role not as providing long-term support that would create systematic change but as a temporary gap-filler in unanticipated emergencies. Pierce directed World Vision's financial support through two main channels: "the needy National and the unsung missionary hero."[19]

Pierce's primary means of meeting needs was to visit personally. As he uncovered ministries of mercy carried out by nationals and missionaries, he rushed to the rescue, aiming to stabilize funding and "scale up" their work by generating donations through lavish stateside publicity. Pierce did not have to look far to find emergencies to alleviate. He encountered faith missionaries whose financial support was spotty, overextending themselves to take in orphans or nurse the sick. He met conservative denominational missionaries who assuaged suffering "on the side" without direct mission board support for that aspect of their ministry.

One of the first missionaries Pierce met was fellow Californian Beth Albert, who ran a home for lepers through the China Inland Mission, a prominent faith mission. Although Albert's stated purpose was evangelism, she spent most of her time treating leprosy, teaching brickmaking as a vocational skill, and caring for the orphans she had taken in. Deeply moved by Albert's lifestyle, Pierce wrote in *Youth for Christ Magazine*, "Work among lepers is a thing of joy. Beth Albert is no weird ascetic. She didn't flee to China in order to escape the eyes of Occidental civilization. Beth Albert is a normal, enthusiastic American girl. . . . Beth Albert loves the lepers because she has found the will of God for her life."[20] Pierce then went on to exhort Western young people to perhaps "find the will of God for their life" by going to work with lepers. This article, with its accompanying graphic pictures of leprosy's grotesque ravages, surely stood out, appearing in a magazine that catered to carefree young people seeking a style of Christianity congruent with their interest in patriotism, wholesome dating, and popular music.

In Japan, Pierce encountered Irishwoman Irene Webster-Smith, who ministered to young girls in prostitution; she lost her funding with the Japan Evangelistic Band when she started an orphanage. Pierce later lionized her in his best-selling 1959 travelogue, *Let My Heart Be Broken*. In Taiwan, he found an important ally in Lillian Dickson of the Canadian Presbyterian Church. Dickson doctored, trained, evangelized, and educated the shunned aborigines living in the remote highlands. Her denomination looked askance at her "extracurricular" works of mercy, as though such vigor from a missionary wife was out of place.[21] But Pierce described her to his American audience in almost hagiographical terms as the "valiant missionary-saint of Formosa whose compassion for the souls of lepers, babies, orphans, prisoners, and mountain tribes has added many more names to the Lamb's Book of Life."[22] For more than ten years she appeared as a frequently publicized heroine in World Vision material.

Pierce never lost an opportunity to affirm virtuous missionary self-sacrifice and often cited the committed spiritual fervor of those he supported in order to motivate further donations. For example, when Pierce met the famed Gladys Aylward,[23] who ran a children's home in a remote corner of China, he asked, "Why are you—a single woman, far from home—why are you here in this remote region of China?" She replied, "Because you aren't."[24] After telling an inspiring story of a Korean Christian woman who gave the $1,500 she received as compensation for her son's death to aid World Vision orphans, Pierce exclaimed, "God could trust the Christians of Korea with the test of martyrdom, because they have perhaps the strongest spiritual structure of any church in the world."[25] While these heroic portraits of missionaries and national Christians were typical, the way in which Pierce highlighted their practical ministry to the poor served to validate it in the eyes of the American Evangelical public.

It is important to notice that all of the aforementioned examples are not of heroes but heroines, which reflects, in part, the greater proportion of women on the mission field. But the preponderance of World Vision collaborators was greater still: more than 80 percent of the missionaries that Pierce publicized in early World Vision letters and periodicals were female. The fact that ministries such as those of Lillian Dickson, Beth Albert, and Tena Hoelkeboer were the dominant force drawing Evangelicalism back toward supporting missions to the poor suggests that the Great Reversal was much stronger among male theorizers than female practitioners. This observation parallels mission historian Dana Robert's findings in her analysis of nineteenth-century missions: while often men dominated the discourse and formal theology, women enacted countertheories born of their relationships and the exigencies of daily life in the field. As Robert summarizes: "Women missionaries in practice usually rejected mission theories that called for radical separation of the spiritual and the physical. . . . In conservative theological circles . . . women excelled in founding and sustaining 'ministries of compassion' such as orphanages, clinics, and schools for the poor."[26] Perhaps one of Pierce's main contributions was his promotion of such female-led efforts that were common in practice but had been marginalized from the "official policy" of the male-dominated agencies.[27]

Ironically, if this were the case, Pierce seemed unaware of it. One of the few times he addressed gender dynamics was to plead for more male missionaries. As he wrote in an article on promoting missions in Sunday schools, "Remind the boys in your Sunday School that men can be missionaries too! Perhaps our failure to do this is one reason for the all-too-prevalent male response to the missionary call: 'Here am I, Lord—send my sister!'"[28]

Ministries of Compassion

World Vision's support of "emergency needs" was as vast as the ministries that Bob Pierce encountered, including widows' homes, a hospital, and leprosaria. Leprosy, in particular, frequently drew the attention of conservative missionaries, due to the grotesque suffering of the disease and its prominent mention in the Gospels. Pierce met needs in a seemingly ad hoc way, as he was so moved. In his 1965 film *The Least Ones*, Pierce narrates the story of a Korean man who had lost his livelihood as a bird catcher when his net wore out. World Vision loaned him the funds for a new net, which he dutifully paid back at a rate of a few cents each month. In the age of YouTube, many years later, World Vision placed the video clip on the internet, claiming the incident as the origin of its microfinance work—yet another major program with roots in a serendipitous, spontaneous meeting with Bob Pierce.[29]

But the needs of orphans moved Pierce most deeply, and this ministry came to define World Vision. Pierce found that his experience with White Jade was not at all uncommon; missionaries and national Christians frequently and often without fanfare found ways to take in orphans, especially in the wake of the Korean War. At first, World Vision set about vigorously building, funding, and expanding orphanages in Korea, but by 1965 they were operating in more than twenty countries. In order to more effectively raise funds, Pierce instituted a sponsorship mechanism in 1953,[30] and the reported number of orphans supported grew from about two thousand in 1954 to more than twenty thousand in 1965.[31] It is not surprising that Pierce was drawn primarily to orphans, since evangelical work among the poor often focuses on needy children. As a biblical people, evangelicals have always been especially sensitive to the needs of orphans, whose plight is repeatedly remembered throughout the Bible.[32] For example, the magisterial historian of early evangelicalism W. R. Ward playfully but insightfully suggested that eighteenth-century evangelicals could be essentially defined as "those who felt spiritually bound to create Orphan Houses."[33] Focusing on children sidestepped a traditional Evangelical impediment to caring for the poor, that is, the strong value they placed on individual responsibility. Perhaps one could ignore a poor man's poverty as being his own fault through laziness or intemperance, but a child's innocence spoke volumes.

During its early years, World Vision films, fundraising letters, and periodicals painted a stark picture of raw, physical needs that emphasized intense or grotesque suffering caused by leprosy and starvation. When Pierce encountered poverty in Asia, it was those who suffered pitiably in public that most struck him (he was initially there to preach, not to seek out the hidden poor), and these were the people he determined to bring to the attention of American Christians back home. To a shocked audience of American teenagers Pierce's traveling companion wrote, "You can find a man or woman or child dying on those streets [of Kunming, China] just about any day you choose. . . . One man, whose face was full of sores, looked at us with warm eyes; he cannot smile. . . . Arms and legs completely gone, the poor chap rolled in the dust, crying for alms as he churned slowly on his way."[34]

Along with physical suffering, Pierce did not spare his audience the emotional distress of those he met in Asia. For example, one appeal letter included a photo of an emaciated orphan child with the following description: "Perhaps even more heartbreaking than his obvious physical need was the fact that this little fellow apparently had been taught—the hard way—never to cry aloud. He had begun to cry, and our hearts ached as we saw his pathetic little body wracked with awful, silent sobs. We took his thin little hand to comfort him, and found it felt more like the claw of a bird than the hand of a child. I confess that we focused through our tears as we took his picture."[35]

Most nongovernmental agencies (NGOs), including World Vision, would later condemn this graphic approach as exploitative, even labeling it as "poverty porn." However, in analyzing its early material one does not get the sense that World Vision was seeking out the worst cases in order to maximize revenue, but rather that Pierce—an intensely emotional man—simply wrote about what moved him.[36]

In describing the physical needs of victims, World Vision rarely considered their suffering in the aggregate or poverty as a broader phenomenon. Rather, it focused overwhelmingly on individuals—usually individuals personally encountered by Pierce himself. The face-to-face encounters that had so provoked Pierce during his Youth for Christ days provided the touchstone for World Vision's discourse during its early period. Ten years after meeting White Jade, Pierce wrote in an appeal to potential sponsors, "I could have turned down an orphanage as being too big. But I couldn't refuse one orphan."[37] Indeed, Pierce's act of compassion that day—sponsoring an individual child—continued to be the central means through which World Vision sought to involve Americans in mission to the poor.

World Vision's individualistic ethos under Pierce precluded any serious or systematic study of the structures that caused world poverty. Despite its growing income and impact, the organization essentially existed in order to offer as many Americans as possible the same opportunity Pierce had to make a difference in the life of one needy child.[38] Consideration of World Vision's individualistic bent gives further insight into its preoccupation with orphans and lepers. Cut off from the ties of family and society through death or disease, they were—tragically—the quintessential individuals within their societies. Involvement in their lives did not require complex interactions with the intricacies of Asian cultures but only compassionate attention to their considerable personal needs. In fact, during the 1950s it was difficult to even promote concern for poor children who had parents. As one popular history of World Vision puts it, "Sponsors wanted an orphan. If the child had a mother, North American sponsors reasoned, 'let her go to work.'"[39]

World Vision's emphasis on the most vulnerable was sharpened by describing them in scriptural terms. One passage used in this regard, Matthew 25:31–46, is perhaps the single most quoted biblical text in World Vision's discourse. In it, Jesus as judge of all humanity surveys the hungry, the thirsty, the naked, the refugees, and the prisoners, pronouncing that "whatever you did for one of the least of these brothers and sisters of mine, you did for me" (Matt.

25:40). This striking passage, which has always been important in Catholic social ethics but had been de-emphasized among conservative Protestants (perhaps because it seemed to imply salvation by works), inspired the title and theme for one of Pierce's films, *The Least Ones*.[40] Pierce was paraphrasing this passage when he constantly referred to the poor as "the little ones of the earth."

In response to the urgent physical and spiritual needs of poor individuals, World Vision called for compassionate action. Once again, this call was modeled on Pierce's personal response to the poverty he had encountered. Near the end of his life, Pierce singled out his emotional response to poverty as the key to World Vision's impact: "I became part of the suffering. I literally felt the child's blindness, the mother's grief. And there was no way that I could walk among the lepers and not feel as lonely, as cut off, as abandoned, as brokenhearted, as debased and humiliated as they were; I wept over the poor little orphan children."[41] Pierce characterized Asian unaccompanied minors in sentimental terms as "mercy's children" or "lovable little darlings."[42] World Vision often prominently placed in its material photographs of Pierce embracing "rescued" children, a motif also employed by a host of Evangelical "relief and development" organizations in later years.[43] Thus the emotionally driven compassionate paternalism of Pierce's experience was writ large in its calls to action directed at the American Evangelical public.

World Vision's basic, central request was for donors to sponsor a needy individual. In so doing World Vision emphasized that potential donors were entering into a relationship with an orphan across the world—a striking possibility in a world without internet or real-time cable news updates. As readers perused an advertisement for World Vision in a magazine, for example, they would not be asked to think about issues like war or land reform or injustice but rather to consider "a little girl named Ban Sun Sook, [who] has found happiness in Yo Kwang Children's home—happiness that can continue with your help."[44] World Vision offered sponsors the chance not just to do the right thing or to obey some ethical mandate but to begin an intimate familial relationship: "You can become his (or her) 'Mother' or 'Dad' . . . and have his picture and letters to warm your heart."[45] World Vision's appeals during this era were literally paternalistic.

This emphasis on adoption, belonging, and emotional connection was far and away the most frequent portrayal of the appropriate American response to global poverty, especially in single-page magazine advertisements and mass mail appeals. World Vision frequently used letters that orphans wrote to sponsors (with the careful coaching of staff) to demonstrate the possibility of emotional connection and to supply concrete evidence that one's investment was paying off. The following is a typical example: "Dear My sponsor: I was very glad when I heard that you always love me very much, and thank to God that he gave me good sponsor, who is living very far place across the ocean. My hope is to work for Christ, to devote all my life for Him. Kim Sung Tai."[46]

As part of the paternalistic relationship, World Vision offered Americans the opportunity to meet an Asian child's emotional needs as well as provide food, shelter, education, and spiritual nurture. For example, one brochure featured a Korean toddler reaching out her hand toward the reader with a caption in all caps and a large font, "I WANT TO BELONG TO YOU."[47] American benefactors were promised that their hearts would "be touched by words like these, from a typical letter received by a sponsor: 'tears of thankfulness poured from my eyes when I could have a precious mother who will pray for me.'"[48] Even when World Vision referred to the vast numbers of orphans it supported, it employed the language of family relationship: "Come home to our precious family of nearly thirteen thousand Korean orphans."[49]

World Vision did not hesitate to use guilt as well. Pierce's style was often direct and confrontational in this regard. For example, as he filmed a group of female missionaries on a visit to China in 1949, he turned to the camera and challenged his American audience: "Think of it . . . four white haired old women serving five hundred blind children. What are you doing, buddy? . . . They who have so little sacrificed so much while we who have so much sacrifice so little. . . . What you probably spend on food for a single day can care for a leper for a whole month."[50] Pierce had little patience with those who felt paralyzed by the great needs of the world. He was fond of saying, "Don't do nothing just because you can't do everything."[51] References to the epistle of James often accompanied this sort of exhortation, with its theme that faith must express itself through action. A typical challenge reads, "Today we too must be 'doers of the word' who illuminate the Gospel in such a way that people will have to listen to what we say."[52]

Some of World Vision's most effective communication did not involve any cajoling from Pierce at all but was designed simply to let the words of Scripture directly impact or "convict" the reader. This communication strategy simply placed a biblical text in close visual proximity to a contemporary scene of pitiable suffering. One particularly striking example of this oft-used rhetorical approach utilizes a full-page black-and-white photograph of a thin, sickly boy in a bed; he has a broken arm and is attached to an IV. Superimposed on the photograph above the boy's head is a quotation from Isaiah 58:10 and 12, which reads, in part, "And if thou draw out thy soul to the hungry and satisfy the afflicted soul, then shall thy light rise in obscurity and thy darkness be as the noon day. . . . Thou shalt be called the Repairer of the breach, the Restorer of paths to dwell in."[53] No other words besides the Scripture appear; the challenge to the reader needs no other commentary.

World Vision made a significant impact on the Evangelical worldview because it went beyond merely arguing that concern for the poor should be part of mission in a generalized sense. It effectively convinced individuals that by sending money to World Vision one could in fact *act* as a missionary, although at one remove. Pierce explains in an appeal letter: "Did the Lord say 'heal the sick' to you? No doubt your first reaction is 'no, I'm not a doctor. Neither do I have the gift of healing.' But the Lord did say 'heal the sick' to his disciples, and as His disciples, you and I have a responsibility to the sick. You can fulfill part of your responsibility through World Vision."[54] Using a different biblical theme, Pierce similarly pleads, "Consider Bob Pierce as your emissary representing you as a Good Samaritan giving help to beaten, down-trodden naked homeless humanity."[55] These examples demonstrate that, for donors, giving money was a deeply significant, personal way of being directly involved in compassionate charity. World Vision defined its relationship with donors as involving them in mission— by giving to World Vision, donors could "go overseas by proxy."[56]

In sum, Pierce's compassionate vision for helpless individuals helped to reawaken North American middle-class Evangelicals to the suffering in the broader world outside the shiny new suburbs of the 1950s. This was a monumental achievement, given the prophetic challenge Pierce brought into the churches through his films, radio shows, letters, and speaking tours. Pierce was so successful in part because his vision remained circumscribed by the limitations of the fundamentalist worldview he shared with his audience. Pierce proved unable to grasp the possibility of structural injustice as a primary cause for chronic poverty, except for the pernicious effects of "heathen religion" that, in his view, consigned entire societies to penury. Always patriotic and virulently anti-communist, Pierce failed to understand the ways in which American or European colonial power was complicit in the poverty he saw in nations like Vietnam or India. He viewed American technological and political might as an unvarnished good that only needed to be shared, not critiqued.

World Vision, the Sequel: Samaritan's Purse

So far, this chapter has told the story of how Bob Pierce's World Vision both sparked newfound compassion for the poor and significantly shaped Evangelicals' perception of the poor. In the 1950s and 1960s, Pierce's advocacy was indeed revolutionary among conservative Protestants. But as the twentieth century wore on, many Americans concerned about global poverty became more sophisticated in their understanding of the structural causes of poverty and the long-term solutions necessary to effectively fight it. World Vision itself became a leader in these developments—a story we tell in chapter 4.

Yet in our judgment, most Evangelical agencies that have sprung up in recent years continue to approach the complex realities of poverty through the simplistic lens of extending emergency relief to individuals. "Compassion" remains the default mode for Evangelicals who become aware of poverty and move to act. Although it is impossible to survey or even list all of the Evangelical organizations, missions, churches, and ministries who limit their focus to individualized compassion, we close this chapter with a brief survey of the largest and most influential organization that (quite literally in this case) followed in Bob Pierce's footsteps.

In 1967 Bob Pierce resigned the presidency of World Vision. Tension mounted with the board as Pierce proved unable to adapt his personal, spontaneous approach to the needs of a growing, increasingly professionalized organization. Graeme Irvine, a later president of World Vision International, summarizes his view of this tumultuous time: "By the middle of its second decade, World Vision was in trouble. . . . Without Bob Pierce World Vision would probably not have been born. It is equally true, in my opinion, that with him it probably would not have survived."[57]

After leaving World Vision, Pierce was still eager to serve. Like a true entrepreneur, he simply began anew. In 1969, Pierce took leadership of a small, moribund missions agency, renamed it Samaritan's Purse, adopted the same vision statement he had used at World Vision, and continued to disburse emergency aid to missionaries scattered around the globe. More than anything, Samaritan's Purse was an attempt to recreate the World Vision of the 1950s. Pierce rejected the growing professionalism of the 1970s

World Vision as unspiritual: "Nothing is a miracle until it reaches the area where the utmost that human effort can do is not enough and God moves in to fill that space between what is possible and *what He wants done that is impossible*—that is 'God Room.' . . . Without that miracle quality, you can get your life and business down to where you don't need God. You can operate exactly like Sears & Roebuck or General Motors or IBM—but the blessings will all be gone."[58] Even though Pierce reaffirmed his time-honored principle of individual charity motivated by spontaneous compassion, by this time those efforts had the feel of an older man trying to hold on to a time that had passed him by.

Under Pierce, Samaritan's Purse failed to gain the degree of influence that World Vision had. The budget never topped $100,000 annually, and their biggest grant was only $1,000.[59] Pierce's vision might have died with him, the relic of a pioneer period in Evangelical concern for the poor that had since developed in new directions, but he was able to pass on his particular vision to the next generation of leadership—remarkably, to the son of his generation's most influential evangelist.

Franklin Graham was a stereotypically rebellious preacher's son until, at the age of twenty-two, he threw out his cigarettes, gave up his scotch, and returned to the faith of his famous father, Billy Graham. About a month later, in the summer of 1974, he met Bob Pierce, his father's old Youth for Christ associate. Pierce, knowing Franklin's love of piloting small aircraft, invited him on a two-month tour of remote mission sites in Indonesia, China, and India. Pierce's adventurous approach to missions was immediately appealing to the young man with a penchant for thrill-seeking. For the next three years Pierce mentored Graham and groomed him as his successor. As Graham later said, "Next to my own father, Bob Pierce has most influenced me and set the course of my life."[60]

Like Pierce, Graham rejected the movement toward long-term development projects and pursued an organizational strategy that can only be described as missionary adventuring. Graham parachuted fearlessly into conflict zones like Lebanon, Haiti, and Ethiopia, exuding enthusiastically about his unique muscular Christianity on behalf of the poor: "There's no excitement and thrill like the complexities of war. It heightens perceptions. The smell of gunpowder. The sound of shrapnel hitting a building. . . . War satisfies my need for danger. . . . I love to go places where bombs blow up."[61]

In the initial years of Graham's leadership, Samaritan's Purse primarily specialized in distributing relief supplies in war zones. In its public communication, the organization highlighted the swashbuckling exploits and heroism of Graham even more than the needs of the poor themselves. Graham portrayed his interventions as thrilling and personally fulfilling: "I turned my desire for excitement to good works. I'd go to wars to help people. I got it both ways. People praised me, and I had fun doing it. I do everything I want to do. People think if you give your life to Christ it's a dull life. But . . . I fly planes, shoot guns, go to wars. When I die I'll go immediately to the presence of God, and yet in life I had a blast."[62] For Graham, the needs of war victims were often subjugated to his desire to portray faithful Christian service as manly and exciting. Despite Graham's admiration for his mentor, this approach diverged sharply from Pierce's efforts to publicize not his own heroism but that of unsung and unknown female missionaries.

Besides war relief, Samaritan's Purse pursued a wide variety of projects in the 1980s, including funding a health clinic, distributing clothing to itinerant evangelists, and plotting an improbable (and unrealized) scheme for resettling Hmong refugees at the Guyanese compound that had been the site of Jim Jones's Peoples Temple massacre.[63] Each endeavor was undertaken with the same spontaneous faith Graham had learned from Pierce. Franklin Graham firmly identified Samaritan's Purse as a "missionary" organization: "We are not just a Christian relief organization. We are an evangelistic organization that takes the Gospel to the ditches and gutters."[64]

Providence continued to guide the spontaneous acts of faith that guided Graham to intervene in disaster situations. A skeptically minded reader of Samaritan's Purse's annual ministry reports might conclude that the organization's involvements were randomly scattered around the world, with an emphasis on war zones. But for Graham, each opportunity to provide emergency aid was the result of divine appointment. For example, when a top general from the CIA-funded Nicaraguan Contras called asking Samaritan's Purse to aid his troops, Graham was reluctant: "I had heard both sides of the issue, but I didn't know what to believe. . . . I had been glad not to be involved."[65] But Graham told God that if God would send a Spanish-speaking evangelist, Samaritan's Purse would send the aid. Upon visiting Central America, Graham met Ruben Guerrero from Dallas, Texas, who was in Honduras seeking to evangelize the Contras. Graham exulted, "God had answered my fleece with what I felt was a firm 'yes' that we should be involved. And the fleece now had a name—'Brother Ruben.'"[66] Graham's experience of guidance led Samaritan's Purse to send extensive material support for the Contras and to train an Evangelical chaplain corps for the army: thus did Samaritan's Purse provide spiritual backing for the Reagan administration's covert operations in Nicaragua.

Buoyed by a timely appearance on Jim and Tammy Bakker's PTL Club[67] and the Graham family name, Samaritan's Purse rapidly began to increase its funding base. Between 1978 and 1995 Franklin built the tiny organization into a $32 million-a-year operation. The new millennium brought more boom times, and the organization reached $200 million in donations in 2004.[68] By the turn of the twenty-first century, Samaritan's Purse had vaulted into second place (after World Vision) among the largest Evangelical poverty relief organizations. In some ways, Samaritan's Purse changed with the times. Franklin Graham completed an MBA at Appalachian State University,[69] and the organization professionalized its accounting standards and logistical operations for distributing clothes, food, and emergency shelter. Samaritan's Purse broadened its reach by offering abstinence-focused curriculum on HIV/AIDS to pastors in the Global South; it sent hundreds of American doctors on short-term mission trips and annually flew a handful of children with rare heart conditions to the United States for surgery, an effort called the Children's Heart Project.[70]

On the whole, however, Samaritan's Purse retained many of the organizational distinctives that Pierce bequeathed it. More than ever, it was an organization totally dependent on the charismatic persona of its president. Much of the notoriety Samaritan's Purse achieved was due to the Graham family name, and the organization eagerly exploited it. Franklin Graham *was* Samaritan's Purse. His name was prominently displayed on all its communication, and ministry reports looked like a photo essay for a Graham travelogue.

Yet he was a polarizing figure. For his supporters, Graham was a worthy heir to his father's throne. Franklin picked up where his father had left off as a chaplain of American civil religion, delivering the benediction for the 1996 and 2000 Republican national conventions and for George W. Bush's inaugural address in 2001. He began to embrace crusade preaching, devoting 10 percent of his time to evangelism and finally ascending to leadership in the Billy Graham Evangelistic Association—a reversal of Billy Graham's previous decision that his son would not succeed him. But to Franklin Graham's detractors, he was a magnet for controversy. During the first Gulf War, he earned General Norman Schwarzkopf's public rebuke for sending tracts into staunchly Muslim Saudi Arabia. In the wake of the September 11 attacks, he stirred up a firestorm of protest by calling Islam "a very wicked and evil religion" on national television,[71] and has continued to escalate his anti-Muslim rhetoric, even calling for a total ban on Muslim immigration to the United States.[72] Because of his aggressive stances on evangelism, he received criticism from the media for receiving United States Agency for International Development (USAID) grants and was denounced by Catholics in El Salvador who claimed they were pressured into attending Protestant services in order to receive earthquake relief.

When Graham is not making headlines, Samaritan's Purse has given priority to exporting around the world a potent mix of evangelism and consumer goods through its headline ministry, Operation Christmas Child. Every December since 1993, volunteers from across the United States have packed shoeboxes full of small gifts like candy, school supplies, mittens, and a gospel tract. Samaritan's Purse then distributes the boxes to poor children around the world—thousands of the boxes at the beginning of the ministry, with annual numbers rising to four million in 2000 and over ten million in 2014. Samaritan's Purse proudly reports that three US presidents have packed a shoebox.[73] For the last twenty years Samaritan's Purse has devoted the majority of its funding to this single annual dose of holiday charity.

The fundraising material Samaritan's Purse uses for Operation Christmas Child follows a simple, two-step formula. First, it relates a story of how shoeboxes packed by rich Westerners have providentially provided for an individual's urgent needs. Second, it tells how compassionate charity sparks Christian conversion. The formula is exemplified in Graham's small children's book *Miracle in a Shoebox*, which tells the story of a war-weary Bosnian Muslim family in the 1990s. On Christmas Eve, when the father sees a Samaritan's Purse truck full of gifts, "he felt hopeful for the first time in months" and recalled "the prayer he had prayed late one night in prison: God, if you're out there, show me you care." The family collects its Samaritan's Purse shoeboxes, and each of them finds that the gifts are exactly what they had wanted—a doll for the daughter in her favorite color dress (she had "dropped hers in the street as they ran from a sniper's bullets") and a scarf that "fits just right" for the son. Finally, the tracts packed by Samaritan's Purse do their work: Christmas Day breaks as the family bows their heads in prayer to Jesus for the first time. The father reflects, "Our friends in America have shown us they care by sending these wonderful gifts. But God has given us the greatest gift of all: his Son . . . tonight we will put our faith in him."[74] Providentially guided compassion, "warming the hearts of children,"[75] makes these shoeboxes sources of spiritual connection rather than simply a matter of material exchange.

These rhetorical framings of the problems of and solutions to poverty illustrate how Franklin Graham has translated Pierce's emphasis on compassion for individuals into one of the most popular means for American Evangelicals to relate to the global poor. The fact that packing a shoebox at Christmas time has become a holiday ritual for millions of families shows that singular acts of compassion for individuals remains the primary lens used by many Evangelicals to understand and do justice.

The Power of Personal Relationship

As I (Gary) reflect on the story of Bob Pierce, I am struck first of all by how much his whole life's work was driven by experiences with individuals. From his initial encounter with White Jade to the heroic female missionaries he lauded and the scores of "the least of these" he traveled tirelessly to meet in person, Pierce was a man of personal relationship. In this way he is a perfect fit for the Evangelical tradition he helped to shape. Scholars often comment that American Evangelicals have created one of the most individualistic subcultures on the planet. According to these scholars, "society" has very little substance in the Evangelical mind-set: society is merely what you get when you add up all the individuals who belong to it. Consequently, social structures are nothing more than the sum of their parts.

Nevertheless, Evangelicals do *not* think individuals are meant for isolation or autonomy. Individual human beings exist for relationships, and the most important decisions an individual makes are relational. Most importantly, the Evangelical view of God is essentially and deeply relational. When preachers invite people to come to faith, they offer them "a personal relationship with Jesus." As a high school student, I may have been disgusted with religion, but I was hungry for the love of God. I was deeply moved when I heard in an Evangelical youth group that "even if you were the only person on earth, Christ still would have died for you."

This emphasis on personal relationships extends to how Evangelicals hope to change the world. In one of the most insightful reflections on Evangelicalism I have read, Christian Smith describes the tradition's undying commitment to what he calls "the personal influence strategy."[76] The basic idea, according to Smith, is that the key to changing the world is simply to impact people's hearts one at a time through personal relationships with them. As someone who became an Evangelical at the age of sixteen, I was a full-grown adult before I even knew that any other theories of social change existed.

When Bob Pierce set about reversing the Great Reversal, it is no surprise that he instinctively used the language of personal relationship. It was not reading the Bible privately or reflecting on ethics in a seminary class or hearing economic analysis of Third World poverty that led him to re-call Evangelicals to biblical compassion—it was meeting White Jade. Similarly, the fundamentalist missionary women who were dedicating themselves so fervently to serving the physical needs of the poor were doing so not because their theology directed them to do so but because they had a personal encounter with those lepers and orphans. Perhaps much of the strong fundamentalist rhetoric that sidelined justice concerns as a distraction from God's mission was less influential in actual practice. According to Chuck Van Engen, "Missionaries found that as they fell in love with the people to whom they had been sent, they yearned to help them in any way they could and ended up bringing education, medicine, agriculture, translation, and other things. . . . On the mission field many . . . found themselves far more socio-economically and politically active than they would have considered being in North America."[77] Personal relationship was trumping theology.

Pierce's recovery of justice through compassionate personal relationships is inspiring and helpful in many ways. It prevents us from ever forgetting the ultimate value of individuals. Doing justice means loving flesh-and-blood people, not abstract concepts such as "the poor" or "the oppressed." Those who have been touched by Pierce's personalism avoid reducing people to mere statistics. The power of compassionate personal relationship also protects us from turning justice into merely a cause that we "like" on Facebook.

However, when the personal influence strategy is the only tool in one's justice toolbox, the results can be troubling. Pierce's individualism never allowed him to perceive widespread, chronic injustices—only individuals with emergencies like leprosy or the loss of parents. It is hard to imagine Pierce having anything constructive to say about sexism, racism, or colonialism. If he could have seen those realities, I think he would have sided with the oppressed. But his vision was limited by an individualistic lens that simply screened them out.

Perhaps the greatest shortcoming of individualistic compassion can be seen in the popularity of Operation Christmas Child. Obviously, distributing millions of gift boxes produces happy moments and exposes some children to Christian faith for the first time—an infinitely good thing! Nevertheless, development practitioners of all kinds are nearly unanimous in their critique of such giveaway campaigns.[78] While this is not the place to rehash those evaluations, I am concerned that reducing the encounter between rich and poor to a single, sentimental moment can seriously distort our perception of what it means to do justice.

At their best, individual personal encounters with those who are poor lead to a deeper understanding of the oppressive social structures that make poverty intractable. But by framing poverty in such simplistic and sentimental terms, programs for mass-produced holiday handouts may actually make it *harder* to see the complexities of poverty. If the hopelessness of destitution can be solved simply by trusting God to providentially guide just the right toy into a child's hands, there is less urgent need to engage the bewildering issues of chronic hunger, disease, illiteracy, and political oppression.

Such an approach sends the message that fighting poverty is not just an easy fix, but a quick one too. When Pierce's heart was broken by meeting individuals in need, he extended charity to them by finding sponsors and long-term solutions to struggles. But by making Operation Christmas Child its flagship ministry, Samaritan's Purse has reduced Pierce's enduring commitments to individuals to a single, fleeting moment of ripping open a shoebox. By providing a one-time dose of Western consumerism, suburban Evangelicals may feel satisfied that they have now helped the disadvantaged and may believe that they have indeed done what justice requires.

But for the generation of World Vision's leadership that followed Bob Pierce, his call for compassion was not an excuse to be satisfied with charity, but rather an invitation to explore other ways of doing justice that better address the tangles of oppression. And that is the next chapter in our story.

PART 2

Justice Is Public and Prophetic

3

World Vision
and the Work
of Prophetic Advocacy

One July morning in 1988, the Slum Clearance Board of Madras, India, rounded up six thousand low-caste homeless people and forcibly "relocated" them to an inaccessible flood plain on the outskirts of the city with no housing, infrastructure, or government services of any kind. Fortunately, Saeed Rallia-Ram, executive director of World Vision India, had set up a community organizing project called Organizing People for Progress (OPP) the year before.[1] As a result, when local Indian World Vision employees began to investigate the people's plight, they were ready to respond. After consulting with Robert Linthicum of World Vision International's Office of Urban Advance, OPP followed traditional community organizing principles by first listening extensively to the concerns of the community and then challenging chosen leaders within the community to take specific action to solve their problems. The women of the community were especially responsive. Over five hundred mothers flooded the local government official's office and refused to leave until he promised to provide services. After the youth of the community "sat in" on major highways to block traffic, the government agreed to build homes that each family could legally purchase in affordable installments. Further pressure tactics achieved water access, paved roads, sanitation, bus service, and even a park and library—an astronomical achievement for a group of low-caste homeless people. While the total cost to the government was $1.5 million, World Vision paid only $25,000 to its organizers for its catalytic part in the triumph.

Just as White Jade symbolized the most typical Evangelical response to global poverty (see chap. 2), OPP's decisive actions in Madras represent a strikingly different approach, which began growing in influence among Evangelicals in the late 1970s. Once again, World Vision was the pacesetter. Despite its continued commitment to relief work and its effective use of individualized compassion in marketing, World Vision began to focus on long-term development and political advocacy on behalf of the oppressed and marginalized. Such initiatives required a much more sophisticated understanding of the interlocking political, economic, cultural, and spiritual structures that perpetuated poverty and demanded holistic responses that took into account not only the needs but also the strengths of the poor. One could almost characterize these changes as a fundamental shift in worldview. This chapter tells the story of that shift—from individual compassion to prophetic justice.

The Evolution of World Vision

From the mid-1970s to the mid-2000s, World Vision underwent tremendous organizational change. During the waning years of Pierce's presidency, World Vision's involvement was already beginning to shift away from Korea[2] (which was in the midst of a rapid economic ascent) and toward Southeast Asia. This process accelerated until, by 1974, one-third of all World Vision's work was in Vietnam, Cambodia, and, to a lesser extent, Laos.[3] But as World Vision staff fled ahead of the Communist governments taking hold of the former Indochina, nearly thirty thousand sponsors lost touch with their sponsored children.[4] Just as a huge portion of ministry investment vanished overnight, World Vision's revenue skyrocketed, so the organization immediately searched out new venues for service. They found them in Latin America, South Asia, and Africa.[5] The children sponsored in these regions tended to be street children, victims of famine, and dwellers in urban slums—all carrying with them complexities different from that of war orphans. By the twenty-first century World Vision had truly lived up to its name; the scope of its service grew from forty countries in 1979 to one hundred in 2003.[6] In 1978 World Vision reflected its global reach in a new internationalized corporate structure, becoming a confederation of national entities instead of an organization run from the United States.

After nearly a decade of successful fundraising through cutting-edge TV telethons, World Vision's gross income topped $65 million in 1980.[7] But its financial expansion was just beginning. By 2005, the US branch of World Vision received more than three-quarters of a billion dollars annually in contributions—more than the total income of the next five largest Evangelical poverty-oriented organizations combined.[8] It began to proudly claim that it was "the largest privately funded relief-and-development agency in the world."[9]

In order to lead what was now a significant multinational corporation, World Vision chose leaders with different skill sets to guide them through this season of dramatic growth and change. Stanley Mooneyham, who succeeded Bob Pierce in 1969, was a man whose gifts were in many ways similar to his forerunner's. Ordained as a Baptist minister, he rose through the Evangelical ranks as a successful denominational leader, evangelist, and missions organizer for the Billy Graham Evangelistic Association. Mooneyham was first and foremost an evangelist; as president of World Vision he emulated Pierce's practice of leading large evangelistic crusades in far-flung parts of the world. He continued to closely associate with the Evangelical missions movement, playing a key role in the Lausanne Congress and the movement that followed.[10]

After Mooneyham's retirement, World Vision for the first time chose leaders who were not evangelists or clergy. In early 1987 Robert Seiple began his eleven-year tenure, coming to World Vision with a background in university administration at Brown University and Eastern College and Seminary.[11] In 1998 Seiple was appointed by President Clinton as the State Department's first Ambassador-at-Large for International Religious Freedom. World Vision next turned to Richard Stearns, a business executive who had been president of Parker Brothers Games and CEO of the tableware company Lenox. Both Seiple and Stearns were committed Evangelicals and high-performing, well-rounded leaders with Ivy League degrees, selected primarily for their business and administrative skills, which were important for the sprawling organization. Although Seiple was not an evangelist, his leadership credentials as president of a major Evangelical college and seminary made him familiar with the world of parachurches. But Stearns, although a committed layman, had been fully shaped by corporate business culture. Consequently, the learning curve was steep; Stearns knew very little about poverty when he reluctantly took the job. As he acknowledged, "The first thing the World Vision staff wanted to do was to get this silly president into the field."[12] On his inaugural trip to Uganda, he realized that he had never even considered that the AIDS epidemic had left behind orphans. Nevertheless, during the last third of the twentieth century, Stearns and everyone associated with World Vision had to navigate a steep learning curve as they added structural development and political advocacy to the child sponsorship programs that had previously defined the organization.

"Development" Develops in the 1970s and 1980s

World Vision's most far-reaching changes came from its movement beyond rescue of individuals to a greater engagement with structural aspects of poverty. Since the late 1960s various national offices had engaged in intermittent, ad hoc development projects. For example, the regional director for Indonesia provoked wonder by suggesting a duck-raising project. The initiative went ahead but was not widely imitated. As an Indonesian associate observed, "It sure is a lot harder to raise money for development than for child care and other projects. The emotional tug just isn't there."[13]

Nevertheless, several factors fostered a growing interest in development among World Vision practitioners. As World Vision gained experience with larger-scale disaster relief, it became clear that follow-up after the initial phase of the emergency was necessary. Within its ministry to children, growing awareness of development sparked important changes. World Vision broadened its focus to include needy *children* rather than just *orphans*. This seemingly minor shift actually reflected a growing realization that legitimate poverty could be caused by more than just the loss of parents. Adding ministry to families was a recognition that poverty ensnared more than just helpless individuals but also larger social units, and indicated the beginnings of a more structural approach to thinking about poverty.

In addition to World Vision's internal structural shift, the organization began to shift toward the smaller-scale development projects seen among other humanitarian organizations. Western development experts, both secular and religious, were increasingly turning to poor individuals and communities as the locus of their concern. Previously, the macroeconomic foci of the wider development sector had been completely incongruous with Evangelical individualism. But by the late 1970s, the two sides seemed to meet in the middle: Evangelicals began to think more structurally, and the rest of the development world (generally speaking) began to focus on supporting neighborhoods and villages.

A watershed moment came in 1978 when more than fifty World Vision staff attended a five-week training session sponsored by the Institute of Rural Reconstruction.[14] The experience heavily influenced World Vision's approach and provided many opportunities to interact with other major organizations involved in development. The conference was a landmark not only for World Vision's work on the ground but for the way it presented itself to the public. In a 1979 *World Vision Magazine* article, Bryant Myers, who would later become the organization's chief theorizer on development, enthusiastically summarized the conference for his American readers, promising that development would be a major direction "for the next 10 years"; he declared that the agency would hitherto commit 75 percent of its funding to development.[15] This article was the earliest recognition in World Vision's public discourse of significant non-Evangelical influence on its work, signaling its integration into the growing movement of humanitarian groups who were becoming known as nongovernmental organizations (NGOs). During the late 1980s the agency established official links with the World Health Organization, the United Nations Children's Fund (UNICEF), and the United Nations High Commissioner for Refugees, among others.

World Vision's newfound openness to learning from "outsiders" also sped up its shift away from the Evangelical missions community. Myers acknowledged that World Vision "didn't know a lot about development ourselves then. It was sort of like the teacher who keeps one page ahead of the student."[16] Yet the organization was eager to share its emerging practices with other Evangelical agencies concerned about poverty. In 1979 World Vision, along with seven smaller organizations, founded the Association of Evangelical Relief and Development Organizations (AERDO).[17] This alignment reflected a significant shift in identity: "instead of defining itself as a *missions agency that did social service*, World Vision was now a *relief and development organization that did evangelism.* To be sure, traditional missions retained an important role within World Vision, but became one aspect of its operations—a department (called MARC)—rather than the unifying force of its organizational vision."[18]

World Vision's growing commitment to long-term development was undergirded by an increasingly structural understanding of poverty. The organization's changing mentality can be clearly seen in its attempt to educate the American Evangelical public in the 1970s about chronic poverty and hunger. The first evidence that a new worldview had emerged can be seen in World Vision's heavy citation of statistics and surveys to describe poverty as a pervasive, global phenomenon. Litanies of data on population, food consumption, trade patterns, and protein intake punctuated World Vision's analysis of food insecurity. President Mooneyham presented the complexities of global hunger in public addresses, books, magazine articles, and intensive church programs. Ever aware of his audience's attention span, Mooneyham attempted to help people relate to the welter of data in more manageable terms: "Did you know that if the world's population were cut down to 100, seventy-five of us would live in want? Seventy-five of us would know hunger at bedtime night after night. Seventy-five of us would live in the dust, the filth, the cold, the need, the sickness that are everywhere in Asia, Africa, and South America."[19]

World Vision's leadership understood that part of their calling was to keep the chronic nature of the hunger problem before a fickle public's attention: "Our World Vision staff often discusses . . . when the media gives high visibility and attention to the food problem . . . many people became concerned and involved. But when a continuing crisis is ignored by the press and the electronic media, many so readily forget."[20] The irony is unmistakable: World Vision was now critiquing the secular media's tendency to present hunger as a series of emergencies, just as World Vision itself had frequently done in the past.

The organization went beyond merely widening its audience's perspective on the magnitude of suffering; it applied structural analysis to the deeper causes of poverty and to its solutions—a comparative rarity within Evangelicalism up to this point. In the past, individual charity involved only meeting immediate needs. Hungry people needed food, and refugees needed a new place to live; orphans needed a new "family." World Vision's new structural model, armed with a statistical big picture, asked *why* the hungry had no food.

So in the 1970s and '80s World Vision mostly emphasized the long-term needs of the poor; it was primarily concerned with determining the factors that led to poverty. One of the most frequently cited factors was the lack of Western technology; traditional methods and ways of thinking were seen as part of the problem, not the solution. As World Vision explained to its donors, "There is the need for long-range education. Farmers need to be taught to use deep-cutting plows. . . . Farmers need to learn to use fertilizers and insecticides."[21] Another magazine article told its readers that in the Central African Republic, "Farmers are locked into traditional farming methods, so a World Vision agricultural specialist has begun working with them . . . to provide improved seed, tools and fertilizers."[22]

Although these solutions seem simple or even banal, explaining the need for such long-term development projects was somewhat risky in the Evangelical world of the 1970s, when some donors were still suspicious of expanding child sponsorship beyond orphans to other needy children. Additionally, World Vision was keenly aware that development aid did not have the emotional traction of child sponsorship. Therefore, when fundraising for rural development projects World Vision utilized strategies to help the donor quantify the tangible results of each contribution: "Your gift of $5.00 will provide 50 pounds of fertilizer. $10.00 will give an African farmer 75 pounds of seed. . . . $100.00 will help drill a well to bring life-saving water to all the families in a village."[23]

One final insight into World Vision's changing worldview can be gleaned from its use of technology in agricultural development, which implied that technology and proper training would be enough to enable a village or family to become "self-reliant."[24] Gone was the 1950s emphasis on "heathen religion" causing poverty—now technology provided solutions, heathen or not. Of course, as good Evangelicals, they vehemently affirmed that this was not enough—that even wealthy people who had been lifted out of poverty still needed Jesus. But now the poor could begin the process of development even before their conversion.

Development Transformed: 1990s and 2000s

By the 1990s World Vision's primary emphasis shifted solidly to "lasting, community-based transformation."[25] World Vision proudly announced that even when media attention inevitably fades after earthquakes or famines, it remains on-site to work for long-term change because "tragedy [doesn't] take a vacation."[26] Development workers, who only a few years earlier struggled to convince World Vision headquarters to embrace a small duck-raising program, became involved in a dizzying variety of projects—drilling deep bore wells, agronomics, forestry, rotating livestock programs, development of fish ponds for protein, public health campaigns, primary education of children, vocational training for adults, microloans, and vaccination programs, to name a few of the most common.

In order to work at a high enough level to integrate these various interventions, World Vision shifted its strategic focus to geographic areas such as urban slums and clusters of rural villages. These regionally based efforts, called Area Development Programs (ADPs), enabled World Vision to engage the complex, interlocking social structures that entangled the poor. Instead of rescuing needy individuals such as orphans or offering preset interventions like fertilizer for farmers, the first step in the creation of an ADP was to listen to a community's perception of its needs and strengths. Through consultation with noted development experts like David Korten, John Friedman, and Robert Chambers, ADPs strove to become spaces for "people-centered development" that were "consistent with [the poor's] own aspirations" through the promotion of their own preexisting movements for justice.[27] ADPs attempted to respect the community's indigenous knowledge and acknowledge that they already knew how to survive.[28]

During this time, Bryant Myers described World Vision's ongoing relationship with the community as one of *mutual learning* and *mutual transformation*, recognizing that Western development professionals had much to learn from the poor. The agency's involvement commenced at whatever entry point was determined by the community's participation.

Naturally, this new approach to development deeply influenced the way World Vision portrayed "the poor" to its potential donors. Instead of defining the poor in terms of their suffering, needs, and deficits, the emphasis in the 1990s shifted overwhelmingly to the potential of the poor. This is perhaps most obvious when one looks at World Vision's photographs of the poor: nearly all of them are smiling. After a brief period following the Ethiopian famine in the mid-1980s, it became almost impossible to find images of extreme suffering in World Vison media. Gone were the leprous limbs and the tear-stained countenances. In their place were vibrant, happy faces brimming with joy.[29] In one representative example, a World Vision periodical contains thirty-four photographs of poor people; twenty-nine of them were smiling broadly, and the rest wore expressions of concentration as they busily worked, played, or studied.[30] Even the way World Vision depicted the dress of the poor changed. African traditional dresses, Bolivian wool sweaters, elegant South Asian saris—the vibrant colors jumped off the glossy pages of World Vision's magazines and the glowing screens of its website, replacing the muted rags worn by the poor since the 1950s.[31]

World Vision journalists and leaders spoke of the poor as responsible agents who were fully capable of improving their lives if given a fair chance. They were partners, not merely beneficiaries. The following example is typical. One participant in a World Vision microfinance program came from a family that had been destitute for generations, but she was able to break through gender stereotypes that had prevented her from becoming a carpenter: "In Cuzco, Peru, Maria Lourdes de Ortiz had a hammer, a saw, a square and a ruler. With a loan from World Vision and training in business administration, she built a dream."[32] Note the structure of the final sentence: World Vision was relegated to the dependent clause, and Ms. Ortiz was the subject: "*She* built a dream."

While World Vision still showcased the generosity of its donors, it also regularly narrated stories emphasizing the generosity and gifts of the poor—they too could pass on the blessings of development. World Vision highlighted the story of the Zambian woman, Margaret Phiri, who tripled her farming output during World Vision field trials of a new agricultural method. She was selected as "lead farmer" and charged with "offering help and advice on every conceivable agricultural problem to 300 farmers in her community. Men who weren't thrilled about taking direction from a woman were soon silenced by the runaway success of the methods she promotes."[33]

World Vision president Robert Seiple illustrated this same point with his unfamiliar exegesis of the now-familiar good Samaritan parable: "The parable does not tell of the casual philanthropy of a wealthy businessman, but the sacrificial giving of a poor person . . . who knew he could make a difference personally."[34] In Seiple's rendition, the good Samaritan is no longer a well-meaning American who comes to rescue victims from the Global South; instead, the Samaritan is a poor person from the Global South who demonstrates true sacrificial compassion.

World Vision's optimistic perspective was not merely the power of positive thinking but a theological imperative: "God blesses us with a glimpse of heaven because we see people as God intended: *in the light of their potential.*[35] In theological terms, one might say that in its history, World Vision's portrayals of the poor moved from a focus on the suffering and brokenness brought on by the fall to an emphasis on the image of God that is present in every human being.

Advocacy for Justice

Just as the experience of working in emergency zones led World Vision to take the next step toward development in the 1970s, so its attempts to tackle root causes of poverty in development work led it to become increasingly involved in "advocating for justice on behalf of the poor."[36] World Vision gradually realized that local, long-term development projects did not address the oppression of dictators or international superpowers; that type of aid required politics.

World Vision founder Bob Pierce had been enthusiastically patriotic, vociferously anti-Communist, and highly optimistic about the impact of American technology and political power on the Global South. However, besides tacit support of the status quo, Pierce disavowed any direct political involvement. His successor Stanley Mooneyham also preferred to evangelize rather than politicize. Ironically, it was evangelism that led Mooneyham to draw World Vision into its first tentative steps toward political advocacy. During a 1971 evangelistic rally in Burma, Mooneyham met leaders from the majority Christian Kachin ethnic group who were reluctantly growing opium poppies to finance their independence efforts. In response to their request for support, Mooneyham promised to inquire about drug eradication funds from the US government. After returning to Washington, Mooneyham lamented, "It took a day just to find out to whom I should talk. It was my first real encounter with government bureaucracy, and it was worse than I imagined."[37] The request was denied.

Four years later, World Vision's deepening response to famine in Africa and South Asia led Mooneyham to reenter the political arena, this time with more encouraging results. He and World Vision board member Senator Mark O. Hatfield attempted to raise consciousness among the American public and its elected political leaders about hunger. They created Project FAST (Fight Against Starvation Today), a media campaign kicked off by a luncheon on Capitol Hill at which members of congress were fed the same food offered to famine victims at World Vision's relief centers in India. This campaign, informed by Mooneyham and Hatfield's frequent public disapproval of America's gluttonous consumption habits, indicated a new willingness to criticize Western culture generally and its political leaders specifically—a striking departure from Pierce's warm and uncritical patriotism.

In 1975 Mooneyham also released his signature book *What Do You Say to a Hungry World?* Though he does not frequently discuss politics, when he does it sounds surprisingly like a left-wing radical. He writes, "The heart of the problem of poverty and hunger are human systems which ignore, mistreat, and exploit man. . . . If the hungry are to be fed . . . some of the systems will require dramatic adjustments while others will have to be scrapped altogether."[38] While this (vague) statement illustrates Mooneyham's structural approach to the issue, it is unclear just who is at fault or what can be done. Nevertheless, Mooneyham sharpens his rhetoric by referring to "the stranglehold which the developed West has kept on the economic throats of the Third World."[39] Mooneyham's indictment of the West reaches its apex with the following assertion: "The hungry nations have suffered long with 'aid' that isn't, with discriminatory trade policies, with the rape of their resources. . . . I can tell you this much—if the roles were reversed, we would have repeated long ago on a worldwide scale the revolution of 1776."[40] Mooneyham does not go on to specify what kind of "aid" was unhelpful, which trade policies were unjust, or how exactly the West exploited the rest, nor does he seriously advocate for the Global South to unite in armed rebellion. Yet for a typical Evangelical reader in 1975, these words would have sounded strange indeed. Asking people in the pew to consider trade policy and the morality of government aid was a worldview away from asking them to sponsor one child.

By the late 1970s, World Vision's forays into advocacy became more frequent. In one press release, Mooneyham broke new ground by declaring that he was "very much concerned with the American level of foreign aid—through government, church, and private agencies."[41] In his publications and weekly television shows, Mooneyham spoke *as an American* and claimed that all segments of American society had a national responsibility to the poor. He defended the political rights of refugees, excoriating governments (including America's) that chose not to provide asylum or to protect refugees against attacks in international waters. Immediately following the Khmer Rouge's takeover of Cambodia, Mooneyham argued vigorously for international intervention but was dismayed to find the West's appetite for involvement in Southeast Asia waning. In his book *Come Walk the World*, he laments his lost hope that "a caring world will rise in moral indignation against the inhuman practices of Khmer Rouge taskmasters. How do you tell such gentle and trusting people that the United Nations is too busy . . . to bother with a mere six million Cambodians?"[42]

This kind of criticism reached a climax in 1979 when Mooneyham became concerned about the plight of the Vietnamese "boat people" as they fled their homeland under threat of storms, piracy, and unwelcoming shores. In a scene reminiscent of World Vision's founding myth,[43] prominent African-American pastor E. V. Hill, who was associated with World Vision's training center in Watts, California, showed Mooneyham a newspaper with a picture of "a Vietnamese mother, cowering under a canvas in the bow of a boat." Hill asked Mooneyham, "What are you going to do about it?"[44] First, Mooneyham tried political persuasion. According to later president Graeme Irvine, "World Vision urged governments and the

UN to rescue refugees from the dangerous pirate infested waters. No one was interested."[45] Next, Mooneyham enacted Operation Seasweep: he chartered World Vision's own relief vessel to bring aid to those drifting on the South China Sea and stridently censured US government inaction in the Evangelical and mainstream press.

Under Mooneyham's watch World Vision's justice advocacy extended not only to the government but also to World Vision donors. While most charities attempt to raise money by appealing for small, painless contribution—which are emotionally satisfying for the giver—World Vision challenged its public to repent by recognizing their complicity in the injustices and turning away from them. The most frequent admonition was that Americans should modify their consumption patterns. In a typical press release, Mooneyham asked, "We all have to re-examine our own lifestyles. At what point do we have too much? As concerned Christians, can we continue to live in prosperity while millions are dying in poverty?"[46]

Because Evangelicals were highly conscious of world hunger, it is not surprising that gluttony was the target of many attacks on American lifestyles. In a second press release Mooneyham excoriated the massive waste of food in America: "Food portions served in most restaurants far exceed the quantity we need. The amount of uneaten food we send back to restaurant kitchens could feed millions of hungry people."[47] In *What Do You Say to a Hungry World?*, Mooneyham posits a causal connection between the over-eating rich and the starving poor: "We have a choice: change our lifestyles a little or watch millions die of starvation."[48] Influential World Vision board member Senator Mark Hatfield concurred: "We should renew the Christian discipline of fasting as a means for teaching us how to identify with those who hunger, and to deepen our life of prayer for those who suffer. . . . We can drastically alter our consumption of meat, and the money we save we can give to alleviate world hunger."[49] Hatfield gave his call to abstinence a deep spiritual foundation, linking the traditional spirituality of fasting, intercessory prayer, and almsgiving with vegetarianism.

In addition to pronouncements, World Vision created programs that raised awareness of world hunger, with the hope of leading people to change their lifestyles. Perhaps the best-known initiative was World Vision's Planned Famine curriculum, which brought together church youth groups for a forty-hour, overnight experience comprised of games, activities, and Bible studies that asked pointed questions about opulent American lifestyles in the face of global poverty. The program's signature angle was that students were expected to fast for the duration of the activity in order to personally experience hunger; the money they saved by not eating during that time was given to World Vision's famine relief programs. At the conclusion of the event, students were encouraged to take the Shakertown Pledge, in which they committed (among other things) to "lead an ecologically sound life," to "lead a life of creative simplicity," and to "share [their] personal wealth with the world's poor."[50] The program challenged students to spend less money on themselves "as an expression of a personal commitment to a more equitable distribution of the world's resources . . . as an act of solidarity with the majority of humankind, [and] . . . as an act of returning what was usurped by us through unjust social and economic structures."[51]

One of Mooneyham's last acts before he resigned in 1982 was to commission a study concerning how a biblical perspective on justice should inform World Vision's work. By aiming the organization in a new direction, Mooneyham embraced (with unprecedented force) the necessity of working for justice at the political, structural level. The move was not without resistance, as a minority within the organization worried that political involvement was indicative of secularizing drift; others were concerned that political engagement was outside World Vision's realm of expertise. Despite opposition, the new focus gained momentum within the organization, and soon political advocacy was just as much a part of the organization's work as relief and development. World Vision International president Graeme Irvine stated the new consensus: "World Vision does not have a political agenda. We have a Christian and humanitarian agenda. But the political consequences of that agenda cannot and must not be avoided."[52] Building on Mooneyham's ad hoc attempts to gain political attention for the plight of the "boat people," World Vision began intentional advocacy efforts in the mid-1980s.

Since the organization itself had grown in stature to become a significant player in the global development community, World Vision attempted to leverage its standing to advocate for justice issues that it felt competent to address. For example, in 1989 World Vision capitalized on its longstanding commitment to Cambodia by publically denouncing a former Khmer Rouge leader as the representative of Cambodia in the United Nations. In this case, World Vision's voice was part of a coalition that successfully pressured the United Nations to declare the seat vacant, leading to free elections in 1993. By the new millennium, World Vision leadership regularly testified before Congress as expert witnesses in an attempt to influence legislation.[53]

Besides direct lobbying, in the 1990s World Vision began to rally its huge donor base for grassroots political action campaigns. Often these campaigns grew out of field experience; justice issues were frequently brought to World Vision's attention through personal contact with sponsored children. Bonded child labor in South Asia and sex trafficking in Southeast Asia were the most common and egregious injustices encountered by development workers, and these campaigns became the front line of World Vision's advocacy work.

A seminal experience in this regard occurred in Thailand when a sponsored fourteen-year-old girl was deceived into leaving her village and then forced into a brothel. World Vision staff were able to locate her and secure her release for $640. Although the child was safe, it was obvious that what was needed was "the enactment and enforcement of protective law."[54] World Vision eventually became deeply involved in supporting legislation in various countries to prosecute Western child sex offenders for abuses committed in developing countries. It supplemented this legislative lobbying with a public information campaign. Beginning in 2004, prominently placed billboards appeared around the world in areas known for sex tourism; the signs warned would-be predators (in English), "Abuse a child in this country, go to jail in yours."[55]

World Vision's most successful and best-known political advocacy campaign was perhaps its most risky. President Richard Stearns courted controversy by directing World Vision's development work to prioritize the global AIDS epidemic. While most Evangelicals did not subscribe to the view of strident right-wing voices like Jerry Falwell, who famously said that AIDS was God's punishment for any society that tolerated homosexuals, they tended to "pass by on the other side" when encountering those afflicted with AIDS. In 2001, a Barna research survey sponsored by World Vision found that only 3 percent of Evangelical Christians were willing to "donate for international AIDS prevention and education," a figure significantly lower than that of non-Christians.[56] Earlier in the 1990s, anti-AIDS prejudice was likely even higher. Yet World Vision began to engage AIDS as early as 1990 in Uganda and Romania, and gradually ramped up its advocacy at global, national, and local levels.

In 2000, World Vision launched its large-scale, heavily publicized Hope Initiative, touring across the United States with a three-thousand-foot multimedia exhibit educating viewers about the global prevalence of AIDS and asking them to sponsor "Hope Children"—children who were HIV positive. World Vision also worked closely with Irish rock star Bono of U2 to raise the profile of the initiative; in a radio spot, Stearns compared Bono to the good Samaritan for his work raising awareness about AIDS in Africa.[57] In 2004 a follow-up Barna survey found that 14 percent of Evangelicals were willing to donate to AIDS work,[58] and by 2006 nearly four hundred thousand Hope Children had been sponsored.[59]

Many other issues taken up for public advocacy followed from World Vision's development emphases. The agency energetically brought before the public eye such issues as female genital mutilation, inequities in pay, nutrition, health care, and domestic violence. Toward the end of the twentieth century, the advocacy department gained even greater mindshare within the overall organization, and the scope of issues they tackled expanded apace. World Vision became involved in coalitions to ban land mines and the sale of "blood diamonds" in the United States, among other campaigns. In 2004, World Vision launched its new website, www.seekjustice.org. Interested donors could find information on the issues World Vision was tackling, learn how to effectively contact their elected representatives, and send pre-scripted letters and emails.

Despite the fact that World Vision was tackling the grimmest injustices on the planet, an optimistic tone suffused its communication with donors. Instead of the radical calls to repentance that had characterized the organization in the 1970s, *hope* became the main theme by the turn of the century. World Vision was concerned that increased awareness of the depths of injustice might inculcate a sense of despair and resignation, a phenomenon often called "compassion fatigue."[60] In this context it attempted to reestablish hope with the message that "you can make a difference."

World Vision drew on the fame of wealthy philanthropists like Bill Gates and Warren Buffett to encourage its more modestly endowed readers: "You can do the impossible—make the difference of a lifetime—anyone can be a philanthropist."[61] Another version of this message took a different tact, explaining that even a young boy could sponsor a child with his paper route money, enabling him to "discover a world of need beyond his own comfortable backyard—a world where even a child can help make a lasting difference."[62] Even the familiar invitation to sponsor a child was recast in empowering terms of structural change. The following advertisement for a World Vision 30 Hour Famine fundraiser translates the same message of hopefulness into a teenage idiom: "Tyler Burke survived 57 clothespins clipped to face. Saved no one. Ali Manzano survived 30 hours without food. Helped save an entire village."[63]

Indeed, World Vision was beginning to offer its would-be donors and followers hope for more than just impacting individual lives—they could become part of a movement for sweeping change. Whereas in the 1970s the call was to be part of a faithful remnant, now donors could become part of the issues and causes that were gaining momentum and popularity. In the realm of this style of discourse, merely sponsoring a child might seem too small—now World Vision spoke of ending poverty entirely.

Transformational Development

By the late twentieth century, World Vision leaders from every corner of the organization were eager to integrate their dizzying array of relief, development, and advocacy efforts into one theoretical framework, which they called "transformational development." Transformational development emphasizes that the spiritual, emotional, social, and political brokenness brought on by poverty must be met with a structural approach that addresses all of these areas. Transformational development is perhaps most fully articulated by Bryant Myers in his influential 1999 book, *Walking with the Poor*. Myers retells the entire biblical story using the transformation motif, integrates the thought of progressive development scholars and justice-minded theologians, and argues that World Vision's holistic approach continues to be evangelistic because of its effective demonstration of the gospel.

While *Walking with the Poor* became a go-to resource for many Evangelical development workers, World Vision's army of journalists and media experts were perhaps even more influential in transmitting the idea of transformational development to the American Evangelical public. Because donors had been conditioned by World

Vision itself to focus on the emergency needs of isolated individuals, writers frequently utilized emotionally warm stories about sponsored children as a hook to draw donors into more complex issues. One representative article tells the story of a South Asian girl freed from child slavery and empowered through a World Vision sewing class.[64] Once the emotional impact of the story has been made, the article explains that the class was attended by 530 local women as part of an ongoing, community-wide effort to provide women with more vocational choices. A sidebar on the same page encourages readers to avoid buying clothing brands that use sweatshop labor and urges them to lobby their congressperson about labor justice.

This story alerts readers to the interrelated factors that kept one girl in slavery, including gender discrimination, lack of vocational training, and cultural norms. It also demonstrates World Vision's holistic response, which engages all of these factors at once, and invites the reader not only to donate money but also to act politically. Through countless articles, advertisements, and webpages of this kind, World Vision strives to change the way Americans think about changing the world.[65]

Compassion International

While World Vision is the largest and almost certainly the most influential American Evangelical organization to model holistic engagement with the complex, structural realities of poverty and injustice, other NGOs have moved in a similar direction. This chapter closes with a case study of Compassion International's "holistic child development" approach, demonstrating that it is possible to integrate very sophisticated, holistic thinking about poverty into strong Evangelical convictions about the primacy and priority of the individual.

Compassion International's early history closely parallels that of World Vision, albeit on a smaller scale. Founded by a traveling evangelist in Korea (see chap. 2), Compassion initially supported Asian orphans through child sponsorship. Like World Vision, Compassion's experience administering orphanages in Korea taught the organization that many of the sponsored "orphans" were actually children abandoned by destitute families in the hope that life in a Western-backed institution would be an improvement. In response, Compassion instituted its Family Helper program in 1968, which expanded the sponsorship mechanism to include children of widows or handicapped fathers. Soon Compassion's focus shifted to providing for the educational needs of sponsored children under its new School Project program. By 1981 its director of program development reported, "At this point the majority of Compassion's involvements are essentially scholarships for children to attend Christian schools."[66]

By the 1980s the trajectories of World Vision and Compassion clearly diverged. Although Compassion dabbled in various development projects, it remained an intensely child-focused organization. While Compassion did begin to incorporate the language of development, such language was applied on an individual scale. Compassion was beginning to identify as a "child development agency."

From 1984–2005 Compassion International was an extremely stable organization, with little change to report except for constant, even spectacular growth. In 1982, 68,000 children received support; more than a decade later the total had multiplied almost tenfold, reaching 611,000 in 2004.[67] Their funding tracked a similar path, peaking at $166 million in 2004, ranking them consistently in the top four among Evangelical NGOs.[68]

Holistic Child Development

Compassion International's version of holistic child development provides a striking counterpoint to World Vision's expansive approach. Compassion uses the language of holism to articulate a more sophisticated, multifaceted approach to ministry to children. Guided by executive program director Don Miller and president Wess Stafford, both of whom graduated from the Michigan State PhD program in nonformal education in third world settings, Compassion became increasingly aware of the complex, intertwined nature of poverty and the necessity of a holistic approach to engage it. Nevertheless, it remained steadfastly and self-consciously committed to a program strategy of developing individual children, as opposed to broader-based work.

In one magazine issue devoted to explaining "What Compassion Believes," Miller provides such a clear thesis statement for Compassion's holistic child development that it is worth quoting at length:

> Most of the time when people talk about development, they're talking about activities like community development or water projects or agricultural projects. When we talk about development at Compassion, we're thinking of results—improvements in one child's life . . . development occurs within individuals. But individuals interact with their social and physical environment. Human development must address conditions and relationships individuals face within their family, church, and community . . . development occurs holistically.[69]

In this statement, Miller assures donors that he understands other prevalent models of development but seeks to show how Compassion's model is distinctive. He appeals to deep-seated Evangelical beliefs that fundamental societal change must happen "within individuals," yet he presents each individual as the locus within which all the complexities of poverty inhere, since individuals are shaped by their environment. For Compassion, development happens not through modifying the environment but by designing a program that will holistically address all the complex impacts of the environment on individual children.

Compassion also explains its holistic approach to donors by contrasting it with Compassion's own approach in the past. Compassion describes its traditional model as "child care," which is distinguished by "material help in the present, focus on urgent needs, 'doing *for* the child,' and dealing with symptoms." "Child care" views children as "helpless, simple, sick, compliant." Compassion then compares this older approach with "child development," which is characterized as "doing *with* the child, dealing with root causes, and providing ongoing opportunities to learn; its view of the child is 'teachable, motivated, and responsible.'"[70] This holistic model emphasizes the potential of the child to take responsibility for personal growth as she gradually confronts the deep-rooted causes of her poverty, in partnership with Compassion.

Not content to show how Compassion was different from more broad-based approaches, Stafford explicitly argues in "What Compassion Believes" that Compassion's approach is better than the others: "Some development agencies consider child development too narrow an approach for meeting a poor family's needs. Compassion agrees that some problems affecting children are best addressed at a broader level . . . but we have a greater impact on an individual and the family rather than letting the help trickle down through community development. Christ has compassion on the masses, but he helped them one at a time."[71] Stafford frames community-based approaches such as those used by World Vision in Reaganesque, laissez-faire economics terms, claiming that such programs do not "trickle down" to children in the same way that Compassion's careful focus on individuals does. He also subtly implies that Compassion's approach is more Christlike, since it more closely approximates Jesus's own ministry.

Nevertheless, Compassion does not make the larger claim that its holistic model is the path to ending global poverty. (At times World Vision seemed to imply that if it could simply "scale up" enough Area Development Programs, poverty would be substantially eliminated.) Instead, Compassion seems to be content to follow its calling of plucking out individuals from the complex world of poverty and holding them up as shining examples of how recovery could be possible. In the words of former president Wally Erickson, "We have chosen to invest in children because they are our future. We have chosen to minister to them one by one because we are constantly reminded that we may not change the whole world, but we can change the world for one child."[72]

Central to Compassion's holism is its emphasis on the emotional aspects of child development. Whereas World Vision attempts to show the complex technological and spiritual aspects of transformational development, Compassion takes a more personal, psychological approach. According to Stafford, "The presence of Compassion sponsors in children's lives strategically attacks the very root of poverty by giving children a reason for hope. They begin to think 'if they believe in me—value me—why should I give up? I matter to them, and to God, I have worth.'"[73]

Consequently, Compassion constantly encourages its sponsors to write to "their" children. Although there is still an edge of paternalism present, its discourse tends to portray sponsors' emotional support in terms of a life coach or mentor. Again, as Miller writes, "Compassion is not a relief agency. It is a Christian child development ministry, and development takes time. By their actions, sponsors say I will enter into a vulnerable relationship with someone in need, and will commit myself to give to them regularly."[74] Thus, the benefits that accrue to sponsors and their families are not the sentimental, paternalistic emotional satisfactions of years past, but rather the satisfaction of being responsible members of the global body of Christ.

Furthermore, Compassion views its model as a critical plank in the conversion of the world. Agency leaders frequently repeat the following statistics: "Children are a critical group in the Great Commission strategy. . . . 85% of the people who make a decision for Christ do so between the ages of 4 and 14, and nearly half the world's population is under 15 years of age."[75] Thus, the organization emphasizes that its inclusion of Bible teaching and church attendance is merely part of holistically developing the whole child, which includes the child's spiritual life. Conversion is not mandatory or assumed, but all sponsored children are required to receive religious instruction.[76]

Finally, like World Vision, Compassion uses the individual stories of its sponsored children as a way of providing a window into the complex world of poverty in the Global South for American donors. Our examination of Compassion's model closes with a case study of the way in which Compassion links gender discrimination—as an impoverishing force—with the stories of sponsored children.[77]

Beginning in the early 1990s, Compassion regularly dedicated issues of its periodical to explaining how its programs upheld the dignity of its female participants. Compassion claims that its holistic approach effectively improves the status of women and girls, and its approach typically includes three steps. First, at the broadest level, Compassion articles cite reams of statistics and studies on gender bias in order to raise awareness for the readers. Next, it provides scriptural responses to the issue, as the following excerpt illustrates: "Scripture explodes with the wrath of a God who deplores the oppression of the poor and needy. The abuses against this vulnerable population, the daughters of the poor, require God's people to intervene. . . . Jesus affirms women, as with Mary Magdalene and the woman subject to bleeding."[78]

But the key point for Compassion is to show that sponsored girls have great potential to escape the worst effects of gender discrimination, since "learning opportunities are a fundamental benefit afforded to every girl registered for sponsorship. . . . Christian education, which emphasizes a Heavenly Father who loves girls and boys equally, is especially valuable in helping girls see their value and worth."[79] Compassion claims that conversion has powerful holistic effects: "As more families accept Christ, their homes will become more loving and stable. Women will be empowered to become all they can be, and children will be the benefactors."[80] Often stories add drama, as with the account of a fifteen-year-old Indian girl who refused her father's arranged marriage so she could continue her education. The father kicked her and said, "You're just another mouth to feed!" but he relented after the intervention of Compassion staff.[81]

In addition, sponsors are educated as to how their letters can more effectively empower the girls they sponsor. In a sidebar titled "What more can you do?," sponsors are advised to use "encouraging words that affirm her intrinsic worth as a human being" and to include "photos and stories of educated, successful young women in present day society. If you have a daughter, share her dreams about the future."[82]

In summary, Compassion International's holistic model of child development illustrates that it is possible to retain the individualism of Bob Pierce's model while incorporating a great deal of the worldview that characterizes other holistic approaches.

The Complications of Justice

For me (Gary), spending years researching organizations like World Vision and Compassion International was more than an academic exercise in chronicling the past. I wanted to go deeper into what biblical justice is and how to actually live it out. After all the organizational details and historical twists and turns, I can summarize what I've learned in one statement: justice is complicated. World Vision started out as a simple organization with a simple idea: sponsor one child. But if you've made it this far in the book, you now know that World Vision has grown into a huge, complex multinational corporation. I doubt World Vision has taken that path because of ulterior motives like mission creep or institutional ambition. I think it's because justice is complicated.

Justice is complicated, first of all, because injustice is complicated. As World Vision brought compassion into the lives of more and more individuals, it realized that the social structures trapping these individuals were complex and all-encompassing. Simple, pre-scripted interventions, even when motivated by the deepest empathy, are no match for the tentacles of global poverty. Compassion International also has learned that teaching its sponsored kids to read the Bible does not help if they are starving to death; receiving an education doesn't matter if there are no jobs anywhere; and vaccination is useless if one is too hopeless to get out of bed in the morning. These organizations learned to think not just about immediate needs but about why those needs are there in the first place.

Once World Vision saw that injustice embeds itself in political, cultural, and economic structures, it realized that a matching structural response was necessary in order that justice might "roll on like a river" (Amos 5:24). Charity alone was not enough—long-term development and political advocacy had to be part of the equation. Despite resistance from donors and even Bob Pierce himself, World Vision invested countless dollars and hours into learning from the Bible, from the poor themselves, and from the best available scholarship in order to create its transformational development approach.

I believe World Vision's story offers deep insight for those who want to do justice. Too often when successful church planters, authors, or college graduates discover "a heart for justice," they assume that doing justice is straightforward. If they've been successful in other areas, they reason, surely it can't be that hard to help the poor. So they spring into action, armed only with good intentions and zeal—and as often as not cause more harm than good.[83]

But like World Vision, we are called to begin not by seeking simplistic solutions but by holding injustice "clearly, urgently, and unmistakably in our field of vision,"[84] despite how overwhelming it may be. If we want to do justice we must deeply study injustice with the same commitment we give to other spiritual disciplines. For today's evangelicals, this often means investing long, hard hours studying the reality that (in)justice is structural. For some readers of this book, this may spark a realization that attempts to change the world one individual relationship at a time are insufficient. Only by embracing the complex realities that true transformation requires can we see our compassion become fully realized in justice.

Doing justice is also complicated because we ourselves are part of the injustice. As World Vision taught its donors in the 1970s, we cannot fight global hunger with integrity if we don't consider the food we put on our own tables. Too often Evangelicals choose justice issues that they feel do not implicate themselves so that they can safely play the heroic role of rescuer. But doing justice always involves repentance—an acknowledgement that we too need deliverance from the injustice that we perpetuate. Along the same lines, repentance involves turning away from the unjust ways in which we see the poor. World Vision and Compassion International are good models in this regard: compare the way in which early World Vision defined the poor by what they lacked with its later vision of the poor as fully capable and worthy to be listened to and partnered with. Sometimes justice requires prophetic, corporate repentance, as World Vision demonstrated when it challenged its own constituency's bigotry against AIDS and stood against its own nation's indifference toward Southeast Asian refugees. Doing justice means that we must humbly but boldly be willing to speak out against the blind spots and hidden injustices perpetuated by our families or our churches or our preferred political parties.

One final piece must be added to this multifaceted portrait: justice is not just challenging but also joyful. It calls forth in us not only repentance but celebration. As World Vision has emphasized to its donors from the beginning: *we can make a difference.* I believe that this is the most exciting moment in history to join God's plan for justice. Organizations like World Vision and Compassion International have learned much in the struggle against injustice, and we have been given the privilege of standing on their shoulders.

4

Sojourners as a Prophetic Voice for Those on the Margins

Published in 1971, the inaugural issue of *The Post-American* featured several sketches of fists thrust in the air, communicating the fight-the-system ethos that would become *Sojourners* magazine. The initial impetus for the magazine's publication emerged from the theological deliberations of Evangelicals in the Chicago area, many of whom were seminary students at Trinity Evangelical Divinity School.

In 1979, I (Soong-Chan) attended a building dedication of an immigrant church affiliated with a fundamentalist denomination. The pastor charged with dedicating the building pointed toward the vaulted wooden ceiling of the new sanctuary and stated, "If you were to turn the sanctuary upside down, you would find that we are sitting in a ship. That's what the church should be: Noah's

Ark protecting God's people as it floats through a world that is under the judgment of God."

During the 1984 election cycle, Republican presidential candidate Ronald Reagan famously said to a group of conservative Evangelical leaders, "I know you can't endorse me. But I endorse you." In 2004 a BBC report on the recent reelection of George W. Bush noted that "the core of the President's support was Christian conservatives."[1] During the administration of George W. Bush, the president of the National Association of Evangelicals, Ted Haggard, as well as key Evangelical leaders such as Richard Land (the chief ethicist for the Southern Baptist Convention), participated in a weekly call with the president of the United States.

In 2009 President Obama assembled a group of religious leaders to serve as members of the White House Office of Faith-based and Neighborhood Partnerships, signing an executive order to reconstitute the office just two weeks after taking office. At the signing ceremony, Jim Wallis, the president and CEO of Sojourners, stood to the immediate right of the president, with observers acknowledging that Wallis played an instrumental role in the formation of this advisory committee.

Evangelicals have experienced twists and turns in the historical evolution of their engagement with social justice, sometimes placing them on the margins of the political system and other times positioning them as insiders of that same system. The multiple iterations of Evangelical political involvement reflect a changing relationship between Evangelical Christianity and the surrounding culture over the course of the latter part of the twentieth century.

American Evangelicals situate themselves squarely in the stream of historical orthodoxy that traces its roots back to the biblical story. As heirs of this heritage and the bearers of orthodox Christianity, Evangelicals feel a particular pressure to maintain the purity of the church, seeking to preserve the integrity of the gospel in the midst of a changing world. Varying expressions of Christian faith are evident from the earliest colonial times and into subsequent centuries. Divisions based on denominational ecclesiology, geography, views on slavery, even social class were realities of eighteenth- and nineteenth-century American Christianity.

In the latter part of the twentieth century, a distinct sociological Evangelical identity emerged, which is often caricatured as white, middle-class, suburbanite, and Republican. The religious right surfaced as the dominant expression of Evangelical involvement in American society and politics. However, the history of Evangelicalism throughout this time reveals two different trajectories of social, cultural, and political involvement: the religious right (seemingly a much larger segment of twentieth-century American Evangelicalism) and progressive Evangelicals (defined here as theologically conservative evangelicals with a more progressive political agenda, as opposed to the contemporary usage of progressive Evangelicals to indicate theological progressivism).

Both expressions of Evangelicalism draw from a broader definition of evangelical Christianity and reflect the breadth of traditions that make up Evangelicalism (as mentioned in the introduction).[2] Both the religious right and progressive Evangelicalism fit our original definition of Evangelicalism. However, distinctions between these two streams surface in regard to how the respective movements approached the relationship of the church to the culture.

In the twentieth century, the American church was particularly concerned about the preservation of the faith in the face of mounting secularism. Toward that goal, Evangelicals and their fundamentalist forebears exhibited nervousness when the society they had once perceived as a New Jerusalem and had considered to be a city set on a hill now exhibited characteristics of fallen Babylon. The postmillennial optimism of nineteenth-century American Christianity was upended with the advent of modernity, industrialization, urbanization, and immigration. Cities that had been bastions of white, Anglo-Saxon, Protestant faith were now home to Italian Catholics, Orthodox Greeks, and Eastern European Jews. Moreover, the Great Migration, which resulted in a massive influx of African-Americans into urban centers, also challenged the assumption of American cities as expressions of white Protestant superiority. The dominant culture of Western European Protestantism feared a society that was no longer under the dominance of Western Europeans.[3] The Fundamentalist-Modernist Controversy, which found expression in denominations, churches, and seminaries, further exacerbated this fear.

As the culture around them shifted, conservative Protestants rejected the social gospel of their liberal counterparts and opted to pit Christ against the surrounding culture.[4] The activist impulse of fundamentalists to convert others remained intact, but now this impulse was expressed as suspicion of the broader culture while seeking ways to rescue as many souls as possible from the wrecked, sinking vessel of the world. This chapter examines the specific expression of how Evangelicalism intersects with the larger cultural context, especially in terms of how the relationship between church and culture shapes Evangelical involvement in the political realm. Particular attention is given to the emergence of the Evangelical religious right and progressive Evangelicals.

The Rise of the Religious Right

In the latter part of the twentieth century, when Evangelicals began to engage more directly in the political process, the assumption of a fallen world remained entrenched. Twentieth-century Christians embraced the narrative of a world destined for God's ruthless judgment—a perspective that contrasted sharply with previous centuries' eschatological hope of America as a nation favored by God. A desire to return to that idealized version of a Christian America would drive many on the religious right. The Fundamentalist-Modernist Controversy of the early twentieth century derailed that perception, and the religious right would address the belief that something had been lost.

The rapidly changing culture of the latter half of the twentieth century served as an impetus for the formation of the religious right. In *American Grace*, Robert Putnam and David Campbell assert that changing sexual norms, which were particularly evident in American society in the 1960s, contributed to the galvanizing of Evangelicals around conservative politics. Putnam and Campbell claim that the '60s represented a perfect storm for American institutions and lit the fuse for the culture wars of the following decades. The '60s witnessed a seismic generational shift on social issues such as birth control, premarital sex, homosexuality, and abortion. The '60s also marked the decline of religious participation, amplifying the Evangelical perception that American society was deteriorating. Putnam and Campbell argue that concerns about sexual immorality can be closely associated with the rise of Evangelicalism. They further argue that the religious right responded to these concerns effectively, which helped to swell its ranks.[5]

Seth Dowland takes a similar approach by identifying anxiety over changing gender roles as a factor in the rise of the religious right. Dowland attributes the rise of the religious right to its roots in a nostalgic gendered value system, asserting that the religious right galvanized around the Evangelical emphasis on order and authority, which reflects a more patriarchal and traditional model of the family. The religious right's emphasis on family values reveals its insecurity concerning the drastic changes in the culture in the latter half of the twentieth century.[6] Anxiety over these changes spurred the religious right to directly utilize overtly political tools to influence the culture, providing another example of the Evangelical ability to use whatever tools available to further its own agenda. In the same manner that fundamentalists did not hesitate to use the cultural tool of media to communicate the gospel, the religious right did not hesitate to use political tools to influence and shape the culture.[7]

The rise of the religious right was predicated on the increasing anxiety over the changing norms evident in American society. An identifiable enemy was needed in order to galvanize American Evangelicals: the prevailing secular worldview would serve that function. Evangelical Christians would combat that dominant narrative of secularism in American society with their own counternarrative.[8]

The work and influence of Francis Schaeffer served as an important centralizing perspective in the face of a changing world. From his perch at L'Abri Fellowship in Switzerland, Schaeffer began to postulate a narrative of the decline of American society. Schaeffer's work tells of a Christian worldview that was under attack in secular American culture. He asserted that in the past Christianity could depend on society affirming a Christian worldview, but the presuppositions endemic in secular humanism enabled it to operate as a surrogate religion. This reality necessitated the assertion of a Christian worldview.

While lacking formal education and depth in his analysis, Schaeffer exerted considerable influence on American Evangelicalism as one of its key thought leaders. His lectures at Christian colleges made sweeping generalizations about American society that led to apocalyptic conclusions while stirring the hearts of Evangelicals who were troubled by the crumbling of a Christendom they believed had existed at one point in American history. Francis Schaeffer's son, Franky Schaeffer, claims that his own desire to launch a movie career led to the production of movies that would popularize his father's teaching.[9] Francis Schaeffer's lectures and movies provided the intellectual fodder (as shallow as it was) for the Evangelical masses.

The Christian worldview purported by Francis Schaeffer viewed the reality of abortions in the United States as particularly problematic. Initially seen as an issue for the Roman Catholic Church, political conservatives surmised that abortion could serve as a rallying issue for Evangelicals. The image of dolls floating in a lake, used by Franky Schaeffer in a documentary on abortion, sought to portray how far American society had fallen and to what extent a secular worldview had shaped that decline. For

Evangelicals, abortion exhibited the depths of America's fall and became their central political issue. Opposition to abortion served as an identifying marker for Evangelicals who clung to a Christian worldview.

Because the world had fallen captive to secular humanism, Evangelicals needed to hang on to a God-honoring worldview, which they believed was rapidly slipping away. Toward that end, the Republican Party sought out issues that tapped into the Evangelical sense of cultural decline. Conservative positions on abortion, prayer in schools, and the separation of church and state provided the necessary ammunition to bring theological conservatives into the politically conservative camp.

Randall Balmer argues that the 1973 *Roe v. Wade* decision was less critical to the formation of the religious right than the *Green v. Connally* case, in which the IRS sought to deny tax-exempt status to a racially segregated school in Mississippi. Balmer claims that the federal government's power to enforce the Civil Rights Act sparked the early formation of the religious right, and a subsequent case against Bob Jones University's policy of segregation served to further raise the ire of fundamentalist Evangelicals. He maintains that the fear of government encroachment on church rights (including the right to resist racial integration) moved Evangelicals toward the larger agenda of the Republican Party.[10] The formation of the religious right pivoted on a narrative that a Christian worldview must hold fast against the machinations of secular culture.

In response to this potential encroachment, Evangelicals began to utilize the infrastructures of media and education that had grown after the Scopes Trial and over the course of the twentieth century. While the culture may have declined during the twentieth century, the tools of that culture could be co-opted. Evangelical activists found an outlet not only in the task of personal evangelism but also in cultural transformation through political activism. Because evangelicals from George Whitefield (1714–70) and Charles Finney (1792–1875) to Aimee Semple McPherson (1890–1944) and

Billy Graham (b. 1918) had used the tools of culture to advance Christianity, the transition to political activism—one of the most significant tools of culture—to express active, conversionist faith proved to be relatively smooth.

Old-time fundamentalist gospel preacher Jerry Falwell formed the Moral Majority and attempted to use the tools of American politics to impact issues like abortion and prayer in schools. Pentecostal televangelist Pat Robertson ran for president of the United States as a Republican and successfully dabbled in media (*The 700 Club* and *The Family Channel*) and higher education (Regent University) in order to assert that elusive Christian worldview. Throughout the last quarter of the twentieth century, one could argue that the religious right successfully incorporated secular cultural tools into the toolbox of American Evangelicalism to combat what it perceived to be a crumbling culture. The Christian worldview would combat the secular worldview. Christ would stand against the culture, and the church would defeat the culture on its own terms.

An Alternative Narrative: Progressive Evangelicals

The religious right rooted its narrative in the fundamentalist stream of American Christianity. As inheritors of orthodox faith and a Christian worldview, they could stand against the onslaught of the deteriorating culture and the secular worldview. In contrast, progressive Evangelicals differed in how they approached the relationship between Christianity and culture. Progressive Evangelicals could also trace their roots to a larger evangelical ethos and to an evangelical theology distinct from Protestant liberalism. A conservative theology of protest provided the theological undergirding for progressive Evangelicalism. As such, they did not hesitate to identify themselves as Evangelical Christians and would even claim that they were returning to a historical evangelicalism that expressed social concern prior to the twentieth century.

In *The Young Evangelicals*, published in 1974, Richard Quebedeaux situates the burgeoning movement of progressive Evangelicals in the stream of fundamentalism and evangelicalism. While not imprisoning the larger Evangelical movement in the fundamentalist stream that contended with Protestant liberals, Quebedeaux acknowledges the influence and impact of fundamentalism on Evangelicalism. However, by the early 1970s, there emerged a new generation of Evangelical leaders who had been less influenced by the fundamentalism of the first generation of the NAE (see Introduction, p. 11ff). Quebedeaux called these fresh voices "neo-evangelicals."[11] While fundamentalists shaped a significant portion of the self-identified Evangelical population (including neo-evangelicals), progressive Evangelicalism was more profoundly shaped by what Donald Dayton and Robert Johnston describe as the variety of American Evangelicalism.[12]

The movement from fundamentalism to neo-evangelicalism is best exemplified by the story of Fuller Theological Seminary. Fuller Seminary began as a fundamentalist institution founded by Charles Fuller, whose *Old Fashioned Revival Hour* radio program integrated the use of the relevant cultural expression of radio with a fundamentalist and conversionist zeal. Despite its fundamentalist roots, Fuller Seminary began to shift in its orientation, drawing scholars such as George Eldon Ladd, whose work on the New Testament attempted to transcend the barrier of critical scholarship and Evangelical thought. John D'Elia's biography of Ladd, *A Place at the Table*, points to the challenge facing Ladd, who sought credibility from the larger academic community for his work on the New Testament. Despite his failure to break into the academic elite, Ladd represented a new breed of Evangelical scholar who did not eschew the secular academy but rather sought to find a seat at the table beyond the context of fundamentalism.[13]

As George Marsden notes, Fuller Seminary moved away from being the vanguard of fundamentalism to a neo-evangelical institution.[14] The antagonism toward the secular culture that had run rampant throughout mid-twentieth-century fundamentalism gave way to a neo-evangelicalism that sought to effectively communicate to the culture. In an unmistakable shift, culture was no longer simplistically painted as the enemy against which the church stood but as an arena of ministry and even learning.

The sociological shift at Fuller Seminary presented a new branch for Evangelicalism. Neo-evangelicals remained biblicists but not in the strictly literalist manner of fundamentalists. Neo-evangelicals took less of a hard-line stance on biblical inerrancy and were less beholden and captive to the doom and gloom of premillennial dispensationalism. Drawing from the variety of Evangelicalism, not strictly the Reformed branch, neo-evangelicals included the contributions of Mennonites, Anabaptists, Methodists, Pentecostals, and the Reformed camp. The intellectual and ecclesial breadth of neo-evangelicalism served to encompass the coalition of progressive Evangelicals.

One of the early markers for the formation of progressive Evangelicals was the participation of younger Evangelicals in the Evangelicals for McGovern movement during the 1972 elections. Most Evangelicals were supportive of the more conservative Richard Nixon, with his law-and-order point of view. Harold Lindsell of *Christianity Today* essentially endorsed Nixon's candidacy in the pages of the magazine, believing (accurately) that his support echoed the majority of Evangelicals in the United States. Evangelicals for McGovern, however, represented a group of Evangelicals not solidly in the politically conservative camp. From various sectors of American Evangelicalism, a group of younger Evangelicals formed relationships founded on their support of the presidential candidate.[15]

While the 1972 election served as a starting point for the formation of progressive Evangelicals, the 1973 Chicago Declaration of Evangelical Social Concern flirted with the possibility of placing progressive Evangelicals at the front and center of the Evangelical movement. The preliminary meeting was held in the basement of North Park Theological Seminary, and the critical meeting took place during Thanksgiving weekend in 1973 at a Chicago YMCA. The declaration itself was released on November 25, 1973.

The gathering drew participation from a wide cross-section of Evangelicalism, including Evangelical icon Carl Henry; Mennonite and Christian pacifist John Howard Yoder; Richard Mouw from Calvin College, who brought a Reformed, Calvinist perspective and who would eventually join Fuller Seminary; black evangelicals such as Bill and Ruth Bentley, Tom Skinner, and Bill Pannell, who were part of the National Black Evangelical Association (NBEA) but represented different denominational influences such as Pentecostalism and the Plymouth Brethren; and Latin American scholar Samuel Escobar.

Ron Sider, one of the key shapers of the document, pointed toward the Chicago gathering and the subsequent document as the launching point of his organization, Evangelicals for Social Action, which would eventually be housed in Sider's institution, Eastern (now Palmer) Seminary. The Chicago Declaration asserted the necessity of justice and concern for the poor alongside a conversionist perspective of repentance from sin. The document sought to frame the pursuit of social concerns in the framework of Evangelical language.

Eventually, other Evangelicals signed the document, including historian Timothy Smith, Senator Mark Hatfield, and Leighton Ford—Billy Graham's brother-in-law and (at the time) heir apparent. Graham himself did not sign the document but acknowledged the need for greater social engagement by Evangelicals. In the following year Leighton Ford's leadership, along with the influence of Latino voices Samuel Escobar, Orlando Costas, and René Padilla, led the Lausanne Congress on World Evangelization to include a statement on Christian social responsibility in the Lausanne Covenant of 1974 (see chap. 6 for more on this topic).

Both the Chicago Declaration of 1973 and the Lausanne Covenant of 1974 challenged the twentieth-century fundamentalist-Evangelical assertion of separatism from the world. Progressive

Evangelicals were not satisfied with the wrecked-vessel motif and the conservation of a Christian safe haven. They felt that Evangelicalism needed to be shaken free of its captivity to American values, with an activist faith made manifest not only in personal conversion but also in social change.

Progressive Evangelicalism presented a different expression of Evangelical Christianity's relationship to the surrounding culture. Progressive Evangelicals did not believe that the only possible response to a fallen world was to retreat to Noah's ark but would advance the possibility of social change as an expression of Evangelical zeal. One of the most significant expressions of progressive Evangelicalism is evident in the influence of Jim Wallis and Sojourners. The history of Sojourners, covering several decades, provides a road map of a distinctive, progressive Evangelical narrative in the latter part of the twentieth century.

Jim Wallis and Sojourners

In 2011 *Sojourners* magazine celebrated a biblical generation of publication. For forty years, Jim Wallis and Sojourners (both the magazine and the accompanying organization) proffered an alternative political voice for the larger Evangelical movement. Sojourners advocated for US policy that would protect the most vulnerable in society, claiming that budgets were moral documents. The publication also provided a strong voice of political conscience opposing the war in Vietnam, nuclear weapons, and US military efforts in Central America. During that time the ministry of Sojourners shifted from a small group of community activists to an influential political advocacy group. As Wallis gained significant national coverage, notoriety, and political influence, Sojourners increased its capacity to provide that alternative political voice. Any discussion of the impact of Sojourners begins with the central role of Jim Wallis. More than the architect and articulator of the vision, Wallis embodies the story of Sojourners and many like-minded Evangelicals.

Jim Wallis grew up in an Evangelical home in the suburbs of Detroit. Wallis's father, an engineer turned executive, provided an upper-middle-class upbringing for his family, and the theologically conservative and dispensationalist Plymouth Brethren denomination served as Wallis's childhood church home. Detroit proved to be an important locus of learning as the privilege of suburban Detroit provided a sharp contrast to the perils of inner-city Detroit. This contrast led to Wallis's rebellion against a stagnant, middle-America Evangelicalism.[16] Wallis befriended Bill Pannell, a member of a Black Brethren church in Detroit, who became an important mentor to Wallis in regard to racial and economic injustice. (See chap. 5 for more on the story of black Evangelicals like Bill Pannell.)

While an undergraduate at Michigan State, Wallis took a break from Christianity and enlisted in Students for a Democratic Society. Leftist activism, however, proved to be unsatisfying. As Wallis later recounts, "In most cases, the choice for revolutionary struggle was short-lived, and most student radicals eventually found their way into respectable and responsible careers. Some are now teaching courses on the sixties and the New Left in political science departments of major universities. For them, the revolution didn't come, but tenure did."[17]

Upon graduation, Wallis recommitted to Christian faith. "I realized that my evangelical faith, so long captive to America privilege and power, need not be abandoned after all, but rather recovered, rekindled, and restored to its truest meaning. I came to believe that the most radical evangelical impulses, like hot coals on a dying fire, might be fanned back into flames."[18] Wallis, therefore, sought a theological education, a journey that took him to Trinity Evangelical Divinity School (TEDS), an Evangelical seminary in an affluent suburb of Chicago.

Wallis's journey reflects larger issues in Evangelicalism in the late decades of the twentieth century. Wallis considered himself a nineteenth-century evangelical who believed "that most of the important movements for social change in America have been fueled by . . . progressive religion."[19] According to Wallis, revivalism and social justice should be joined in holy matrimony, and nineteenth-century evangelicalism embodied this union. Twentieth-century Evangelicalism witnessed a painful divorce, as fundamentalism prioritized individual spirituality over social transformation.[20] While fundamentalists did not shy away from the exploitation of cultural tools,[21] they emphasized engaging the culture for the sake of saving individuals. As a result, personal evangelism became the primary expression of Christian faith at the expense of concern for social problems.

This narrative served as the dominant perspective of American Christianity as understood by progressive Evangelicals, and Wallis identified the institutional Evangelical church as part of the problem. By ignoring social concerns, the Evangelical church failed to live up to the standards of authentic biblical faith. Wallis labeled this development the American captivity of the church and called for a "post-American" theology, expressed in the nascent ministry of Sojourners.

Sojourners sprang up in the heart of midwestern Evangelicalism. When Wallis arrived at TEDS, the questions that had dogged him early in his Evangelical journey continued to hound him. The idyllic, isolated, and racially homogeneous seminary campus provided a sharp contrast to the economic and racial sufferings in the city of Chicago. A conservative Evangelical seminary, TEDS became an unlikely incubator for the formation of Sojourners.[22]

In the early 1970s, a handful of TEDS students gathered to discuss the relationship between their Evangelical faith and the pressing issues of their times.[23] The seminary students that initiated *The Post-American* publication reflected the inchoate movement of progressive Evangelicals. As Wallis describes their core commitment, "The gospel message that had nurtured us as children was now turning us against the injustice and violence of our nation's leading institutions and causing us to repudiate the church's conformity to a system that we believed to be biblically wrong."[24]

The TEDS students led antiwar demonstrations and protested against the TEDS system, including the distribution of inflammatory edicts.[25] Their actions drew the negative attention of the administration, which was under pressure from alumni to expel the students.[26] These same students helped found *The Post-American*, which served as the precursor to *Sojourners* magazine. Both magazines reflected the discontent of younger Evangelicals, who were reacting against the individualistic, materialistic, nationalistic, sexist, and racist religion that dominated American Evangelicalism at that time.

Similar to the student gathering at TEDS, a growing Evangelical leftist movement began to form on Christian college campuses. In addition to the formation of Evangelicals for McGovern,[27] InterVarsity chapters were established, and new publications appeared. As David Swartz notes, "Key students, faculty, and benefactors [at various Christian] institutions, driven by a rising social consciousness, showed a rather astonishing resonance with progressive and radical politics that would culminate in a 1973 bid in Chicago to capture large chunks of evangelicalism."[28] The Chicago Declaration of 1973 "included confessions of the evangelical community's sins of omission and commission in areas of justice such as racism, sexism, economic exploitation, and militaristic nationalism."[29]

The Post-American found itself in the middle of this rising stream of progressive Evangelicalism. As the publication grew in readership, Jim Wallis expanded his national speaking engagements, which led to his withdrawal from TEDS.[30] At the same time, an intentional living community formed in the city of Chicago around the publication. Within a short period of time, however, the community collapsed. Members later reflected that the community focused too much on conceptualizing the community and finding the right structures and not enough on the quality of relationships with each other.[31] In 1975 the publication moved to Washington, DC, and renamed itself *Sojourners*, launching a new phase of ministry with a new community formed around the publication.

Sojourners Progresses

From the late 1970s onward, the focus of Evangelical political involvement centered on the role of the religious right. Evangelicals received credit for the 1980 election of Ronald Reagan over the Evangelical incumbent, Jimmy Carter. Throughout the 1980s and 1990s, the Moral Majority and its successor, the Christian Coalition (along with Focus on the Family and the Phyllis Schlafly–led Eagle Forum) increased their influence and grip over both Evangelical Christianity and the Republican Party. The 2000 and 2004 elections of George W. Bush cemented this relationship.[32]

While the religious right gained momentum, *Sojourners* continued to publish social justice content for the Christian community. As the media increasingly identified Evangelicals with political conservatism, progressive Evangelicals remained largely out of the spotlight. The *Newsweek* cover story that declared 1976 the year of the Evangelical placed the progressive Evangelical movement at the end of the article.[33] Scholars were intrigued by the story of the religious right. As David Swartz observes, "In the understandable rush to explain the rise of the Moral Majority of the 1980s, the Christian Coalition of the 1990s, and the evangelical language of George W. Bush in the 2000s, scholars have neglected moderate and progressive sectors of evangelicalism."[34]

Sojourners, meanwhile, took on a more ecumenical flavor. Both the editorial board and the readership of the magazine reflected a larger swath of Christianity. By 1979, Evangelicals and charismatics composed only 41 percent of *Sojourners*' readership.[35] Within the magazine, *Sojourners* asserted its own role beyond Evangelicalism.

The November 1977 issue declares, "We are not merely or uniquely an evangelical magazine. . . . There will continue to be those who write for and read *Sojourners* who are deeply Christian but may well be non-evangelical."[36]

As early as 1976, *Sojourners* published a story that warned of "a major initiative by the evangelical far right in this country."[37] In Jim Wallis's 1983 *Revive Us Again*, he deduced that "since the Reagan victory, the political Right has sought to consolidate its gains. Forces both inside and outside the government are moving to define a political consensus further to the right than ever before."[38] Early in 1994, Wallis traced the short history of the religious right and revealed his frustration with the movement, in contrast to the Chicago Declaration.[39] As Wallis puts it, "By 1980 a new evangelical foray into politics emerged, known as the 'Religious Right.' The following years of Jerry Falwells and Pat Robertsons made Evangelicalism synonymous with the political Right. The promise of Chicago was effectively derailed—at least in the public perception—by this development."[40]

In "Beyond the Christian Right," Wallis asserts a claim that served as a common refrain: "Evangelical Christians are not all right wing; in fact, most are not. Changing this perception may be one of our most important political tasks in the raging culture war."[41] *Sojourners* reflected the frustration that the religious right rather than progressive Evangelicals had emerged as representative of Evangelicals.

In 1995 Sojourners launched the Call to Renewal movement "to specifically focus on poverty by uniting churches and faith-based organizations across the theological and political spectrum to lift up those whom Jesus called 'the least of these.'"[42] The movement presented Christian concern regarding the issue of poverty, which was often lost in the rhetoric of the religious right. In *Who Speaks for God?*, which was released in the incipient stage of Call to Renewal, Wallis claims that "the Christian Right does not represent all the Christians in America, or even most of them. The media-created perception of a right-wing evangelical juggernaut is the most tragic misperception in American politics today. It is time to change that perception."[43]

The emergence of Call to Renewal reflected the need to respond directly to the rapid proliferation of the religious right. *Sojourners* increasingly focused on the negative impact of the religious right. In the March/April 1995 issue of *Sojourners*, Jim Wallis, Tony Campolo, Tom Sine, Marian Wright Edelman, and Roberta Hestenes published articles critical of the religious right. The authors accuse the religious right of hijacking American Evangelicalism and draining the meaning of the word.[44] Their message of opposition to the religious right drew national attention to the larger work of Sojourners as it advocated for progressive Christianity on a political level.

The Washington, DC, location bolstered the political work of Sojourners, but the DC location also supported the ministry of the Sojourners community. The national impact of Sojourners depended on the Sojourners community, which grew out of the common work of *Sojourners* magazine. In turn, the magazine relied on the Sojourners community to produce the magazine and contribute stories about community life.[45] Wallis acknowledged that "the relationship between the members of our little group was the foundation for the publication of the magazine."[46]

Prior to moving to Washington, DC, a community had formed in Chicago around the publication of *The Post-American*. That community gradually eroded as they would testify that "we formally dissolved the bonds and commitments that had been between us. . . . The great experiment had failed. Our life together had formally ended."[47] Despite the failure of that initial community, a subset of the group decided to leave Chicago for Washington, DC. The move resulted in a serendipitous contribution to the long-term impact of Sojourners.

The impetus for the move did not arise from a desire to move closer to the center of power. Instead, the move was precipitated by a desire to engage in urban ministry in an inner-city neighborhood.

As Wallis writes, "The big drawback of Washington was that it is the nation's capital and the center of political power, and we didn't want to be in the middle of all that. But we decided to come anyway and live in one of the poor sections of the city. It often amuses me when people think that the reason we came to Washington, like most everyone else here, was to be closer to the center of power, when in reality that fact almost kept us from coming."[48] The community would also move within Washington, DC, to maintain an incarnational presence among the urban poor.

The Sojourners community pursued a model of intentional living community until February 1998. "The community lived together in common households, had a common purse, formed a worshipping community, got involved in neighborhood issues, organized national events on behalf of peace and justice and continued to publish the magazine."[49] In the fifth anniversary issue of *Sojourners*, the lead article describes the community as a cluster of households that function as "an extended family unit. . . . The household has also become a place where poor and homeless people can be incorporated into our life."[50] As late as 1987, the Sojourners community financial report showed that the community continued to pool its resources and shared expenses.[51]

Wallis recognized the important role of the Sojourners community in his publishing success. The introduction to 1981's *The Call to Conversion* acknowledges that "thanks for this book must go to the whole Sojourners community. It literally grew out of our life together and was, indeed, a community endeavor."[52] The community life of Sojourners served an integral role in the social justice work of Sojourners. A regular column called the "Euclid Street Journal" appeared in the pages of *Sojourners* magazine and provided snapshots of the Sojourner community, and the urban location of the community proved to be an essential factor of its success. "Our community makes its home in the 14th Street 'riot corridor,' one of the sections of Washington that burned during the riots following the assassination of Martin Luther King, Jr."[53]

By presenting stories of the community life, Sojourners spearheaded the organization of other intentional communities. Letters poured into *Sojourners* seeking to join the Sojourners community, asking for assistance on starting intentional communities, and seeking to network with other intentional communities.[54] Another regular column in *Sojourners* magazine provided advice to other intentional communities. The Sojourners community emerged as an exemplary community for progressive Evangelicals. Not only did the magazine advocate for the poor, but also the Sojourners community embodied real-life ministry to the poor.

Sojourners impacted its local DC neighborhood, but its broader, national influence depended not only on the distribution of the magazine but also—maybe more importantly—on the popularity of Jim Wallis's books. One book in particular thrust Wallis and Sojourners onto a much larger platform. *God's Politics* arrived at the right moment in American Evangelical political history. Because the religious right had dominated the conversation regarding the Evangelical role in American politics, conservative politics went hand in hand with conservative theology. Written after the second George W. Bush election, *God's Politics* declared the end of the conservative monologue and the beginning of a genuine political dialogue among people of faith. In the book, Wallis avers that neither the religious right nor the secular left understands the role of values in politics.[55]

Prior to the release of *God's Politics*, Sojourners engaged more explicitly in national politics. The February 2004 issue of *Sojourners* attached a voter registration application.[56] The October 2004 issue featured an article by Jim Wallis titled "The Religious Right Era Is Over." The article declares that "God is not a Republican. Or a Democrat. . . . Jerry Falwell, Pat Robertson, and other extreme fundamentalists are losing credibility among the faithful by putting loyalty to party before loyalty to scripture. . . . A backlash has begun, even among evangelicals."[57] The culmination of this explicit campaign in opposition to the religious right was the release of *God's Politics*.

The success of the book propelled Jim Wallis into media-star status. Wallis made a well-received appearance on *The Daily Show with Jon Stewart*, where the usually cynical and snarky Stewart warmed up to Wallis. Politicians—even Democrats—reached out to him. During this time, Wallis fostered a burgeoning friendship with a young Illinois state senator named Barack Obama, who later presented a key speech on his own faith at the 2006 Call to Renewal conference. Wallis would later state that while presidents had become his friends, Obama was the first friend to become president.

If Sojourners' prophetic challenge to the agenda of the religious right proved to be its Mount Everest, then the election of Barack Obama was K2. Both moments represented heights that may never be scaled again. Jim Wallis and Sojourners reached this pinnacle by precipitating the demise of the religious right and spurring the Evangelical shift toward Barack Obama. The election of Obama cemented Jim Wallis's role as an Evangelical political influencer.

The impact of *God's Politics* reached beyond the secular media and politics to the audience that Sojourners started with: Evangelicals. As Jim Wallis made the circuit of both the secular halls of power and Christian institutions, his positive reputation grew among Evangelicals, particularly younger Evangelicals. A whole new generation of Evangelical Christians discovered Jim Wallis and Sojourners. The emerging church looked toward Sojourners to guide its inquiry into postmodern and post-Evangelical expressions of faith,[58] and *Sojourners* increased its web presence with sojo.net. The *God's Politics* blog attracted younger writers and a younger readership. Younger Evangelicals conferred Wallis with rock-star status as he made the rounds of Christian colleges and seminaries. Even TEDS invited him back to speak at its chapel. As more and more Evangelicals embraced Wallis, Wallis embraced them back.

Following up the politically focused *God's Politics*, Wallis wrote *The Great Awakening*, in which he sounds a hopeful note linking spiritual revival with political change: "I'd like to report that many Americans, and in particular many people of faith in this country, believe we can do better with both our religion and our politics. . . . We may be approaching a new 'revival' of faith. . . . Personal transformation is necessary for social movements, and social movements are necessary to transform politics."[59]

In *The Great Awakening*, reflecting the language of revivalist Christianity, Wallis employs the heritage of spiritual revivalism to inoculate social justice with Evangelical language. After the book's publication, Sojourners launched a series of Justice Revivals that were modeled after the Billy Graham crusades. Pastors and Christian leaders from a particular city worked together to host a Justice Revival with Wallis as the keynote speaker. Harking back to his Evangelical roots while maintaining his progressive Evangelical agenda, Wallis used altar calls as a way to call participants to social justice activism.

From Wallis's perspective, his message had been consistent for the past three decades. For some reason, it rang true at that particular moment. Wallis continued to oppose the American conservative captivity of Evangelicalism and asserted a progressive Evangelical position on concern for the poor. He raised the flag for biblical social justice yet retained a strong sense of Evangelical revivalism.

One major difference between the earlier expression and the latest incarnation of Sojourners, however, was the change in the Sojourners community. The central and primary role of the intentional community that had so deeply shaped Sojourners in its first few decades had dissolved by the close of the twentieth century. The intentional, incarnate households in an inner-city DC neighborhood no longer defined the Sojourners community. The formerly "war-torn" Columbia Heights had evolved into a gentrified neighborhood, and the neighborhood-based grassroots ministries of the Sojourners community had given way to a more national political advocacy approach.

The May/June 1995 issue featured an advertisement for a Sojourner "National Organizer to join its Washington, DC staff." The position required "coordinating a network that provides an alternative to the Religious Right. . . . [The National Organizer will] help create and implement press strategy, and will represent Sojourners in national coalition and networks."[60] Instead of advertising for a community organizer that would work in the local Fourteenth Street neighborhood, the position called for a national presence that leveraged Washington, DC, as a location of power and influence. The new millennium saw the evolution of Sojourners as a ministry that embraced the power politics of the nation's capitol.

Sojourners acknowledged that "today, the community context has shifted away from an intentional model; rather we are a committed group of Christians who work together to live a gospel life that integrates spiritual renewal and social justice."[61] The days of community meals and shared bank accounts had passed. In the July/August 1998 issue of *Sojourners*, Jim Wallis acknowledged, "It's been awhile since we've reported much to our magazine readers about Sojourners Community. . . . It's been some years since we all lived in large households and shared a common purse."[62] Wallis compares Sojourners to Dorothy Day's Catholic Worker, which she described as a school where individuals would come and go. In the article, Wallis describes Sojourners as

a dispersed community, a Diaspora, scattered across the country and around the world. . . . The "school" has been much wider than those who have had direct contact with the community in Washington, DC. For almost 30 years, people around the world have told me how much they feel connected and a part of Sojourners, just by consistently reading the magazine. They tell me that Sojourners has been their community, even though they have never lived as part of it. Thousands, of course, have visited the community, and tens of thousands have participated in Sojourners events.[63]

The casual, plaid-shirt-and-jeans environment of the Sojourners community had given way to dress shirts, ties, and business attire. The unheated back porches that served as makeshift production rooms and the dilapidated buildings that had been home to house-hold communities had been replaced by space in a professional building with cubicles and private offices. The 1998 article reveals that "'community' is understood more broadly today than it was in the days when it was defined as more intentional and residential."[64] Broadening the original definition of community, Sojourners asserted that community should encompass a larger national network of like-minded individuals. The ministry of Sojourners had expanded beyond the Columbia Heights neighborhood to encompass a community no longer defined by a specific location or specific group of people.

Sojourners experienced numerous twists and turns in its first forty years of public ministry. A radical incarnational community that worked with the powerless evolved into a Washington, DC–based ministry working with the politically powerful. The White House that arrested the radical activist members of the Sojourners community now proved to be an ally that created scheduling conflicts as a result of the number of meetings it requested with Jim Wallis.

The story of Jim Wallis and Sojourners reveals the larger narrative of progressive Evangelicalism, which emerged from the larger story of American Evangelicalism. The activist impulse that had been directed almost exclusively toward personal evangelism would now be directed toward political involvement, and progressive Evangelicals were not alone in this movement. The religious right also followed this trajectory, as both expressions of Evangelicalism attempted to address the question of the church's relationship to culture.

Jim Wallis and Sojourners held the conviction that the religious right had infiltrated Evangelicalism by posing as a wolf in sheep's clothing. The religious right did not represent the perspective held by the majority of Evangelicals. Wallis believed that progressive Evangelicalism more accurately reflected the Evangelical story. Sojourners' confidence in the rightness of its position drove the organization to stand against the religious right, even as the religious right encompassed a larger swath of Evangelicalism. For their part, progressive Evangelicals sought God's kingdom on earth. The culture could be redeemed through a proactive involvement in both politics and the community. Toward that end, Sojourners engaged in the embodiment of incarnational communities to contribute to the kingdom.

Progressive Evangelicalism, however, may have become a victim of its own success. A grassroots movement that at times seemed to be on the fringes of Evangelicalism was catapulted into the spotlight as Sojourners shifted from a grounded, grassroots community working with the marginalized in a specific DC neighborhood to a nationally focused and professionalized advocacy group that thrived in Washington politics. The counterculture revolutionaries who espoused revolutionary change received validation from the establishment they battled.

The journey of Jim Wallis and Sojourners may simply reflect the larger narrative of America after the Vietnam War. The financial success of the '80s and '90s tempered the radicalism of the '60s and '70s. Hippies evolved into yuppies. Countercultural prophets became spiritual advisers to the king. The ultimate outsiders realized the benefits of insider status.

The trajectory of Sojourners as an extended national community that seeks advocacy for the poor on the level of national politics holds potential. The Sojourners community, however, incurred a high cost. The dissolution of the intentional community that ministered to the poor is a contributing cause and a casualty of this transformation. The question lingers as to whether the benefit of a national platform compensates for the loss of a local community.

Sojourners made a broader impact on Evangelicalism and American society by providing an important perspective within the American political landscape. Using the platform of the *Sojourners* magazine, books, conferences, and personal relationships built over the years, Sojourners presented an alternative voice to the religious right. The organization's strong advocacy for the poor emerged from on-the-ground work in a particular neighborhood. The community could speak for the poor because they lived among the poor. Advocating for the poor is challenging work, particularly when we are disconnected from the life of the poor. Sojourners' prophetic challenge found greater validity in its connection to the real-life stories of the poor.

Sojourners did not waver from the important role of prophetic advocacy. While broadening its constituency beyond the stereotypical Evangelical subculture to include mainline Protestant and Catholic allies, Sojourners continued to claim an Evangelical identity. Even when the Sojourner community moved out of a specific DC neighborhood, the voice of Sojourners continued on behalf of the poor. Positional improvement did not cause the organization to turn its focus inward, and Sojourners' advocacy proved its willingness to speak on behalf of others, particularly the very "least of these."

An Immigrant Evangelical's Sojourn

The story of progressive Evangelicalism resonates with this immigrant Evangelical (Soong-Chan), whose own narrative and worldview never jibed with the privileged narrative of the religious right. The religious right often seemed to be an attempt by the dominant culture to maintain centrality and privilege. If Evangelicalism were to be defined exclusively in the domain of white, suburban Republicans, then I did not fit within the movement. My own journey as an Evangelical aligned more with the progressive Evangelical trajectory, and the lessons I learned arose from my intersection with this community.

The year of my Evangelical discontent dawned in 1990. Having recently completed my undergraduate education, I languished in a secure federal government position while faithfully serving my church on the weekends. Deeply rooted in the evangelical theology of the Korean immigrant church, I could not imagine ever turning in my metaphorical Evangelical membership card. But I struggled with the shallowness of American Evangelicalism.

My youth group, the locus of my Evangelical conversion, focused on my personal spiritual growth. Evangelicalism was reduced to an individualistic expression, and my ticket to heaven was punched with the required purchases of the Scofield Bible and *Evidence That Demands a Verdict*. My years as an undergraduate in New York reintroduced me to a world that I had abandoned since my family moved out of inner-city Baltimore to a Maryland suburb. The jarring juxtaposition of my secular education on the border of Harlem with my comfortable suburban church could not be reconciled. My church offered the power of Christ's resurrection only to call believers to go apple picking with their small group. My new, late-model import car failed to provide me with the expected satisfaction of having arrived into middle-class America at such a young age.

In the midst of my Evangelical angst, I stumbled across the *Sojourners'* article "The Second Reformation Has Begun." During college my InterVarsity staff worker referenced *Sojourners* magazine as a good resource. Most Evangelicals in my circle were either unfamiliar with the magazine or steered me away from it, but that particular article proved revelatory. No longer could I reduce my faith to multiple trips to the altar and a feel-good, individualized faith. Suddenly, my Mazda 626 represented oppression rather than triumph.

My personal Evangelical angst reflected the years of confusion and division within evangelical history itself. My immigrant family had emerged from poverty and marginalization, and with my graduation from an Ivy League school I had achieved middle-American success. I conjectured that I could proceed to law school, make a lot of money, and relish my role as a faithful church tither, but what difference would my faith have made in that scenario? Was I simply called to be a good person who would focus on my family? Sojourners challenged my American Evangelical assumptions and redirected the trajectory of my life. Progressive Evangelicalism resonated with my desire to bring the biblical values of compassion and justice to the world rather than run away and hide from the world. Progressive Evangelicalism engaging in an active faith that sought to positively transform the world was a viable alternative to the dominant culture's insistence on maintaining the status quo for the benefit of the already privileged.

In 1999, I stood in the basement of a Washington, DC, church nursing my rapidly cooling cup of church percolator coffee. Having just arrived at the Call to Renewal conference sponsored by Sojourners, I was looking for a friendly face. I turned around and nearly collided with Jim Wallis. I didn't think he would remember me, but his face lit up in recognition. He warmly embraced me and welcomed me to the conference.

A few months earlier, I had met Jim Wallis for the first time. In 1996 my wife and I planted a multiethnic church in an inner-city neighborhood where we attempted to embody the values of Sojourners. One of my church members who served as a teaching assistant for Wallis's Harvard Divinity School class arranged the meet. We chatted about the urban ministry work of my church, and he shared stories from his own journey. I inquired about the difficulties of raising a family in the urban context, and he excitedly produced pictures of his newborn son. As our conversation progressed, he invited me to the upcoming Call to Renewal conference and expressed interest in mobilizing Asian-American pastors for the movement. He challenged me to raise the flag to see who rallied around it. I sent out emails to all of my Asian pastor friends. None of them attended the conference.

I came to the conference in search of like-minded individuals. While our church had reached a comfortable level of attendance, the church down the street that ignored social issues was expanding at a faster rate. The conference touched on many issues that our church faced, such as ministry with at-risk youth and community organizing. I met participants from historic black churches, mainline congregations, and a few Evangelicals. The conference confirmed my commitment to pursue justice in the urban context. Our church did not stand alone. At the same time, the conference felt like a small and ghettoized movement on the margins of Evangelicalism. On my return flight, I perused my copy of *The Washington Post*. The only article referencing Christianity focused on the increasing influence of the religious right. In the eyes of the media and many of my Evangelical colleagues, progressive Evangelicalism was not the winning team.

In 2009, I sat in a Starbucks in northwest Washington, DC, one block away from the Sojourners offices on Fourteenth Street. I cradled my four-dollar latte and acknowledged various Sojourners employees stopping by for their daily caffeine. I stepped out of the Starbucks and looked around the neighborhood that was Sojourners' home for many years. A fancy new shopping complex had opened across the street. Uptown Cafe and The Heights Restaurant served the gentrifying population in the neighborhood, featuring yuppie fare such as "Spinach and Goat Cheese Quiche" and "Crispy Tofu in Coconut Green Curry"—items I doubt appeared on the menu of Martha's Table Soup Kitchen several blocks up the street.

A few years earlier, I had joined the board of Sojourners, and in subsequent years, I joined the boards of the Christian Community Development Association and World Vision. My involvement in urban and social justice ministry led me to positions of influence within Evangelical circles. Upon Obama's election, Jim Wallis asked me to join a convening of faith leaders that would provide a Christian voice to the new administration.

Recently promoted in my new role as a seminary professor, I anticipated my tenure review in a few more years. As I transitioned to my role at the seminary, I moved away from the on-the-ground ministry of the urban church I helped plant. I had entered into a new phase of ministry. My work involved training others to do actual ministry, but I did not feel that my work was any less important. But I longed for the days when riding around in the back of a police car and visiting gang youth was the highlight of my week.

At each step of my Evangelical journey, Sojourners played an important part. At a time when I had grown frustrated with the narrow fundamentalism of my youth, Sojourners provided a biblical perspective that broadened by Christian worldview. As a young, church-planting pastor who was committed to many of the same values as Sojourners, the writings of Jim Wallis and *Sojourners* magazine provided encouragement to continue to faithfully pursue God's kingdom values. Even as I entered into phases of ministry where security and comfort proved to be strong temptations, Sojourners maintained its radical edge despite learning to play in the adult world. In each step of my Evangelical journey, I have learned the value of a progressive Evangelicalism that engages the culture rather than eschewing it.

PART 3

Justice Confronts Power in Community

5

African-American Evangelicals and the Challenge of True Racial Reconciliation

The striking figure of Tom Skinner approached the podium at InterVarsity Christian Fellowship's 1970 Urbana Student Missions Conference. His appearance puzzled many in the predominantly white Evangelical college student audience who had gathered for one of the most significant student mission gatherings in North America. During a time of great turmoil in American society, Skinner preached a landmark sermon titled "The U.S. Racial Crisis and World Evangelism." The sermon would strike at the heart of Evangelicalism with a prophetic challenge to confront aspects of racism found in American society and American Christianity.

Skinner's rousing rhetoric captured the imagination of the Evangelical students. When Skinner closed out his sermon with a resounding proclamation—"The Liberator has come!"—his audience erupted in a thunderous and sustained ovation. Carl Ellis, a key African-American InterVarsity student leader at Urbana 1967 who had staged a protest and subsequently negotiated for Skinner's inclusion in Urbana 1970, recalls the prophetic power of Skinner's words and the sense that people were shaken to their foundations.[1] William Pannell, who served with Tom Skinner Associates and would eventually join the faculty of Fuller Theological Seminary, described the scene from his perspective on the platform as "dynamite." "I have never seen such an explosion of joy and acceptance in response to a sermon."[2]

The 1970 Urbana Student Missions Conference became a benchmark event for African-American Evangelicals in both positive and negative ways. Skinner's presentation signaled the increasing prominence and the fresh prophetic voice offered by black Evangelicalism. However, Skinner also represented a prophetic voice that made many white Evangelicals nervous. The story of the emergence and eventual decline of African-American Evangelicals in the 1960s and '70s reveals the myriad challenges American Evangelicals face as they engage the issues of race, racism, and racial reconciliation.

At the close of the twentieth century, American Evangelicalism identified overwhelmingly with white Christians, and North American church history focused the Evangelical story on those of European, particularly Anglo, descent. The defining face of late twentieth-century American Evangelicalism can be identified as an educated, upper-middle-class, fifty-year-old white male living near a seminary in an exurb community.

Historian Donald Dayton challenges the dominant motif of the Evangelical story by calling attention to the Evangelical diversity that is present outside the Calvinistic Presbyterian and Baptist networks that have often defined Evangelicalism.[3] Dayton confronts the scholars who have helped to limit the boundaries of American evangelicalism. To Dayton, those scholars "have focused mainly in their writings on the movement's intellectual leaders, usually privileged white men with Calvinistic worldviews and cultural pretensions that put them at odds with the vast majority of their followers."[4]

A narrow reading of Evangelical identity has resulted in the exclusion of the story of nonwhite evangelicals. Nonwhite evangelicals have often had difficulty finding acceptance in the dominant white Evangelical culture. In the twentieth century, the domination of the white Evangelical story has specifically resulted in the exclusion of African-Americans from the white Evangelical mainstream. A 1979 work on Evangelical theology by John Woodbridge, Mark Noll, and Nathan Hatch offers only passing references to black Evangelicalism. As the text states, "The cornerstones of the inarticulate black theology were for the forgiveness of sins, awe of God, religious ecstasy, self-respect in Christ, ethical earnestness, and hope."[5] In the subject index, "Black Christians: and other evangelicals" yields a total of five pages in a 253-page work, and the entry "sovereignty of God" yields eleven pages of references.[6] Even the story of self-identified Evangelicals in the black community and their attempts at integration with the larger white Evangelical movement remains severely underreported. For example, one of the most extensive archival collections on American Evangelicalism, the Billy Graham Center Archives at Wheaton College, has one folder on the entire history of the National Black Evangelical Association.

For most of American Evangelical history, the black church was excluded from categorization as Evangelical. In 2006, journalist Ed Gilbreath reported that

> recent studies by sociologists and political scientists estimate the number of evangelicals in the United States at 25 to 30 percent of the population, or between seventy and eighty million people. However, these estimates usually separate out nearly all of the nation's African American Protestant population (roughly 8 or 9 percent of the US population), which . . . is typically pretty evangelical in

theology and orientation. Indeed, 61 percent of blacks—the highest of any racial group, by far—described themselves as "born again" in a 2001 Gallup poll.[7]

In spite of similar theological stances, there exists a lack of connection between white Evangelicals and the black church. As Oberlin College church historian A. G. Miller notes, "Most scholars who study the evangelical phenomenon have had a difficult time situating black Evangelicalism historiographically and tracing its development as a movement."[8]

The focus of this chapter is the development of a uniquely African-American Evangelical identity in the 1960s and '70s. The formation of this identity emerged from a strong black identity (the black nationalist movement and civil rights movement of that era) engaging with a conservative Evangelical theology, which arose from the context of the larger Evangelical movement. While the prophetic presence of these African-American Evangelicals had the potential to make a great impact on the larger movement of Evangelicalism, numerous factors consistently undermined the influence of black Evangelicals. Three different examples—the National Black Evangelical Association, Tom Skinner, and Circle Church—provide insight into mainstream Evangelicalism's resistance to prophetic challenges.

The Formation of the National Black Evangelical Association[9]

The initial failure to see the black church as an expression of evangelical faith has yielded an unnecessary gulf between white and black Evangelicals. From the very beginning, the black church reflected an evangelical ethos. As William Pannell notes, "The origins of the black Christian experience in America were evangelical in nature. Some elements of evangelicalism could be found in the early attempts of the Church of England to convert and baptize blacks."[10] The black church, while holding to an evangelical theology, developed a particular expression that served the particular cultural context of African-American Christianity. "African American Protestantism evolved as a special hybrid of black culture and international evangelicalism. Rooted deeply in the Bible and empowered by the Spirit, black faith was facilitated initially by evangelical witness."[11]

The exclusion of the traditional and historical black church from the larger Evangelical movement meant that in the latter half of the twentieth century, a new category needed to emerge to intersect with white Evangelicalism. One expression of that emergence is the National Black Evangelical Association (NBEA). While not all black Evangelicals during this time were associated with the NBEA, the NBEA stands as an important institution that facilitated the rise of a black Evangelical identity. Founded in 1963 at a conference in Los Angeles and originally known as the National Negro Evangelical Association (NNEA), the NBEA's story reveals four different formative threads. While several threads were sometimes present in the same individual, each of the four distinct influences contributed to the formation of the NBEA.[12]

The Nottage brothers of the Plymouth Black Brethren make up the fundamentalist thread,[13] which is one of the four key influences of the NBEA. The Nottages converted to Christianity in their native island of Eluthera in the Bahamas. After immigrating to the United States, the Nottage brothers aggressively pursued evangelistic efforts throughout the urban African-American community and established a number of churches in various cities across the United States. These churches formed a cluster separate from the association of white Plymouth Brethren.[14] While organizationally separate from the larger white denomination, they continued to reflect the conservative fundamentalism of their white counterparts in the middle of the twentieth century. Both the theology and the eschatology of the Nottages aligned with the theology of fundamentalists.[15]

The fundamentalist strain of the NBEA (having emerged out of the context of the black church in the Caribbean rather than the historic black church in the United States) also provided a contrast to the influence of the historic black church, often resulting in conflict and suspicion.

> The modern black evangelical movement, as it developed, placed more emphasis on the propositional aspects of faith than on experiential and ecstatic elements. This caused some strains between the black evangelical movement and the traditional black church, leading some black evangelicals to characterize the historic black church as "apostate" and "unbiblical." Conversely, some in mainline black churches labeled black evangelicals as doctrinaire and schismatic "fanatics."[16]

The fundamentalist thread, particularly through the influence of B. M. Nottage, is evident in NBEA leaders such as "Marvin Prentis, the first president of the NBEA; William Pannell, professor of evangelism at Fuller Theological Seminary; and Howard Jones, the first black associate of Billy Graham."[17]

African-American Pentecostals account for the second thread—specifically the trinitarian Pentecostal tradition, which includes the Church of God in Christ and the United Pentecostal Council of the Assembly of God. William H. Bentley, who became one of the most important voices within the NBEA, emerged from this thread, and his wife, Ruth Bentley, not only served an important role in the formation and establishment of the NBEA but also continued to uphold the work of the NBEA after her husband's passing. William Bentley served as the president of the NBEA from 1970 to 1976 and proved to be an important consensus builder for the organization. Bentley also self-published the NBEA's only self-reported historical document: *The National Black Evangelical Association: Evolution of a Concept of Ministry*. The Pentecostal thread differed from the fundamentalist thread in that many of the black Pentecostals emerged from traditionally black denominations free of white control. As a result, the Pentecostals within the NBEA represented a middle way between the fundamentalist thread of the NBEA and the traditional black churches.

The third thread emerged out of the growing number of African-Americans graduating from Evangelical institutions. After World War II, a number of African-Americans attended Evangelical educational institutions such as Wheaton College, Moody Bible Institute, Trinity Evangelical Divinity School, and Fuller Theological Seminary. Though influenced by these educational institutions in relatively small numbers, these pioneering African-Americans provided a significant base of leadership for black Evangelicalism. The conservative teaching of Evangelical institutions took root in these African-American Evangelical leaders, and since their theological framework arose from white Evangelical Christianity, an organization like the NBEA was able to foster contextual reflection on the social and racial reality of the African-American experience. Part of the role of the NBEA was to develop a uniquely black theological reflection in addition to the conservative theological framework that these African-American Christians had received in Evangelical educational institutions.

The connection between black Evangelicals and predominantly white institutions extended into African-American involvement in parachurch organizations, such as InterVarsity Christian Fellowship, Youth for Christ, and Campus Crusade for Christ. The 1960s and '70s began to see an increasing involvement of black Evangelicals in white Evangelical institutions. However, these black Evangelicals were increasingly frustrated in the face of white Evangelical racism. As one of the few ethnic minority organizations in predominantly white Evangelical institutions, the NBEA provided a venue for black Evangelicals to engage with one another as they faced these challenges.

Black Evangelicals often found themselves frustrated during the early stages of the white Evangelical movement. "This tension primarily sprang from what blacks perceived as the white Evangelical indifference toward and lack of sympathy for the evangelistic needs of African-Americans. Eventually, some black Evangelicals charged their white counterparts with a spiritual 'benign neglect,' a charge that evolved into a stronger allegation of racism."[18] The NBEA gave black Evangelicals the opportunity to connect with one another and to develop an Evangelical theology that incorporated greater sensitivity to the African-American community.

African-American evangelists—whose expressions of evangelistic ministry mirrored those of white Evangelicals, including crusades, altar calls, and the prioritizing of personal salvation—account for the fourth thread of the NBEA. Because of the emphasis on personal evangelism, many of these evangelists received sponsorship and support from white fundamentalists and Evangelicals. The aforementioned Ralph Bell was a black evangelist. Howard Jones, an evangelist, and Jimmy McDonald, a musician, both served with the Billy Graham Association. Jones frequently appeared on the radio in Billy Graham's stead.

But the most notable African-American evangelist was Tom Skinner, who represented the Harlem Evangelistic Association (which eventually became Tom Skinner Associates). Skinner was a nationally recognized evangelist who possessed a gripping testimony that appealed to both blacks and whites. But his entrance into the NBEA represented more than the presence of black evangelists: Skinner's involvement led to the introduction of the "young turks" into the NBEA. The "young turks" included Tom Skinner, Carl Ellis, Columbus Sally, and others who were more holistic in their approach to evangelism. Some of the fundamentalist roots of the early NBEA eventually came into conflict with the social justice emphasis of the younger black Evangelicals. At the 1969 NBEA conference held in Atlanta, William Bentley notes that "the lines were clearly drawn between those Blacks who were identified with a more socially conservative bent, and who, on account, some felt, enjoyed close relationships with the white Evangelical establishment, and those Blacks who felt that more conscious efforts ought to be made to actively accept our own culture and carefully relate the Gospel claims within that context."[19]

The emergence of this social justice emphasis and a strong black identity provided a balance to the strongly personal evangelism emphasis that characterized the early years of the NBEA. "As a result, for the first time in the history of the organization, the position was unequivocally expressed that white methods to reach Black people had been historically proven to be inadequate."[20] As awareness grew regarding the shortcomings of white Evangelical methods applied to the African-American context, the NBEA became a safe haven for African-American Evangelicals to explore issues specific to their own community and to develop their own theological framework and Evangelical identity. However, the formation of a unique, black Evangelical identity meant the diminishing support of the white Evangelical community, which is exemplified by the story of Tom Skinner.

Tom Skinner and the Challenge to Evangelicalism

In many ways, Tom Skinner's story mirrors the trajectory of the NBEA. Skinner was an Evangelical through and through, yet his message was not considered to be within the bounds of mainstream Evangelicalism. Not only was his initial foray into Evangelicalism rooted in his ability to share his personal conversion story and speak about his individual salvation journey, but this ability to powerfully communicate an Evangelical gospel message caused many in both the white and black communities to take notice. In *The National Black Evangelical Association*, William Bentley observes the following about the emergence of Tom Skinner: "Young and captivating, charismatic and capable, Tom expanded the mental and spiritual horizons of what Black ministry could be. His rare gifts of communication made him, even then, a figure to be reckoned with. . . . With [his first book], *Black and Free*, he became an overnight sensation and to many, 'the' major voice of Black Evangelicalism."[21] Though Skinner provided the best of what white Evangelicalism sought from black Evangelicalism, he also came to exemplify white Evangelicalism's inability to deal with black Evangelicalism.

Skinner was the son of a Baptist preacher, born in Harlem, New York. His family pushed Skinner toward an intellectual engagement with the world around him. In an interview for the Billy Graham Center Archives, Skinner reveals, "My father . . . placed a strong emphasis on the mind. So my father urged us . . . to read very early. By the time I was twelve, thirteen years old I had read five or six of Shakespeare's plays. I had read Othello and Macbeth and Hamlet, Julius Caesar. . . . He believed that the way black people overcome is that you just have to be educated."[22]

Skinner was a good student, "president of his high-school student body, a member of the basketball team, president of the Shakespearean Club, and an active member of his church's youth department."[23] At the same time, Skinner was also the leader of the Harlem Lords, one of the most feared street gangs in New York City.

Skinner expressed disgruntlement with a distant God who seemed removed from the sufferings of his community. In *Black and Free*, Skinner writes, "As a teenager, I looked around and asked my father where God was in all this? I couldn't for the life of me see how God, if He cared for humanity at all, could allow the conditions that existed in Harlem."[24] Skinner states that he felt "it was necessary for me to disavow religion, Christianity. I could not reconcile the things that I was hearing in church with what was going on in the street. The violence, the hunger, the poverty, the oppression."[25]

Skinner voiced disenchantment with white Christianity's inadequate gospel. "There were whites who made a lot of noise about how God was the answer to all our problems and how the Bible was our hope. . . . Basically, this individual had a half dozen Bible verses for every social problem that existed. If you went to him and told him that a place like Harlem existed, he would say, 'Well, what those people up there need is a good dose of salvation.' That all sounded well and good, except for the fact that I never saw the fellow actually in Harlem administering that 'dose of salvation.'"[26]

Disappointed with the black church of his father's generation, Skinner lived a double life as the good church kid and the violent gang leader. The night before a big gang fight that could have established Skinner as one of the major gang leaders in New York, Skinner was converted by an unscheduled gospel radio broadcast. As Skinner puts it in *Black and Free*, the broadcast featured a preacher whom Skinner characterizes as emotional, uncouth, and uneducated, but Skinner "got a spooky feeling this guy was talking right to me."[27] Skinner experienced a personal, spiritual conversion.

Ed Gilbreath notes the supernatural experience of Skinner's departure from the street gang.

> Few had voluntarily left the Harlem Lords without losing their lives. So when Skinner went to his 129 fellow gang members to announce he was quitting, he knew he would probably not leave the room alive. Terrified, Skinner informed the gangbangers that he had accepted Christ into his life and that he could no longer be a member of the Harlem Lords. Not one sound came from the bewildered gang. Skinner turned to leave the room. Still, no response. To his astonishment, Skinner left the room a free and unharmed man. Later, the gang member who had been Skinner's second-in-command told him that he wanted to kill him that night but that a strange force prevented him.[28]

Upon his conversion at the age of seventeen, Skinner left the street gang and embarked on the path of becoming an evangelist.

Skinner began to preach on the streets of Harlem, attracting crowds and winning converts. The formation of the Harlem Evangelistic Association led Skinner to schedule a major crusade at the world-renowned Apollo Theater in Harlem. The crusade cemented Skinner's reputation as a powerful evangelist, as more than 2,200 people responded to Skinner's preaching during the Harlem crusades. Skinner's oratorical gifts were recognized by all who heard him preach, including prominent white evangelists. In the early years of his ministry, Skinner worked with the white evangelist Jack Wyrtzen, who set aside one of the seven nights of crusades for Tom Skinner to preach. Oftentimes, Skinner's night was the most popular. As Skinner's profile rose with the backing and endorsement of many white Evangelicals, he began making appearances on Moody Radio and speaking at evangelistic crusades both around the country and across the Caribbean islands.

Skinner's appeal to the broader spectrum of Evangelicals came from telling his powerful personal testimony. The story of a tough gang member converting and becoming a crusade evangelist was irresistible to many white Evangelicals. But Skinner's testimony did not emerge out of a vacuum. His evangelistic efforts were in the shadow of a growing black nationalism and the civil rights movement. As Skinner's standard testimony about his life story became widespread, he began to move his message beyond the simple story of personal salvation that appealed to white Evangelicals and to incorporate more teachings on the kingdom of God and the necessity of social concern, responsibility, and action.

In 1969 and 1970, Skinner gained larger venues to speak his message to the Evangelical world. Skinner was invited in 1969 to address Wheaton College. In a stirring talk titled "Jesus the Revolutionary," Skinner cemented his move away from the standard Evangelical testimony in his move toward social concerns.

Skinner furthered this type of rhetoric in his sermon at the 1970 Urbana Student Missions Conference, directly challenging white Evangelicalism's failure to address the social sin of slavery. He also confronted an important social-historical foundation of Evangelicalism—its emphasis on individual salvation and piety above social justice:

You must keep in mind that, during this period of time, in general (there were some notable exceptions, but in general) the Evangelical, Bible-believing, fundamental, orthodox, conservative church in this country was strangely silent. In fact, there were those people who during slavery argued, "It is not our business to become involved in slavery. Those are social issues. We have been called to preach the gospel. We must deliver the Word. We must save people's souls. We must not get involved in the issues of liberating people from the chains of slavery. If they accept Jesus Christ as their Savior, by and by they will be free—over there."[29]

Skinner addressed the history of white racism from slavery to Jim Crow laws and used examples from white Evangelical churches. To a great extent, the Evangelical church in America supported the status quo. It supported slavery and segregation; it preached against any attempt of the black man to stand on his own two feet. And where the church did communicate the gospel to black people, it was always done as a way to keep them under control. "We will preach the gospel to those folks so they won't riot; we will preach the gospel to them so that we can keep the lid on the garbage pail."[30]

Skinner confronted the apathy of white Evangelicals who ignored social problems, going so far as to call them cowards. He refused to hold back on his understanding of the intersection between racial justice, social justice, and the gospel of Jesus Christ, masterfully weaving together multiple themes and raising a challenge to the status quo.

The standing ovation received by Skinner signaled a significant moment in African-American Evangelicalism; the response revealed that Skinner's sermons no longer operated exclusively in the realm of individual salvation. At a prominent Evangelical missions conference, Skinner had elevated the need to engage in social justice alongside personal evangelism. As William Pannell notes, "Skinner's speech that night was the climax to a conference that was being refocused. . . . This made some [InterVarsity] leaders very nervous. What would become of 'foreign' missions if students' attention was redirected to the USA and its urban challenges?"[31]

Other concerns emerged as Skinner rose to greater prominence in the white Evangelical community. Pannell recalls conversations with Tom Skinner in 1968 after a series of crusades in Newark, New Jersey, which was still smoking from race riots. Pannell and Skinner began to develop a deeper theological reflection on the kingdom of God that eventually became the focus of Skinner's sermons. Pannell recalls that as Skinner began to speak more about the kingdom of God, he began to be perceived as having a political agenda.[32] "Just as Skinner's ministry was attracting more attention from whites, his outspoken views on issues of social injustice facing the black community intensified (a fact that would lead many Christian radio stations to drop his program due to its 'political' content)."[33]

Pannell recalls that as the crusade's focus began to shift toward a kingdom theology and a more holistic understanding of evangelism, white Evangelicalism became increasingly suspicious. Skinner's increasingly frequent rejection by the broader white Evangelical community came to a head when he divorced his first wife in 1971. In the early 1970s, Tom's ever-growing ministry began to put a strain on his marriage. Tom and Vivian's marital problems eventually led to divorce. His divorce caused many friends to withdraw their support. Now with the rejection from much of the white evangelical community compounded by his divorce, Tom's life went through a significant time of transition.[34]

While Skinner continued in ministry, he did so in a different form after his divorce. Opting to focus on Christian leadership training, he formed a ministry that still bears his name—the Skinner Leadership Institute. Skinner also increased his influence with African-American leadership in other segments of society. He served as the chaplain for the Washington Redskins and worked with the black congressional leadership, where he met his second wife, Barbara Williams-Skinner. By the time of his death in 1994 at the age of fifty-two, Skinner's voice in the larger Evangelical community was considered negligible.

Circle Church and the Test Case for Racial Integration

Our third example of the intersection of black Evangelicalism and white Evangelicalism is taken from the story of a Chicago church attempting racial integration. The tenuous relationship between blacks and whites living out Christian life in an urban church reveals the difficulties of racial integration and the underlying tensions of power, fear, and mistrust that characterized many of the experiences of black Evangelicals in the context of white Evangelicalism.

On the first Sunday in February 1967, Circle Church began in Union Hall on the west side of the city of Chicago. As the founding pastor David Mains describes it in *Full Circle: The Creative Church for Today's Society* (Mains's reflections on the fledgling church, published in 1971), "To the rear of the Union Hall begins Chicago's famous Westside black ghetto with Madison Street, Chicago's Skid Row, snaking along its inner boundaries."[35] Circle Church went against the norm of American Christianity in the latter half of the twentieth century as a church in the urban context. Not only was Circle Church moving into the city at a time when most whites were fleeing the city, but the church also proved to be innovative in many other areas.

Mains viewed this church-planting effort as an important and significant event for the church in America. In *Full Circle* he reveals his desire "that the church is once again setting the precedent for society rather than having society set the precedent for her."[36] This conviction that Circle Church was plowing new ground compelled Mains to write *Full Circle* after four years of the church's existence. The book reveals Mains's frustration with his previous church experiences before Circle Church, many of which centered on rigidity in the worship life of the local church. In describing his previous church experience, Mains uses phrases like "indescribably awful" and "all alike" to describe the worship services. "All of this tended to make me squirm uneasily during the ensuing hour and a quarter."[37] Going against the grain, Mains sought to innovate a different type of church on multiple levels.

Full Circle reveals Mains's priorities for Circle Church in its nascent stages. Started when Mains was just thirty-three years old, Circle Church became the venue through which Mains expressed his vision of the church in the United States. "David Mains was an optimist with God-given gifts which were fully exercised in seeing his dream come true."[38] The church became known as a place for innovation and pioneering ministry. In particular, Mains had a passion for creative worship and ministry, and one of his key concerns in founding Circle Church was his desire to see innovative and dynamic worship services.

As the church grew, Mains sought to develop curriculum to be used by other churches that would foster creative worship. By the mid-1970s Mains was exploring the hiring of staff to roll out what would come to be known as "Step Two."[39] Step Two was eventually marketed to other churches that wanted to learn from the creative worship expressions of Circle Church. Mains's lasting legacy would not be the establishment of a pioneering multiethnic church; instead, he came to be known as a pioneer of creative worship.[40] For many, he was most often remembered for being on the radio with "The Chapel of the Air" program for over twenty years. His long-term legacy in the larger Evangelical community focused on his work to help support the local church through church growth, worship, and sermon resources.

In a *Full Circle* chapter titled "Why Do We Have Church Anyway?," Mains outlines his approach to church ministry. The chapter focuses on creative expressions of church ministry and ways in which the local church can function. The following chapter is wholly devoted to a description of the Sunday worship format and logistics. In the worship service context, Mains's priority was the expression of creativity. "Our purpose was to test ideas related to how a local church functions. . . . It is a story of church renewal."[41]

While Mains's book seems to prioritize creative worship, church growth, and renewal, it was the church's multiethnic composition that drew the most attention. Mains was concerned not only about creative worship; in contrast to many of his contemporaries, he was also concerned about the church's response to social issues. In planting the church, intentional choices were made not only to be in an urban location but also to reach the poor and the oppressed and to cultivate a multiethnic congregation.[42] The ahead-of-its-time multiethnic pastoral staff team included, at various stages, a Chinese Filipino pastor (Ka Tong Gaw) and African-American pastors (Mel Warren and subsequently Clarence Hilliard). Even *Time* magazine recognized this unique distinction and featured Circle Church in a December 1969 issue focusing on the diversity of Circle Church: "[David Mains's] team ministry is mixed (a Negro, two whites and a Filipino-Chinese assist him), and the congregation is even more disparate: foreign students from the University of Illinois' nearby Chicago Circle Campus, poor people from the neighborhood, an increasing number of hippies and occasional young whites from the suburbs."[43]

While church members appreciated the value of the creative worship experience at Circle Church, the African-Americans in the church were attracted to the open church concept. "The open church concept basically meant that a multi-ethnic congregation was not to assimilate but rather was to mutually share in the life of the church."[44] Open church provided the grid by which disempowered African-Americans could engage in a church that still maintained a white majority.[45] In an interview with Manuel Ortiz, Clarence Hilliard reveals that "the open church . . . is not assimilation or loss of identity, but a mutual sharing in the privileges and responsibilities of God's new community through the finished work of Christ, in an atmosphere of freedom where differences are accepted and appreciated."[46]

Circle Church was ahead of its time. The late 1960s and the early 1970s witnessed the advent and growing influence of the Church Growth movement. The work of Donald McGavran and C. Peter Wagner focused on principles that eventually led to church growth. One of the key principles of the Church Growth movement is the earlier-mentioned homogeneous unit principle, which began to be applied on a practical level among many Evangelical churches, resulting in a de facto segregation of American Christianity. Circle Church went against the grain by attempting racial diversity in the midst of the strong push for the homogeneous unit principle.

One of the expressions of multiethnicity at Circle Church was the formation of a multiethnic pastoral staff. Mains writes, "Our congregation was very open to hiring a black man. Because we were so young, much of the prejudice and inhibitions an older group might have demonstrated simply did not exist, or if they did, were being dealt with by the individuals who held them. We wanted an integrated church."[47] Mains's perspective demonstrates an approach to ministry that was ahead of its time. His desire for an integrated church bucked contemporary trends but also raised significant challenges.

Circle Church hired Mel Warren as the first African-American staff member in 1968. When Warren left Circle Church, Clarence Hilliard was hired. Circle Church had difficulty keeping blacks at the church. Hilliard initially saw his job as keeping blacks from leaving the church and believed it to be "a 'Mickey Mouse job' for the first couple of years. . . . It was communicated almost as a babysitting job—holding on to the Blacks that attended."[48] Hilliard eventually came to believe that Circle Church was truly interested in becoming a multiethnic church; however, he believed that blacks were leaving because "Circle was too White. . . . Their worship, music, and preaching were not inclusive or representative of the Black community."[49]

Hilliard had been influenced by the ethos of the NBEA, having served the NBEA as the head of the social concerns committee and later as vice president. While holding to an Evangelical theology, Hilliard was a leader in Operation PUSH (People United to Serve Humanity) and reflected a burgeoning conservative African-American Evangelical theology that reflected a high black identity and a deep concern for social justice.

Therefore, Hilliard had a clear sense of calling both to the blacks in the church and to the entire church, whom he wanted to challenge with the theology emerging from the black Evangelical framework. For Hilliard, Circle Church's vision of being an open church provided the motivation and focus for his ministry.[50] Hilliard believed that to be true to the open church concept the church needed to embrace an Evangelical black theology.[51] The priorities of Mains and Hilliard were at odds from very early on in their working relationship, and Circle Church soon became a church with two competing visions. The question as to which vision would drive the church—"Open Church" or "Step Two"—was an underlying conflict between the two pastors.

Circle Church was significant not only as an innovative church but as a church with social-historical importance. As Russ Knight explains, many African-American Evangelicals were watching Circle Church. Was integration possible among Evangelical Christians? Could blacks and whites worship together? Clarence Hilliard's presence raised the stakes for Circle Church. Could a strong black identity be accepted among white Evangelicals?

In the winter of 1975 the young church encountered a crisis that would cripple the church and ultimately alter its course. As a result of the crisis, the church's African-American pastor was fired, the church's only African-American elder resigned, and all of the African-Americans eventually left the church. "The Crisis" (as it came to be known among Circle Church leadership) stemmed from a series of conflicts on the staff, on the board, and in the congregation.

Mains asserted that team ministry was an important element of Circle Church. As Mains writes, "My concept of a team was that of a whole containing equal parts. All of us would be called pastor, with each man having differing areas of responsibility. . . . It would be impossible to overestimate the importance of this team concept."[52] Mains placed a high value on the team concept. The actual application of the concept, however, was much more difficult. As the founding pastor of the church, Mains requested that he be officially established as the senior pastor by the board.[53]

As senior pastor, Mains exerted authority over the Sunday worship, which resulted in conflict among the staff. While Mains did not preach every Sunday, he established an approval process for all sermons that were to be preached at the church. In *Full Circle*, Mains reveals that each sermon was to be "a composite of the thoughts of the other five [staff members]. Whoever preaches goes over his thoughts with another member of the team on Monday. . . . On Tuesday the entire staff hears in summary the emphasis of the sermon."[54]

Both the team concept (as worked out through the Sunday worship service) and the establishment of David Mains as the senior pastor tested the relationship between Hilliard and Mains. Hilliard was concerned that the worship services were too white. Being an open church meant that all the races should be allowed to contribute to the worship service, which meant that blacks should have a significant say in the planning of the worship service.[55] To live into the open church concept, "the Blacks of Circle Church mapped out what they saw as significant [ways] to produce a 'soul experience.' First, they needed a soul choir and a Black choir director. Secondly, they wanted the Black preacher to do more preaching."[56] Mains wanted to maintain authority over the worship service as the senior pastor. Many years after the crisis Mains wrote, "I don't believe Clarence [Hilliard] ever recognized the fact that I was senior minister and the reason he was given opportunity was by my invitation. We were not equals on staff, we didn't receive the same pay, we didn't have the same title. The reason he felt like an equal was because I treated him that way. When you have two senior ministers in any church—red, yellow, white or mixed—you have trouble."[57]

Hilliard, however, diagnosed the source of the conflict as a lack of willingness to adhere to the open church concept. In the fall of 1975, Hilliard proposed to preach a sermon titled "The Funky Gospel."[58] Hilliard wanted to push the congregation toward understanding and even embracing black theology. The sermon referenced James Cone and his work *Black Theology and Black Power*.[59] It boldly proclaimed that "Christ came into the world as the ultimate 'nigger' of the universe."[60] In doing so, Hilliard connected concern for the poor with black theology. "To be black theologically is to join yourself to the Lord Jesus Christ, find your identity with the poor, the powerless, and the oppressed."[61] Hilliard raised the challenge that "one must realize that another gospel is being preached—the gospel of the system, the gospel of the status-quo, the 'honkey' gospel. . . . I seriously question the nebulous, almost contentless 'Lord and Savior Jesus Christ' presented in both the Billy Graham style and the 'four spiritual laws' type of evangelism."[62] "The Crisis" erupted when Hilliard was prohibited from preaching this sermon.

A series of meetings occurred between the staff, the elder board, and certain members of the congregation, and multiple conversations took place concerning "The Funky Gospel" sermon, as well as who had the authority over the sermon, the worship service, and the church.[63] A November 15, 1975, letter from the church elders to the church members describes the emerging conflict. "Two weeks ago, during a time when the elders were re-evaluating the structure of the church, the staff deadlocked over a key issue in the structure and requested resolution of the matter by the elders."[64] David Mains's assertion of senior pastor authority to prevent Clarence Hilliard from preaching the sermon initially raised the issue of church structure.[65]

The letter goes on to state that "issues of staff teamwork relationships, trust, and submission were evident. The elders were also very concerned that David and Clarence were feeling immense pressure from several outside sources that were unrelated to these issues. We felt that it would be more appropriate to deal primarily with the matter of healing for Dave and Clarence and not to only decide on the question of church structure." Both pastors were asked to step back and take a break from all official responsibilities in the interest of their own personal healing.

While the focus of the letter was on the need for Dave and Clarence to rest and receive healing, a specific decision was made about governance over the Sunday worship services.

> We have affirmed that Dave is especially gifted in the areas of preaching and creative worship planning. However, the blackening of Circle, while not the total of what is involved in becoming an open church, has many unique aspects. We feel that the blackening of the church would be endangered if all of the services were under exclusive white authority. We have decided, therefore, that Clarence's services will not be a part of Dave's responsibility nor authority.

At this point in the crisis, there seemed to be an affirmation of the open church concept and Hilliard's authority over select services at the church. In Mains's November 20, 1975, response letter to the elders, he claims "that the relationship with me as your former Senior Pastor has been radically changed. This is so much the case that my old position is almost non-existent. . . . In fact, I bear no 'official responsibility in the church at this time.'"[66]

From late November to early December, a series of meetings occurred between the elders of the church and the Black Fellowship, as well as between the elders and the staff, to gauge the church's next steps. At the December 9, 1975, elders meeting, David Mains stated that he "was unable to see any possible way of staff working together at this point." Clarence Hilliard "felt he could continue to work as a part of staff only if he was free to preach the messages he feels God has given to him and if a situation arises in staff where he feels a need to have additional black input he be allowed to bring additional blacks into the discussion."[67]

For Hilliard, the conflict revolved around the failure of Circle Church to live up to the open church concept. For Mains, the issue revolved around his role as senior pastor. The minutes of the meeting reveal that "a consensus decision was reached by the Elders that the staff is in fact incompatible and should be dissolved. . . . The implications of that decision were not decided on at this meeting."[68]

At the December 15, 1975, elder meeting, "It was decided that the elders should ask for Clarence's resignation and the reason would be because there is a lack of communication and confidence between Clarence and the Elders."[69] The vote was 7-2-1, in favor of asking for Clarence's resignation: seven votes affirmed the decision; two votes abstained; and one vote withdrew.[70]

The elder minutes defined "withdrew" as withdrawing "from the question if you don't feel you can support the decision, but feel it is important enough to make the decision. This would mean you would have to withdraw from the elders."[71] The withdrawal came from Russ Knight, Circle Church's only African-American elder.

A letter dated December 17, 1975, was sent by the elders to Clarence Hilliard.

> Clarence, we love you; so it is with great pain and struggle that we
> have come to the point of believing that we can no longer work
> and minister together. In other words, it is with deep regret that
> we are at the point of asking you for your resignation. We, the
> elders, feel that there is an irreconcilable difference of perspective
> on both the problems involved in this present crisis and the solu-
> tions to those problems.[72]

In response, African-American members at Circle Church sent a letter on December 20, 1975, that challenged the elders' decision.

Signed "Clarence L. Hilliard and The Black Fellowship," the letter challenges the elders' letter to Hilliard: "It is vague, 'irreconcilable difference' needs to be defined and supported by evidence." The letter also questions the authority of the elders: "The elders also shifted from presenting a recommendation to the church to the elders requesting the resignation." Most explicitly, the matter of race is brought up.

> The stated needs of Blacks are still being ignored and the action itself is a racist attempt to make Blacks the scapegoats. It is obvious that the elders never responded in love to the urgent request in the Black Resolution for Black involvement in all meetings dealing with this crisis. . . . To ask Pastor Hilliard for his resignation under the present circumstances without any real effort to get at the bottom of the issues as we see them seems to be a racist attempt to place the blame on the Black pastor for the present status of things and expect to solve the problem by getting rid of him. The truth of the matter is that when the elders intended course of action is complete they will not only have succeed[ed] in getting rid of Pastor Hilliard but will have forced the Blacks out of the church as well.[73]

At the end of the process, Hilliard was fired,[74] despite strong protest by blacks at the church (in the form of an eight-page letter).[75] Mains was reinstated. The decision to ask for Hilliard's resignation was not supported by Russ Knight, the only African-American member of the elder board, who resigned from the elder board after the vote to ask for Hilliard's resignation. In a letter dated January 9, 1976, the Black Fellowship of Circle Church issued the following statement to the elders.

> Our Fellowship is violated by your decision to terminate Pastor Hilliard's employment. We are also convinced that you have officiated over the death of the Open Church at Circle. Therefore we ask that when you terminate Pastor Hilliard's employment that our names be stricken from the records of Circle Church and be

dropped from your mailing list. At that time our involvement in Circle and other related activities will cease.[76]

For many in the African-American Evangelical community, the failure of Circle Church was yet another example of black Evangelicals being rejected by white Evangelicals. To compound matters further, the Evangelicals at Circle Church were the "good white people"; unfortunately, "significant blind spots" remained.[77] Even progressive white Evangelicals fell short in relating to their African-American counterparts. What's more, the reasoning and perspectives that developed along color lines in the context of the crisis were perhaps the most telling. The Circle Church story reveals the difficulty in bridging the great gulf between black and white Evangelicals, even in the midst of positive intentions and great promise. In the face of the twentieth century's dominating homogeneous unit principle, Circle Church's attempt to sustain a healthy multiethnic and racially reconciled church ultimately failed.

The Challenge of True Reconciliation

In each of the examples offered in this chapter, we unearthed different aspects of the discomfort experienced by white Evangelicals in their encounters with strong nonwhite identities. Whether in the strengthening of black identity through the formation of the NBEA, the assertion of a black theology by Tom Skinner, or the proclamation of a funky gospel by Clarence Hilliard, dominant-culture Evangelicalism reverted to the comfort of the existing norms of white Evangelical theology and ecclesiology when challenged. By clinging to the Western, white cultural trappings of American Evangelicalism, Evangelicalism as a whole has often denied itself the gifts that other cultures bring. Rather than promoting a sense of exclusion—a common characteristic of the Evangelical response to nonwhite Christianity—perhaps the next Evangelicalism requires a greater sense of embrace.

This embrace needs to extend beyond those individuals who fit the cultural boundaries of dominant-culture Evangelicalism, which seems willing to support Evangelicals of color as long as they fit the mold that is cast by white Evangelicalism. White Evangelicals were willing to elevate Tom Skinner's message of personal salvation but unwilling to engage his call for racial justice. Clarence Hilliard was considered the black pastor who could keep the blacks at Circle Church but not a pastor who could speak to the issue of racial injustice. Dominant-culture Evangelicalism consistently exhibits a willingness to accept people of color as long as those people accept "our" way of thinking. This preference reveals an inability to allow for nonwhite expressions of faith and theology. In the next Evangelicalism, room must be allotted for people of color to express their own faith in culturally appropriate ways. "It is important to most black Christians *both* to make good on their African heritage (demonstrating that Christianity is not simply a 'white man's religion') *and* to maintain the best traditions of orthodox, biblical Christianity."[78]

The need for the dominant culture to embrace only "acceptable people of color" is an expression of power, that is, the power of privilege to choose with whom to identify and the ability to determine who is in and who is out. In the three cases presented in this chapter, a degree of exclusion was exercised by the majority culture, which had the power to exclude. In the Circle Church example, an unrecognized and even unstated power dynamic existed. African-Americans were drawn to the church by the open church concept, which raised the possibility that the power dynamics of the majority culture would be challenged in the context of the church. However, when a crisis occurred many in the church reverted to existing power dynamics; both the senior pastor and the elders were unwilling to yield power. Instead, there was an emphasis on preserving what they believed to be the important and critical attributes of the church, which were based on Western value systems and priorities. Circle Church's inability to see the extant power dynamic contributed to its downfall.

The end of the twentieth century and the beginning of the twenty-first century witnessed a dramatic change in the face of American Christianity, with a numerical decline of white Evangelicals accompanying a numerical increase of nonwhite Evangelicals. In a 2005 article, *The Wall Street Journal* notes that the "traditional face of American evangelicalism is changing. An ever higher number of US evangelicals—perhaps nearing a third of the total—are Asian, African, Latin American or Pacific Islander."[79] Yet in the same way that American Evangelicalism inadequately understood the integration of races in the latter half of the twentieth century, it continues to struggle with racial integration in the twenty-first century.

Despite the projection of Evangelicalism's rapid movement toward a multiethnic future, the assumption of a white-dominated Evangelicalism remains entrenched. In the same year that *The Wall Street Journal* article announced the changing face of American Evangelicalism, *Time* magazine profiled the twenty-five most influential Evangelicals in the United States. Twenty-three of the twenty-five slots were held by white Evangelicals.[80] While *Time*'s assessment was unfortunate, it was seemingly accurate. Evangelicalism lacks nonwhite leadership in nearly all areas of influence. National Evangelical pastors' conferences continue to be dominated by white leadership. Christian publishers continue to focus on white authors. Seminaries and Christian colleges struggle to hire and retain minority faculty.[81] If Evangelicalism is to be prepared for its next stage, diverse voices need to be represented.

Even as we attempt to address the reality of the changing face of Evangelicalism in the twenty-first century, we are reminded that attempts at inclusion and integration are not merely a twenty-first-century phenomenon. In the latter part of the twentieth century, particularly in the 1970s, the burgeoning movement of African-American Evangelicals made a genuine attempt at reconciliation. These self-identified Evangelicals held to a conservative Evangelical theological framework but were often excluded from key areas of Evangelical leadership and influence.

What needed to change? In our current era, are we prone to repeat the same mistakes of the Evangelical community that came before us? The emergence of African-American Evangelicalism in the 1960s and '70s reveals the complexities of dealing with the issues of race, racism, and racial justice in the American Evangelical context. In the emerging Evangelicalism of the twenty-first century, these questions continue to haunt churches attempting to move beyond the status quo of segregated fellowships. The difficulty of dealing with racial, ethnic, and cultural differences should not be downplayed or underestimated if we are to move toward an authentically reconciled and integrated Christian community.

6

The Fraternidad Teológica Latinoamericana and the Sharing of Power in a Globalized Christianity

Conferences—whether professional, political, or religious—do not generally produce moments of high drama. Attendees usually gather at large chain hotels to network, receive a dose of inspiration, and perhaps skip a few sessions to see the local sights. But when Evangelical missions leaders gathered in Lausanne, Switzerland, in the summer of 1974, submerged controversies burst out into the open, and Evangelicals have been debating them ever since. *Time* magazine's coverage describes the International Congress on World Evangelization as "the widest-ranging meeting of Christians ever held,"[1] and historians generally agree that it represents the symbolic arrival of Evangelicalism as a genuinely global movement. Although more than one-third of the 2,500 or so participants were from the West, for the first time in an Evangelical gathering the majority hailed from Asia, Africa, and Latin

America. In particular, the Latin Americans fanned the flames of upheaval. When two Latin American plenary speakers, C. René Padilla and Samuel Escobar, openly challenged the missiological status quo, they were (in one sense) merely participating in debates that had occupied missionaries for one hundred and fifty years. On a deeper level, however, they were decisively rejecting the missionary paternalism that had labeled them as "natives" from "daughter churches"—they were asserting their right to be heard as full partners in the global body of Christ.

Padilla and Escobar are founding members of the Fraternidad Teológica Latinoamericana (Latin American Theological Fraternity), or the FTL, a tight-knit group of Evangelical theologians gathered from every corner of predominantly Roman Catholic Latin America. This chapter seeks to tell their story and to reflect on what it means for Evangelical Christians to truly embrace their global identity. Unlike the African-American leaders highlighted in chapter 5, scholars have repeatedly and skillfully analyzed the work of the FTL. Nevertheless, seminal figures such as René Padilla and Samuel Escobar remain mostly unknown among younger Evangelicals today. As a seminary professor in both the United States and Costa Rica, I (Gary) have found that even students most committed to justice activism are rarely aware of these key Latin American leaders, who have formed their own progressive Evangelical "family history."

The goal of this chapter is not to retell the entire organizational history of the FTL.[2] Instead, I will focus on two themes. The first theme is the FTL's crucial role in reshaping an Evangelical theology of mission that fully integrates compassion, justice, racial reconciliation, and evangelism. Throughout this book, we have seen that struggles against the Great Reversal were fought on the level of practice (global poverty) and on the battleground of relationships and authority (race). Yet for Evangelicals, for whom the Bible is so central, theology has never been far from the surface. All the leaders profiled in this book are theologians reflecting contextually on their situation in order to recover a more faithfully biblical view of justice. But for those in the FTL, their sphere of engagement is specifically academic theology: they are professionals. While deeply committed to the local church, they address their writings and speeches mostly to other leaders and activists. As a result, their influence has taken root through a "top-down" approach, impacting global conferences (such as Lausanne) and then reverberating back into the congregations of the United States.

Our second theme is also theological, though we approach it from a different angle. God loves diversity in the body of Christ because our different perspectives on the gospel enable us to mutually correct, deepen, and enrich each other's grasp of the good news itself—but only if we listen to each other. It is worth (re)telling the story of the FTL because it is such a heartening example of the church being the church. The FTL's rereading of the Bible's teaching on justice and mission from the context of pervasive Latin American poverty and oppression was just what was needed at a time when individualism, racism, and materialism often went unchallenged in pulpits across the United States. It is a message that North Americans still need to hear today! Many of us have encountered novelists and historians who portray the entirety of missions work in terms of Westerners imposing their cultures on others. But the FTL is an excellent example of what some have called "reverse mission." Latin American theologians who found their voice and North Americans who chose to take their perspective seriously together offer an excellent example of the good fruit borne when those at the "center" listen to those on the "margins."

Missionary Fault Lines

Before our story can begin, we need a better sense of the theological landscape in which the FTL found itself. As we have seen throughout this book, the pioneers of Evangelical social justice activism worked in an atmosphere of suspicion and resistance, which was propagated by conservative Evangelicals who still saw the world through the lens of the Great Reversal. This was certainly true in the restless world of Evangelical missionaries, strategists, theologians, and administrators, all of whom were striving to preach the gospel to the entire world. Theological controversy has been part of the Protestant missions enterprise ever since William Carey kicked off the movement in 1791. In particular, missionaries have debated the relative priorities of evangelism (preaching the gospel) and social concern (demonstrating the gospel). In the nineteenth century this argument was often framed in terms of "Christ and Civilization." Western missionaries almost universally assumed that their culture was normative—hence, Christianity and civilization went together. While some argued that "heathen" people needed to be converted through preaching before their cultures could become "civilized," others thought the reverse was true: only when non-Christian cultures were leavened by Western cultural patterns did conversion become possible. Despite paternalistic assumptions, there was at least widespread acknowledgement that both preaching and holistic concern for the structures of society were legitimately part of Christian mission.

Paralleling the creeping influence of the Great Reversal in the United States, this holistic approach to mission began to bifurcate after the turn of the twentieth century. Mainline Protestant missionaries under the influence of the social gospel, liberal theology, and resurgent faiths like Hinduism, Buddhism, and Islam began to question the validity of trying to convert people of other faiths. Instead, they worked to coax non-Western societies along the same trajectory of economic and political development that the West had undergone. As colonialism crumbled, more and more "liberal" missionaries supported national movements for independence and liberation.

In reaction, newly founded fundamentalist missions agencies redoubled their commitment to preaching the gospel. In fact, it became common to define "missions" simply as evangelism and church planting. At best, any entanglement with justice or compassion was a distraction from the main task of missions; at worst, it was a compromise with the dreaded liberals. Many conservative missionaries were fundamentally motivated by Matthew 24:14, in which Jesus predicts that the end of the world will come after the gospel has been preached to all nations. For missionaries striving to save eternal souls and hasten the second coming of Christ, offering a cup of cold water seemed insignificant indeed.

This line of thought reached its most influential form in the Church Growth school of thought. The father of Church Growth was Donald McGavran (mentioned in chap. 5), who served as a missionary in India for many years before becoming a celebrated professor of missions at Fuller, Evangelicalism's flagship seminary. In India, McGavran observed that churches grew fastest when castes did not mix—that is, when entire people groups converted en masse. Generalizing this insight, he notes in his book *Understanding Church Growth* that "people like to become Christians without crossing racial, linguistic, or class barriers."[3] Therefore, he argues, missionaries ought to gather together churches of homogeneous "target groups" that are comfortable together. This simple strategy was known as the homogeneous unit principle (HUP), which became a central tenet of many North American Evangelical missions agencies. As discussed in chapters 1 and 5, by the 1980s the HUP was the basic approach for the most successful megachurches in the United States.[4]

The homogeneous unit principle assumes that the goal of missions is to plant churches as rapidly and successfully as possible. It does not reject the importance of Christians being influential in their societies or building relationships with other Christians across the lines of class or race. However, it relegates these endeavors to a secondary phase, after churches have been planted. Church Growth theorists assumed that once homogeneous churches had been planted, the new converts would inevitably develop a broader social concern. That being said, social justice was clearly not a priority of mission itself. Therefore, as an especially developed expression of the Great Reversal, the Church Growth school became the primary foil for FTL leaders as they entered the global Evangelical scene.

Latin American Protestant leaders in the late 1960s experienced divisions that ran along similar fault lines as those in the United States. On one side, groups like Iglesia y Sociedad en América Latina (ISAL) strongly identified with the liberal World Council of Churches and the growing liberation theology movement, which sought to address social and political injustice by reading the Bible through the lens of Marxist categories. On the other side, Evangelicals found their roots in fundamentalist churches planted by agencies such as the conservative Central American Mission. However, the situation was not as simple as this binary division. In the late 1960s the Latin American Mission (LAM), arguably the most influential Evangelical missions agency on the continent, began to reorganize in order to vest more authority in Latin American leadership. Similarly, the International Fellowship of Evangelical Students (IFES), an international affiliate of InterVarsity, created a number of leadership positions for Latin Americans desiring to reach their university campuses for Christ. These new leadership opportunities created more space for Evangelicals who wanted to transcend binary *gringo* divisions and reflect theologically on their own societies from an authentically Latin American perspective.

A Third Space Emerges

René Padilla and Samuel Escobar were two of the most important leaders in the emergence of this third space. Both were born in the early 1930s—Padilla in Ecuador and Escobar in neighboring Peru. Padilla was one of the first Latin Americans to graduate from Wheaton College with a master's degree in theology. He later completed a doctorate in New Testament at the University of Manchester in the United Kingdom, where he read evangelical scholars (such as George Eldon Ladd) who were reemphasizing Jesus's teaching on the kingdom of God (a term previously neglected by Evangelicals because it was so popular among Social Gospelers). Escobar studied in Peru, absorbing the radicalism that pervaded college campuses at that time; he later wrote his doctoral thesis at the University of Madrid on famed liberationist Paulo Freire. The goal of both men was to bring the good news to Latin America, so in 1958–59 they began crisscrossing the continent, planting campus chapters for IFES; Escobar also maintained close links with LAM. Ten years later, a conference that proved unable to impose its orthodoxy on leaders such as Escobar and Padilla provoked the founding of the FTL.

In an era without email, Skype, or the blogosphere, international conferences were an important forum for Evangelicals to build their identity as a movement and share their perspective with the world. In 1966 the Billy Graham Evangelistic Association (BGEA) sponsored the World Congress on Evangelism in Berlin; its goal was to validate the centrality of proclamation evangelism. The BGEA considered the event a stunning success in terms of promoting its vision of missions among global Evangelical leaders. In a typical statement Graham declared, "I am convinced that if the church went back to its main task of proclaiming the gospel and getting people converted to Christ, it would have a far greater impact on the social, moral, and psychological needs of men than any other thing it could possibly do."[5] Respected English Anglican John Stott, who was emerging as a global leader of Evangelicalism, was even more blunt: "The mission of the church . . . is exclusively a preaching, converting, and teaching mission."[6] For the next several years the BGEA sponsored similar regional conferences in Asia and Africa; in 1969 it decided the time had come for a Latin American conference.

North American organizers attempted to exercise strict control over the Latin American Congress on Evangelism (Congreso
Latinoamericano de Evangelización, or CLADE), held in Bogotá,
Colombia. They were especially concerned to keep out a long list
of "undesirable" Latin American leaders who had any connection with liberation theology or the World Council of Churches
(WCC). One organizer assured Billy Graham that they would not
invite those "that we know are cooperating with the Communist
forces, are extremely liberal in theology, or would in any other way
be a complete detriment to the cause of evangelism were they to
attend the conference."[7] In practice, that meant excluding from the
podium such highly respected theologians as José Miguez Bonino
and Mortimer Arias simply because of their links with mainline
denominations. Despite René Padilla's stature, he was not asked
to speak. As Padilla later reflected, "What surprised me the most
was how the intention was to bring a pre-made package to Latin
America so that Latin America would have an evangelistic strategy
but without any real and effective participation of Latin American
people . . . typical of the way in which work was done sometimes
in the conservative sector."[8]

Samuel Escobar, however, did offer a plenary address, and his
message entitled "The Social Responsibility of the Church" unleashed a firestorm of approval from nearly a thousand delegates.
Parts of his address read like a declaration of independence from
the very Evangelicals who had organized the conference: "Economic
and political solutions from an Anglo-Saxon background simply
do not work in this explosive situation. . . . Anglo-Saxon missions
resulted in the concept that the Christian life is completely separate
from the world."[9] He spoke boldly against "the imitation of the
missionary, so that people speak with his linguistic defects or hold
slavishly to the same opinions about economics and politics. We
must learn to be men of our own country and our own generation."[10]

Escobar repeatedly hammered home his theme that North
American influence had truncated the Evangelical gospel, making

it irrelevant to the social issues that most concerned Latin Americans: "Churches and denominations have concentrated their efforts on the growth of ecclesiastical machinery, shutting off their eyes to the needs of the world, and neglecting compassion in typical bourgeois fashion."[11] Furthermore, he accused the North American missionary establishment of "a naïve anti-Communism lead[ing] them to close their eyes to misery and injustice and be suspicious of anything that speaks of change."[12] Nevertheless, Escobar later reflected that his comments were not motivated by "a gratuitous anti-Americanism nor an adolescent rebellion."[13] Rather, he was searching for a genuinely "indigenous"[14] gospel that saw Jesus through Latin American eyes, as one who himself was born as a "member of an ill-favored social class in a country exploited by colonialism."[15]

The ferment unleashed by Escobar created momentum for a permanent organization that could represent a Latin American Evangelical theology unhindered by North Americans. Before CLADE was over, planning for the FTL had already begun. One year later, twenty-five theologians met near Cochabamba, Bolivia, for the inaugural meeting of the FTL. Instead of repeating rigid North American definitions of orthodoxy, the group hoped to create space for "cross-fertilization of minds . . . born out of profound reflection in the midst of [Latin America]."[16] Samuel Escobar was selected as its first president. But the Latin American struggle with North American hegemony was an issue even at the FTL's first meeting. Since the group had gained funding from a North American donor with links to the right-leaning organization Campus Crusade for Christ, several leaders who later became cornerstones of the FTL were not even invited because they threatened conservative *gringo* sensibilities.[17] C. Peter Wagner, whose influence in the Church Growth school was second only to McGavran's, attended the meeting, bringing with him a "suggested" draft of the new group's constitution. Wagner also tried to mandate what would be included in the FTL's initial theological statement and, when he did not get his way, wrote an incendiary article in *Christianity Today* insinuating that the FTL was not fully orthodox.[18]

Nevertheless, throughout the 1970s the FTL marked out an increasingly clear space for a "third way" between liberation theology (appreciated for its attention to biblical themes of poverty and oppression but critiqued as too beholden to Marxism) and North American Evangelicalism (appreciated for its attention to biblical themes of evangelism but critiqued as too beholden to capitalism). What makes the FTL relevant for North American Evangelicals today is the fact that it was influential not just in Latin America but perhaps even more so among progressive Evangelical circles in the United States. Due to their Western education and connections, Escobar and Padilla were essentially bicultural (Padilla was married to a North American he met at Wheaton). For that reason, their addresses at conferences in the United States and Europe had the largest impact; their writings in English found even more readers than did their publications in Spanish.

After CLADE, Escobar made frequent trips to the United States. He struck up a friendship with progressive Evangelical leader Ron Sider while speaking at Messiah College, and in 1973 Sider invited him to the Thanksgiving meeting that resulted in the Chicago Declaration (see chap. 4). Escobar was the only representative of the Global South to sign the Chicago Declaration—a document that many see as the charter of North American progressive Evangelicalism in the twentieth century. Escobar gave plenary addresses at InterVarsity's Urbana Student Missions Conferences in 1973 and 1970, where he shared the stage with Tom Skinner (see chap. 5). Escobar's sojourns in the North convinced him that the FTL was not alone in its vision for a renewed Evangelicalism. He later reflected: "It became evident to me that there was growing awareness among evangelicals around the world that the evangelistic and missionary zeal of the evangelical tradition needed to be matched with an equal concern for justice in society."[19] Both he and Padilla began to publish frequently in the journals of progressive Evangelical organizations, such as *Sojourners* and *World Vision Magazine*.

A Global Voice Emerges

Yet it was not until 1974 that Padilla and Escobar became truly global Christian leaders. As mentioned in the opening paragraphs of this chapter, the International Congress on World Evangelization in Lausanne, Switzerland, was to be Evangelicalism's largest and most representative post–World War II missions conference. As with previous conferences, Lausanne was instigated by Billy Graham, and to his credit, Graham requested that "national representatives of the younger churches"[20] contribute significantly to the planning. As a result, both Escobar and Padilla were selected to write papers that would be distributed before the conference, and their plenary speeches would then respond to comments sent in by participants. As it happened, their papers were "probably [subjected] to more comment than all the other papers put together."[21] Even before delegates arrived in Switzerland, it was clear that Lausanne would do more than repeat long-established missionary platitudes.

Although Lausanne aspired to make a comprehensive statement regarding missions that all evangelicals could affirm, Padilla and Escobar were catalysts in unleashing the conference's most significant outcome: the creation of a new stream of "holistic mission" that challenged the conservative status quo propagated by the Great Reversal.

However, for the North American–dominated missionary establishment, especially the Church Growth school, Lausanne was a landmark as well. Propelled by Fuller professors Donald McGavran and Ralph Winter, Lausanne served as a powerful springboard for their claim that "unreached people groups" deserved top priority in mission work. Building on the concept of the homogeneous unit principle, they argued that it no longer made sense to think of missions frontiers as comprising geographical or political boundaries. In other words, the goal should no longer be to take the gospel to "deepest, darkest Africa" or to nation-states like China or India. McGavran and Winter rightfully pointed out that it made little sense for evangelism to continue to concentrate on parts of the world that were already familiar with the gospel (even if they had not accepted it). Instead, missionaries should identify and immerse themselves in culturally homogeneous groups that lacked a vibrant Christian witness. For that task, Church Growth proponents offered reams of computer-generated data and technologically driven strategy. When it came to evangelism, theirs was an insight of enduring value.

However, for the Church Growth school, social justice essentially remained a sideshow. In McGavran's plenary address, he argued that although social justice was not an essential part of mission, it would eventually take care of itself: "Of course Christians engage in social action. . . . Christians have always done this, are doing it, and always will."[22] He saw no shortcomings in the social activism of Evangelicals. His concern was that Evangelicals were not sufficiently prioritizing the very heart of mission: converting those whose cultural and social location denied them access to the gospel.

The next day René Padilla took the stage. His message, simply titled "Evangelism and the World," was a prophetic challenge to the Evangelical missionary establishment, but at a deeper level he took aim at the Great Reversal itself. He argued as a theologian and biblical scholar, but his scholarly tone belied its revolutionary content. In contrast to what he called the "truncated" gospel of the Great Reversal, Padilla offered what he claimed was a truly "comprehensive" gospel. It is important to remember that in 1974 Evangelical platforms were dominated by white, North American men even more than they are today; Padilla represented a breakthrough voice of the Global South. Because his paper offered a theological foundation that has been echoed in countless FTL writings and by an untold number of North American progressive Evangelicals, it is worth taking a bit of time to summarize Padilla's game-changing perspective.

Padilla began with the crucial view of humanity as essentially embedded within social structures: "Man is a social being. . . . There is no possibility for him to be converted to Christ and to grow as a Christian except as a social being."[23] This means that sin not only is the result of wrong ethical choices by individuals, but it also pervades the very social structures that define human existence. Thus, salvation must deal not only with individual guilt but also with the fallen political, economic, and cultural realities that shape the "world" around us. Turning to the Gospels, Padilla shows that Jesus's ministry seamlessly weaves together teaching, preaching, and compassionate healing, which illustrates the fullness of God's rule.

Likewise, Jesus always links salvation and repentance. For example, the spiritual reality of Zacchaeus's salvation is expressed concretely when he gives lavishly to the poor as restitution for his lifetime of embezzlement. His story is a perfect illustration of how people "are delivered from both the guilt and power of sin . . . in order to form a new humanity."[24] According to Padilla, the salvation that Jesus offers not only includes our intellectual religious beliefs or an experience of forgiveness in our souls but also inevitably impacts how we spend our money and how we align ourselves with political power. In response to one participant who asked how involved Christians should be in politics, Padilla replied, "Whether we like it or not, we are already involved. . . . Since we are in fact involved, how can we make sure that our involvement is faithful to our Lord Jesus Christ?"[25]

Padilla summarizes his holistic view in the following way: "The New Testament knows nothing of a Gospel that makes a divorce between soteriology and ethics, between communion with God and communion with one's neighbor, between faith and works."[26]

If salvation for Jesus and Paul is holistic, then it does not make sense to define mission only in terms of verbal preaching. Rather, "a comprehensive mission corresponds to a comprehensive view of salvation. Salvation is wholeness. Salvation is total humanization. Salvation is eternal life—life that begins here and now."[27]

Compared to the all-encompassing portrait of mission Padilla found in Scripture, Evangelical theology in the wake of the Great Reversal looked to Padilla like a shallow caricature. In stark contrast to McGavran, who was confident that individualized, spiritualized gospel preaching would inevitably result in robust social concern, Padilla argued that Evangelicalism was producing converts who could not even conceive what it would look like for the gospel to impact the socioeconomic world around them. And if Evangelicals could not see social structures as part of the gospel's "sphere of influence," then they could only further reinforce the sin-soaked status quo. Padilla thundered: "A truncated Gospel . . . can only be the basis for unfaithful churches, for strongholds of racial and class discrimination, for religious clubs with a message that has no relevance to practical life in the social, economic and political spheres."[28]

But what stirred up the most controversy was Padilla's claim that in the United States the inability to critique social structures in light of the gospel had led North American Evangelicals to identify the gospel itself with "the American Way of Life." Although Evangelicalism was highly successful among middle-class whites, the church had "forfeited its prophetic role in society" by confusing "Christian orthodoxy with socio-economic and political conservatism." Instead of radical disciples who fundamentally challenged North American social evils, the typical image of the Christian life was that of "a successful businessman who has found the formula for happiness."[29]

Most galling for Padilla, North American Evangelicals had exported a distorted gospel to Latin America and the Global South through their missions methods. Padilla claimed that because the homogeneous unit principle was so obsessed with making conversion as easy as possible, it drew more inspiration from North American capitalism than from biblical religion: "It is not enough to turn the gospel into a product; it also has to distribute it among the greatest number of consumers of religion. . . . [It is] a question of mathematical calculation. The problem is to produce the greatest number of Christians at the least possible cost in the shortest possible time, and for this the strategists can depend on the work of the computer."[30] Padilla was not against technology per se, and of course he shared the Church Growth school's concern for spreading the gospel as widely as possible—he simply disagreed with them on the fundamental issue of *what the scope of the gospel is*. In perhaps his most memorable quote, Padilla mourns, "There is no place for statistics on 'how many souls die without Christ every minute' if they do not take into account how many of those who die, die victims of hunger."[31]

Padilla had offered an alternative vision—not just of mission strategy but of the gospel itself—and his presentation deeply divided the delegates. Progressive Evangelicals and many leaders from the Global South rallied to his message, but many North Americans shunned him. Several friends never spoke to him again, and some even cynically attributed his critique of the missions establishment to marital strife with his North American wife![32]

Two nights later, Samuel Escobar took up the baton. While Padilla emphasized theology and biblical exegesis, Escobar stressed empirical realities, both contemporary and historical. He critiqued the Church Growth gospel on pragmatic, not theological grounds. When Western missionaries ignored the pressing realities of "over-population, hunger, oppression, war, torture, violence, pollution, and the extreme forms of wealth and poverty" and offered only spiritual consolation in the next life, Escobar was not surprised that many would-be converts in the Global South "suspected the whole task of evangelization . . . [to be] only an 'imperialistic plot,' a Western way of manipulating people."[33]

Escobar pointed out that the Christian faith originally spread from a persecuted, marginalized Jewish community dependent on charity from its cosmopolitan, hellenized daughter churches. In the 1970s, however, the situation was reversed; North American hegemony was spreading alongside the leading edge of missionary effort. In this situation, Escobar urged privileged Evangelicals to "express concern for justice through active involvement in lobbying, revision of investment, and working through international control organizations. Christians in the West can do all that without in any way decreasing their missionary and evangelistic fervor."[34]

Escobar then cited a litany of progressive Evangelicals from the past (William Wilberforce and John Wesley) and present (including the Sojourners community and World Vision board member Mark Hatfield) who illustrated the way justice activism enhanced and did not distract from evangelism. While many delegates feared that social justice would totally displace eternal concerns (which they believed was the case for liberation theologians), Escobar asserted that "the heart which has been made free with the freedom of Christ cannot be indifferent to the human longings for deliverance from economic, political, or social oppression."[35]

In order to capture the momentum Escobar and Padilla had created, more than five hundred leaders, mostly younger and from the Global South, spontaneously gathered for a late-night strategy session. That evening the Radical Discipleship Group, as they called themselves, agreed that the Holy Spirit was doing something both new and old: bringing fresh perspective to the missions status quo and recovering aspects of the biblical witness that Evangelicals had once grasped but had since forgotten. They affirmed that "there is no biblical dichotomy between the Word of God spoken and the Word made visible in the lives of God's people. . . . We repudiate as demonic the attempt to drive a wedge between evangelism and social action." They lamented the malignant effects of neglecting God's commands to do justice: "We . . . have failed to condemn societal and institutionalized sin, especially that of racism. . . . We have sometimes so identified ourselves with particular political systems that the Gospel has been compromised and the prophetic voice muted. We have frequently denied the rights and neglected the cries of the underprivileged and those struggling for freedom and justice." But they also rejoiced in "the prophetic voices of our brothers and sisters at this Congress, with whom we go forth in humility and hope."[36] Through this group of leaders, a new voice in global Evangelicalism had emerged.

Within the larger conference, tensions simmered. Leaders had committed to draft a consensus statement that could represent the worldwide Evangelical missions movement, but rather than cementing the party line, the Congress had only created new fault lines. Thankfully, John Stott (who has since been described as the closest thing Evangelicals have had to a pope) skillfully mediated between North American conservatives and progressives from the Global South. Stott personally knew many campus ministry leaders such as Escobar and Padilla, and he was sympathetic to their position. Stott worked feverishly for two nights to incorporate the concerns of the Radical Discipleship Group into the language of the official consensus document.

The final version of the Lausanne Covenant, signed by more than 80 percent of delegates, expressed a holism that had been missing among mainstream Evangelicals since the First World War. As the covenant puts it, God's missional concern includes "justice and reconciliation throughout human society and the liberation of men from every kind of oppression"; therefore, "evangelism and socio-political involvement are both parts of our Christian duty."[37] For the last forty years, the Lausanne Covenant has served as an influential marker of centrist and progressive Evangelical identity.

However, even Stott could not heal the divisions that had emerged. Many voices within the Radical Discipleship Group felt that the covenant still waffled in its commitment to social justice. On the other hand, as one historian notes: "How far Stott and the Lausanne Covenant had really carried the Evangelical constituency has been doubted: to the right of Stott there were two for every one who joined him."[38] Billy Graham even worried that Lausanne had been a regrettable diversion from the task of evangelism. The Great Reversal had, and continues to have, significant staying power within the kaleidoscope of Evangelicalism.

Speaking Truth to the North

In the decades that followed, Padilla, Escobar, and other FTL theologians continued to advocate for justice as an aspect of God's mission, sharpening their critique of North American forms of Evangelicalism that were spreading around the globe. While they have written widely in English and Spanish, follow-up consultations and conferences that sought to develop and debate the themes of Lausanne proved to be especially effective platforms for their message. Of particular interest to readers of this book is the way these theologians have held up a mirror to North American Evangelicals, who are unaware of the degree to which racism, materialism, and consumerism have infiltrated the church.

Since we all have blind spots, it is essential to hear from believers of different cultural and class contexts because they notice things we don't. We have often so habituated ourselves to our cultural environment and the compromises the church has made in regard to the status quo that we are like fish swimming in water without realizing that they are wet. I would like to offer three brief examples of Padilla's work that vibrantly illustrate the FTL's enduring relevance.

The first symposium after Lausanne afforded Padilla the chance to offer a prophetic challenge to consumerism in the church—a problem that, unfortunately, is still applicable today. At the symposium, Padilla expanded his earlier emphasis on St. Paul's concept of principalities and powers. For North Americans wedded to individualism, the idea that evil spiritual forces are capable of shaping "institutions and ideologies that transcend the individual and condition his or her thought and lifestyle" is strange, though biblical.[39] While everyone can agree that it is wrong to be greedy, Padilla asserted that a biblical critique of consumerism involves more than just condemning excessive avarice in individuals. In some ways, consumerism is more like a poison in the air that gets into our bloodstream and shapes everything we do. As Padilla puts it, "Consumer society has imposed a lifestyle that makes property an absolute right and gives priority to money over people and production over nature. This is the form that 'the present evil world' has taken, the system in which the powers of destruction have organized human life."[40]

Padilla came to this insight by reflecting on Scripture from the perspective of his social location amidst the extreme inequalities of Latin America. Observing that consumerism has been exported to the *favelas* of Brazil and the *precarios* of Costa Rica, Padilla writes that it "has even invaded the areas where poverty reigns."[41] Padilla's work reveals that a sole focus on personal morality fatally impoverishes the church; it is impossible for the church to transform society because society has already transformed the church. In his words, "the church . . . becomes merely another reflection of society and another instrument that society uses to condition people to its materialistic values."[42]

In 1977 Padilla traveled to Fuller Seminary for yet another round of debates with the Church Growth school. The thoughts he offered there need to be heard by the entire church, not just those interested in missiological minutiae. Ever the biblical scholar, Padilla argued persuasively that the entire New Testament portrays the community of believers as a reconciling force. He claimed that the breaking down of the dividing wall between Jews and Gentiles was a *defining* aspect of the church. Since "there is neither Jew nor Gentile, neither slave nor free, nor is there male and female, for you are all one in Christ Jesus" (Gal. 3:28), racial reconciliation should not be reserved for politically correct left-wingers, but should be the passion of every Christian.

Padilla argued that to center a method of church planting on the commonplace desire to be comfortable around "people like us" flies in the face of what God has done in Christ: "Whether a person likes it or not, the act that reconciles one to God *simultaneously* introduces one into a community in which people find their identity in Jesus Christ rather than in their race, culture, social class, or sex."[43] Padilla insightfully showed that minimizing the importance of diversity within the church has led inevitably to culpable silence about the social problems that haunt us most: "What can this missiology say to a church in a North American suburb in which the bourgeois is comfortable but remains enslaved to the materialism of a consumer society and blind to the needs of the poor? What can it say to a church in which a racist feels at home because of the unholy alliance of Christianity with racial segregation?"[44]

The final example is this: in 1980 Padilla traveled to England for a conference on the most controversial clause in the Lausanne Covenant. In fact, Ruth Graham (Billy Graham's wife) publically refused to sign the covenant because of the following two sentences: "All of us are shocked by the poverty of millions and disturbed by the injustices which cause it. Those of us who live in affluent circumstances accept our duty to develop a simple life-style in order to contribute more generously to both relief and evangelism."[45] Many Evangelicals simply ignored this clause or rejected it as too intrusive and legalistic, but voices like Padilla and his close friend Ron Sider believed it to be an essential part of discipleship and mission. As Padilla puts it, "Solidarity with the poor on the part of the rich is not a mere option but an essential mark of participation in the life of the kingdom."[46]

Once again, Padilla emphasized biblical passages that are all too often censored in North American pulpits. While most Evangelical sermons on money focus on giving to the church, responsible saving, or the blessings of prosperity, Padilla pointed out that the New Testament's strongest themes address the potential danger of wealth when it is not shared with the poor: "Rich Christians ought to see themselves as no more than stewards of God's gifts summoned to live in the light of God's generosity toward all and his special concern for the poor."[47]

As the Lausanne Movement began to lose steam in the late 1980s and 1990s, the FTL found other avenues in which to share its voice with its northern siblings. Samuel Escobar joined Ron Sider on the faculty of Eastern Seminary in Philadelphia, where he published a number of highly regarded books on missions. After twenty years at Eastern, he joined the Facultad Protestante de Teología UEBE (Unión Evangélica Bautista de España) in Madrid. From his home base in Buenos Aires, Padilla created the Kairos Foundation, which promotes much-needed theological publishing in Spanish. Kairos also encompasses a tight-knit church community that practices what the FTL preaches by welcoming people of all social classes, from professors to prostitutes. In his later years, Padilla has been instrumental in forming the Micah Network,[48] which supports evangelical organizations across the globe who share the FTL's vision of holistic mission.

FTL leaders like Padilla and Escobar have called their perspective *misión integral* because of their emphasis on the role of radical discipleship in shaping all aspects of our spiritual, social, and physical life. *Misión integral* translates awkwardly as "integral mission," which is sometimes used in English, along with "holistic mission" or "transformational mission" (World Vision's preferred term).[49] But I prefer sticking with the Spanish. When I lived in Costa Rica, I thought of the term every time I ate whole wheat bread, or *pan integral*. In whole wheat bread, all of the ingredients are integrated yet retain their integrity, and in the same way *misión integral* challenges our church-shopping, pick-and-choose approach to faith. It calls us to a life of discipleship that truly forms us *and* transforms our society.

Today's Voices of Global Evangelicalism

In the 1970s, missions conferences served as temporary zones of engagement where global Evangelicals could meet and find their voice. Friendships were maintained through arduous air travel and handwritten letters that often arrived weeks after being sent. In today's Evangelicalism, it is much easier to encounter diversity right where we live. While calling the United States a nation of immigrants may be a cliché, it has never been more accurate. Most of us know that each year more immigrants arrive in the United States than any other nation on earth. However, the religious makeup of newcomers is less understood. Many white Americans think of immigrants as exotic or strange and perhaps fear the presence of militant Islam in our midst. Scholars have frequently studied Buddhist, Muslim, and Hindu immigrant groups in order to emphasize the religious diversity they bring.[50] But in fact, about three quarters of immigrants to America are Christian when they arrive, and others convert later. As sociologist R. Stephen Warner observes, "Immigration is not so much creating new diversity in American religion as new diversity within American Christianity."[51]

Until recently, immigrants primarily formed communities in the large "gateway cities" where they first arrived—such as Los Angeles, New York, Miami, and Chicago.

But within the last ten years, immigrants have scattered from gateway cities to every corner of the United States in a trend that sociologists call "secondary migration." In the whitest state in the union, Maine, the tiny town of Lewiston has attracted more than a thousand Somalis. When psychologist Mary Pipher decided to write a book on refugees called *The Middle of Everywhere*, she focused on Lincoln, Nebraska, because of its tremendous diversity. When I moved to the gateway city of Oakland, California, in the late 1990s, I got to know many Bosnian Muslim immigrants who lived in my apartment complex. Unfortunately for me, our friendships were cut short when nearly everyone moved to Idaho—not typically thought of as a hotbed of cultural diversity.

The ubiquity of the global church was brought home to me when I worked at the Emmanuel Gospel Center in Boston. Boston is known as a bastion of New England indifference to religion; it seems like closed or dying historic churches can be found on every corner. But when the Gospel Center carried out a simple research project, it revealed an entirely new face of Evangelicalism in Boston. Simply by trying to catalog basic information about every congregation in the city, researchers discovered there to be more churches than ever, and the great majority of them were immigrant churches led by bi-vocational pastors who met in storefronts or in the basements of historic churches.[52] In only thirty years the number of Haitian Evangelical churches skyrocketed from near zero to more than sixty. So no matter where we live, it is increasingly possible to encounter global Evangelical voices as we walk across the street, drive across town, or intentionally meet the other congregation that meets in our church building.

In addition to proximity, immigrant churches also bring vitality to the United States. At Lausanne in 1974, white Evangelicals spoke about participants from the Global South as coming from "the younger churches" in part because they viewed themselves as mature, experienced leaders whose voices should take precedence. Although an entitlement mentality is still commonplace among majority-culture Evangelicals, in the last forty years the center of gravity in the global church has shifted. As North America and Europe have secularized, new believers in Africa, Asia, and Latin America more than make up for the losses in the West. Scholars of global Christianity have long predicted what many American Evangelicals refuse to believe: the lifeblood of the global church now flows from places outside Christendom's heartlands. As missiologist Dana Robert puts it, "Interpretations of Christianity by people in Latin America, Africa, and southern Asia are coming to the fore. . . . The future of world Christianity rests with the so-called 'younger churches' and their daily struggles."[53]

Just as conservative Evangelicals needed to hear Escobar and Padilla's call to *misión integral* in the 1970s, today's majority-culture Evangelicals desperately need the voices of their immigrant brothers and sisters. Although we must be careful when generalizing about a group of people with cultural roots that span the globe, I know that as I have been mentored by immigrant Evangelicals, I have repeatedly learned valuable lessons that have shaped my practice of God's mission. I would like to focus on three gifts I believe immigrant Evangelicals bring to the church in the United States.

First, as Soong-Chan mentioned in his own story (see chap. 1), immigrant Evangelicals are frequently more comfortable with evangelism than are those in the mainstream church. At the time of this writing, one of the largest waves of refugees to the United States are of Chin, Karen, and Karenni ethnicity, from the highlands of Burma. North Americans often assume these nationalities are Buddhist, but more than 90 percent are Christian; many can trace their Baptist heritage back two hundred years. Jenny Hwang Yang, who works for the resettlement agency World Relief, writes that refugees from Burma are marked by "a depth of theology and a fire for evangelism when they arrive in the USA."[54] I confess to feeling intimidated on several occasions by the missionary zeal of Karen Christians I have met. Even in Oakland, my Muslim neighbors initiated more conversations about religion than I did, and I am no longer surprised when someone in my Mexican-American neighborhood in Denver talks to me about Jesus on the street. Many world cultures do not place religion in a private sphere, thinking it is too embarrassing to expose in polite conversation. This is a deeply valuable perspective; unlike many who participated in the Lausanne Congress, majority-culture Evangelicals today are more likely to dread evangelism than to reject social justice. To be fully missional, we need both.

Second, life as an immigrant in the United States demands constant cultural negotiation. Every day immigrants move back and forth between the worlds of mainstream culture and their own culture of origin. Children of immigrants must develop "triple consciousness,"[55] adding their own hyphenated American identity to that of their parents and North American culture. Like René Padilla and Samuel Escobar, immigrant Evangelicals have the advantage of being freed from one particular cultural captivity of the gospel. Because they must be fluent in two or more cultures, they are less likely to be trapped by the theological blind spots that tend to fester among Christians of mainstream culture. For the last twenty years I have attended majority Asian-American or Hispanic churches. Because of the friendship and mentorship of my brothers and sisters, I have a much deeper understanding of how my own white culture teaches me to form relationships, resolve conflict, understand society, and see God.

Third, immigrant churches often maintain deep links with the global church. Sociologists observe that immigrants frequently see themselves as "transnational," investing in their new lives in the United States while continuing to cultivate ties in their home countries.[56] Immigrants send money to their families back home, vote in local elections, visit during holidays, and learn of news occurring thousands of miles away in real time. Immigrant congregations pray for their home churches, exchange sermon recordings and books, financially support entire church planting networks, and maintain relationships through what white Christians typically call "short-term missions."[57]

Because of these spiritual, cultural, and relational gifts, immigrant Evangelicals in the United States are well placed to serve as key leaders in the global church. Like Padilla and Escobar, who bridged the gap between North and South America, immigrants can function as networkers, bridge-builders, and catalysts to connect monocultural North Americans with the insights, zeal, and needs of the global church.

But what might this look like in practical terms? While the answer to this question might require a book of its own, let's just consider missions, the subject of this chapter. Think of what usually happens on a short-term missions trip. A monocultural church raises money, reads a book or two (at best) about their destination, and jets off with matching T-shirts to "save" a place about which they are almost totally ignorant. Photos with exotic people appear on Facebook pages, and high school students are impressed by "how happy they are even though they are so poor."[58] This modus operandi completely ignores the gifts of the immigrant church. But what if monocultural churches invited immigrant leaders to mentor them and asked to participate in the missions work their churches are already doing through transnational relationships?

For years Pastor Soliny Védrine, a key leader among the Haitian churches in Boston, has traveled with Haitian-Americans to the Caribbean to join in solidarity with its thriving churches. But when I and fellow pastors Vince and Diana Bantu asked to accompany him on a trip in support of Haitian sugarcane farmers in the Dominican Republic, we were the first non-Haitians to join him. Before and after the trip our connections with the Haitian church in Boston deepened, and we saw firsthand what *misión integral* looks like in a place that God is lifting out of centuries of slavery and oppression. Even bus rides—in both Boston and Hispaniola—became an opportunity to learn from each other about racial reconciliation. After that experience, I can never go back to the old way of doing missions.

Listening to all of the voices in the global church is not just an issue of political correctness or cutting-edge mission strategy—it is living out the gospel so that we might together carry out the fullness of God's call. As one of my favorite theologians says, this orientation "has the capacity to advance Christian mission in both the Western and non-Western worlds. It opens the dazzling possibility that the fullness of the stature of Christ that, according to the epistle to the Ephesians, is reached as people of diverse ethnicities and cultures are united in the body of Christ, could be realized in our time."[59]

Conclusion

Evangelicalism in the twenty-first century owes a great debt to the forebears who helped to redirect the trajectory of its story. The assumption that twentieth-century Evangelicalism disengaged from social concerns can be answered by several different historical realities. Whether by self-proclamation, theological affinity, ecclesial identity, or sociological identification, Evangelicalism emerged from multiple streams. Inherent within these streams is a sense of identification with the broader narrative of orthodoxy. Even within the commonality of theological orthodoxy, Evangelicals demonstrated a great variety and diversity. To explore the full story of post–World War II Evangelicalism, the full range of the Evangelical narrative must be explored.

In this text, we have offered several snapshots that help to broaden and deepen awareness of activist Christians in twentieth-century Evangelicalism. Evangelicalism should not be limited to a theology of a select group of white, suburban, intellectual elites or the political partisanship and narrow agenda of a select few. Instead, the grassroots movements and parachurch networks that helped to shape the Evangelical ethos not only were theologically committed to a biblical and christocentric faith but also maintained a conversionist and activist ethic that spurred movement toward compassion, mercy, and justice as well as personal evangelism.

Engaging the rich history of twentieth-century Evangelicalism allows us to imagine a hopeful trajectory for twenty-first century Evangelicalism and to understand that the story of American Evangelicalism is not complete. It continues to unfold with new possibilities as the full breadth of Evangelical history is embraced. These new possibilities must include a seat at the table for those who hold a theological affinity, if not necessarily a social or political affinity, with those we consider to be the majority culture. The table should include those who may not have been typically associated with Evangelicalism in the latter half of the twentieth century—either because they were not from the right political party, did not have the right skin color, or were not practicing church-growth principles in the suburbs. The Evangelical narrative finds a more robust expression in the inclusion of voices outside of privilege and triumphalism.

In Evangelical engagement with justice ministry, momentum is amplified by the intentional hearing of the diverse voices that arise from the variety of experiences and backgrounds within Evangelicalism—including non-Western, non-American, non-white, non-middle-class, and non-privileged voices. The power of these stories, particularly those spoken from the margins, challenges the status quo. John Perkins expressed a narrative that questioned mainstream Evangelicalism's allergic reaction to the civil rights movement and domestic urban poverty. Bob Pierce resurrected a passion for justice by telling the stories of fundamentalist women who could not even preach in their own churches. World Vision began by rescuing the poor and ended up learning from them. Black evangelicals, who held the same credentials as white evangelicals, raised the issue of an endemic racism in American Christianity. Latino and Latina theologians offered a fresh perspective on evangelism and missions in the global Christian community.

In the twenty-first century, we have moved past the era of Western, white Evangelicalism. The next stage of evangelicalism must include the voices of the multiethnic community in the United States and the multinational community throughout the world. Through the stories of the previously silenced voices, Evangelicalism creates space at the table and compels Western, white Christians to yield their position of dominance. Stories legitimate the demographic changes already taking place. The primary voice of justice arises from those who have lived through injustice and can lead the way toward a deeper engagement with biblical justice.

These personal experiences of justice move our engagement from abstract, theoretical theology to a lived and embodied ecclesiology. We can no longer employ the language of justice to expand our intellectual capacity and our ministry rhetoric; justice must arise from real experiences. We can no longer simply "like" justice on a Facebook post; we must seek to live into the stories that set an example for us. We need these stories to change us. We are not the saviors of those who are poor and "other." They become our mentors. It is not their needs that drive our justice efforts; rather, our hope rises up in learning from those we deem as the needy other. Engaging in ministries of compassion and justice, therefore, becomes a salvific narrative.

Justice must be a personal reality for the twenty-first century Evangelical. A personal connection to injustice helps make justice real. However, this personal reality must not remain strictly personal. Justice has never been about a personal experience for the privileged. Simply being inspired by a moving story of poverty in Mississippi or India proves to be inadequate because poor people do not exist to make our spiritual lives better. An increasing awareness of injustice in the world should lead to a greater awareness of the systemic and structural nature of injustice. Even as we are moved by personal stories, these stories point to a greater reality. Confronting and advocating for the marginalized and the voiceless requires a structural confrontation, and this confrontation may prove to be costly for those who have invested heavily in the fallen systems of the world. While an American Christian exceptionalism calls us to acquiesce to an American system that benefits the majority culture, engaging the stories of justice challenges us to see God's work on a global scale that neither privileges nor respects the dominant culture.

In recent years, justified and appropriate concerns have been voiced about the future of Evangelicalism. In response, this book offers stories of Evangelicalism that challenge the dominant narrative and remind us of the unfinished business to which we must attend. The inheritance of a biblical orthodoxy compels us to an active faith that has taken many forms. We need to integrate these stories to further advance an active faith in the new century.

The future of Evangelicalism will involve greater diversity in ethnic and cultural makeup. The future of Evangelicalism should move beyond the culturally determined narratives so that we can hear the hidden stories that have been there all along. While holding fast to the inherited orthodoxy of evangelical theology, we must move beyond the trappings of Western Evangelicalism. A full range of stories can only help—not hinder—our move toward the next Evangelicalism.

Bibliography

Balmer, Randall. *The Making of Evangelicalism*. Waco: Baylor University Press, 2010.

———. *Thy Kingdom Come*. New York: Basic Books, 2006.

Bebbington, David W. *Evangelicalism in Modern Britain: A History from the 1730s to the 1980s*. Boston: Unwin Hyman, 1989.

Bentley, William. *National Black Evangelical Association: Evolution of a Concept of Ministry*. Rev. ed. Chicago: self-published, 1979.

Boyd, Gregory. *The Myth of a Christian Nation*. Grand Rapids: Zondervan, 2005.

Carpenter, Joel A. *Revive Us Again: The Reawakening of American Fundamentalism*. New York: Oxford University Press, 1997.

Carpenter, Joel A., and Wilbert R. Shenk, eds. *Earthen Vessels: American Evangelicals and Foreign Missions, 1880–1980*. Grand Rapids: Eerdmans, 1990.

Cerillo, Augustus, Jr., and Murray W. Dempster. *Salt and Light: Evangelical Political Thought in Modern America*. Grand Rapids: Baker, 1989.

Chabbott, Colette. "Development INGOs." In *Constructing World Culture: International Nongovernmental Organizations since 1875*, edited by John Boli and George M. Thomas, 223–48. Stanford, CA: Stanford University Press, 1999.

Chester, Tim, ed. *Justice, Mercy and Humility: Integral Mission and the Poor.* Carlisle, UK: Paternoster, 2002.

Clebsch, William A. *From Sacred to Profane America.* New York: Harper & Row, 1968.

Conn, Harvie M. *The American City and the Evangelical Church.* Grand Rapids: Baker Books, 1994.

Dayton, Donald W. *Discovering an Evangelical Heritage.* Peabody, MA: Hendrickson, 1976.

Dayton, Donald W., and Robert K. Johnston, eds. *The Variety of American Evangelicalism.* Downers Grove, IL: InterVarsity, 1991.

Dayton, Donald W., and Douglas M. Strong. *Rediscovering an Evangelical Heritage: A Tradition and Trajectory of Integrating Piety and Justice.* Grand Rapids: Baker Academic, 2014.

D'Elia, John. *A Place at the Table.* New York: Oxford University Press, 2008.

Douglas, J. D., ed. *Let the Earth Hear His Voice: International Congress on World Evangelization, Lausanne, Switzerland.* Minneapolis: World Wide, 1975.

Dowland, Seth. *Family Values and the Rise of the Religious Right.* Philadelphia: University of Pennsylvania Press, 2015.

Dunker, Marilee Pierce. *Days of Glory, Seasons of Night.* Grand Rapids: Zondervan, 1984.

Ebaugh, Helen Rose, and Janet Saltzman Chafetz, eds. *Religion across Borders: Transnational Immigrant Networks.* Walnut Creek, CA: AltaMira, 2002.

Eck, Diana. *A New Religious America: How a "Christian Country" Has Become the World's Most Religiously Diverse Nation.* San Francisco: HarperSanFrancisco, 2001.

Ellis, Carl, Jr. *Free at Last*. 2nd ed. Downers Grove, IL: InterVarsity, 1996.

Escobar, Samuel. "My Pilgrimage in Mission." *International Bulletin of Missionary Research* 36, no. 4 (October 2012): 206–11.

Evans, Curtis J. *The Burden of Black Religion*. New York: Oxford University Press, 2008.

Gans, Herbert. *The Levittowners: Ways of Life and Politics in a New Suburban Community*. New York: Columbia University Press, 1967.

Gasaway, Brantley. *Progressive Evangelicals and the Pursuit of Social Justice*. Chapel Hill: University of North Carolina Press, 2014.

Gehman, Richard. *Let My Heart Be Broken with the Things That Break the Heart of God*. New York: McGraw-Hill, 1960.

Gilbreath, Edward. "A Prophet out of Harlem." *Christianity Today*, September 16, 1996, http://www.christianitytoday .com/ct/1996/september16/6ta036.html.

————. *Reconciliation Blues: A Black Evangelical's Inside View on White Christianity*. Downers Grove, IL: InterVarsity, 2006.

Graham, Franklin. *Rebel with a Cause*. Nashville: Nelson, 1995.

Graham, Franklin, Estelle Condra, and Dilleen Marsh. *Miracle in a Shoebox: A Christmas Gift of Wonder*. Nashville: Nelson, 1995.

Graham, Franklin, and Jeannette Lockerbie. *Bob Pierce: This One Thing I Do*. Waco: Word Books, 1983.

Griffiths, Brian, ed. *Is Revolution Change?* Downers Grove, IL: InterVarsity, 1972.

Hankins, Barry. *Francis Schaeffer and the Shaping of Evangelical America*. Grand Rapids: Eerdmans, 2008.

Harding, Susan Friend. *The Book of Jerry Falwell: Fundamentalist Language and Politics*. Princeton: Princeton University Press, 2000.

Hatch, Nathan O. *The Democratization of American Christianity*. New Haven: Yale University Press, 1989.

Heltzel, Peter Goodwin. *Jesus and Justice: Evangelicals, Race, and American Politics*. New Haven: Yale University Press, 2009.

Henry, Carl F. H. *The Uneasy Conscience of Modern Fundamentalism*. Grand Rapids: Eerdmans, 1947.

Heyrman, Christine. *Southern Cross: The Beginnings of the Bible Belt*. Chapel Hill: University of North Carolina Press, 1997.

Hudson, Winthrop S. *Religion in America*. 3rd ed. New York: Scribner, 1981.

Hunter, James Davison. *Culture Wars: The Struggle to Define America*. New York: Basic Books, 1991.

———. *Evangelicalism: The Coming Generation*. Chicago: University of Chicago Press, 1987.

Hwang Yang, Jenny. "Immigrants in the USA: A Missional Opportunity." In *Global Diasporas and Mission*, edited by Chandler H. Im and Amos Yong, 148–57. Oxford: Regnum Books, 2014.

Im, Chandler H., and Amos Yong, eds. *Global Diasporas and Mission*. Oxford: Regnum Books, 2014.

Irvine, Graeme. *Best Things in the Worst Times: An Insider's View of World Vision*. Wilsonville, OR: BookPartners, 1996.

Jennings, Willie James. *The Christian Imagination*. New Haven: Yale University Press, 2010.

Kyle, Richard. *Evangelicalism: An Americanized Christianity*. New Brunswick, NJ: Transaction, 2006.

Labberton, Mark. *The Dangerous Act of Loving Your Neighbor: Seeing Others through the Eyes of Jesus*. Downers Grove, IL: InterVarsity, 2010.

Levitt, Peggy. "Transnational Ties and Incorporation: The Cases of Dominicans in the United States." In *The Columbia History of Latinos in the United States since 1960*, edited by David Gutierrez, 229–56. New York: Columbia University Press, 2003.

Linthicum, Robert. "Doing Community Organizing in the Urban Slums of India." *Social Policy* 32, no. 2 (Winter 2001): 34–38.

Mains, David R. *Full Circle: The Creative Church for Today's Society*. Waco: Word Books, 1971.

Marsden, George. *Fundamentalism and American Culture*. New York: Oxford University Press, 2006.

———. *Reforming Evangelicalism*. Grand Rapids: Eerdmans, 1987.

Marsh, Charles. *Wayward Christian Soldiers*. New York: Oxford University Press, 2007.

Marsh, Charles, and John Perkins. *Welcoming Justice*. Downers Grove, IL: InterVarsity, 2009.

Martin, Jim. *The Just Church*. Carol Stream, IL: Tyndale, 2012.

Martin, William. *With God on Our Side: The Rise of the Religious Right in America*. New York: Broadway Books, 1996.

McGavran, Donald A. *Understanding Church Growth*. Grand Rapids: Eerdmans, 1980.

Miller, Albert G. "The Rise of African-American Evangelicalism in American Culture." In *Perspectives on American Religion and Culture*, edited by Peter W. Williams, 259–69. Malden, MA: Blackwell, 1999.

Moberg, David. *The Great Reversal: Evangelism versus Social Concern*. New York: J. B. Lippincott, 1972.

Moeller, Susan D. *Compassion Fatigue: How the Media Sell Disease, Famine, War, and Death*. New York: Routledge, 1999.

Mooneyham, W. Stanley. *Come Walk the World: Personal Experiences of Hurt and Hope*. Waco: Word Books, 1978.

———. *What Do You Say to a Hungry World?* Waco: Word Books, 1975.

Nash, Dennison. "And a Little Child Shall Lead Them: A Test of a Hypothesis That Children Were the Source of the American 'Religious Revival.'" *Journal for the Scientific Study of Religion* 7, no. 2 (Fall 1968): 238–40.

Nash, Dennison, and Peter Berger. "The Child, the Family, and the 'Religious Revival' in Suburbia." *Journal for the Scientific Study of Religion* 2, no. 1 (Fall 1962): 85–93.

Noll, Mark. *The Scandal of the Evangelical Mind*. Grand Rapids: Eerdmans, 1994.

Orsi, Robert. *Gods of the City*. Bloomington: Indiana University Press, 1999.

Ortiz, Manuel. "Circle Church: A Case Study in Contextualization." *Urban Mission* 8, no. 3 (January 1991): 6–18.

Padilla, C. René, ed. *Hacia Una Teología Evangélica Latinoamericana. Ensayos en Honor de Pedro Savage*. Miami: Caribe, 1984.

———. *Mission between the Times: Essays*. Grand Rapids: Eerdmans, 1985.

———, ed. *The New Face of Evangelicalism*. Downers Grove, IL: InterVarsity, 1976.

Pally, Marcia. *The New Evangelicals*. Grand Rapids: Eerdmans, 2011.

Pannell, William. *My Friend, The Enemy*. Waco: Word Books, 1968.

———. "The Religious Heritage of Blacks." In *The Evangelicals: What They Believe, Who They Are, Where They Are Changing*, edited by David F. Wells and John D. Woodbridge, 116–27. New York: Abingdon, 1975.

Perkins, John. *Let Justice Roll Down*. Ventura, CA: Regal Books, 1976.

———. *A Quiet Revolution*. Pasadena, CA: Urban Family, 1976.

Perkinson, James W. *White Theology: Outing Supremacy in Modernity*. New York: Palgrave Macmillan, 2004.

Perry, Dwight. *Breaking Down Barriers: A Black Evangelical Explains the Black Church*. Grand Rapids: Baker, 1998.

Putnam, Robert, and David Campbell. *American Grace: How Religion Divides and Unites Us*. New York: Simon & Schuster, 2010.

Quebedeaux, Richard. *The Young Evangelicals: The Story of the Emergence of a New Generation of Evangelicals*. New York: Harper & Row, 1974.

Rah, Soong-Chan. "The Necessity of Lament for Ministry in the Urban Context." *Ex Auditu* 29 (2013): 54–69.

———. *The Next Evangelicalism*. Downers Grove, IL: InterVarsity, 2009.

———. *Prophetic Lament: A Call for Justice in Troubled Times*. Downers Grove, IL: InterVarsity, 2015.

Robert, Dana Lee. *American Women in Mission: A Social History of Their Thought and Practice*. Macon, GA: Mercer University Press, 1996.

———. "Shifting Southward: Global Christianity since 1945." *International Bulletin of Missionary Research* 24, no. 2 (April 2000): 50–58.

Rohrer, Norman. *Open Arms*. Carol Stream, IL: Tyndale, 1987.

Salinas, Daniel. *Latin American Evangelical Theology in the 1970s: The Golden Decade*. Leiden, Netherlands: Brill, 2009.

Schaeffer, Frank. *Crazy for God: How I Grew Up as One of the Elect, Helped Found the Religious Right, and Lived to Take All (or Almost All) of It Back*. Cambridge, MA: DeCapo, 2007.

Seiple, Robert. *One Life at a Time: Making a World of Difference*. Dallas: Word, 1990.

Seligman, Amanda I. *Block by Block: Neighborhoods and Public Policy on Chicago's West Side*. Chicago: University of Chicago Press, 2005.

Sider, Ronald, ed. *The Chicago Declaration*. Carol Stream, IL: Creation House, 1974.

Silverman, Lori L. *Wake Me Up When the Data Is Over: How Organizations Use Stories to Drive Results*. San Francisco: Jossey-Bass, 2006.

Skinner, Tom. *Black and Free*. Grand Rapids: Zondervan, 1968.

———. *How Black Is the Gospel?* Philadelphia: J. B. Lippincott, 1970.

———. Papers. Collection 430. Billy Graham Center Archives, Wheaton College, Wheaton, IL.

———. "The U.S. Racial Crisis and World Evangelism." Sermon presented at Urbana Student Missions Conference, Urbana, IL, December 1970. https://urbana.org/transcript/us-racial-crisis-and-world-evangelism-1970.

———. *Words of Revolution.* Grand Rapids: Zondervan, 1970.

Slade, Peter, Charles Marsh, and Peter Goodwin Heltzel, eds. *Mobilizing for the Common Good: The Lived Theology of John M. Perkins.* Jackson: University Press of Mississippi, 2013.

Smith, Christian. *American Evangelicalism: Embattled and Thriving.* Chicago: University of Chicago Press, 1998.

Smith, Timothy. *Revivalism and Social Reform in Mid-nineteenth-century America.* New York: Abingdon, 1957.

Stanley, Brian. *The Global Diffusion of Evangelicalism: The Age of Billy Graham and John Stott.* Downers Grove, IL: IVP Academic, 2013.

Steensland, Brian, and Philip Goff. *The New Evangelical Social Engagement.* New York: Oxford University Press, 2014.

Stuckless, Bonita ("Bonnie"). Papers. Collection 415. Billy Graham Center Archives, Wheaton College, Wheaton, IL.

Sutton, Matthew. *Aimee Semple McPherson and the Resurrection of Christian America.* Cambridge, MA: Harvard University Press, 2007.

Swartz, David. *Moral Minority: The Evangelical Left in an Age of Conservatism.* Philadelphia: University of Pennsylvania Press, 2012.

Sweeney, Douglas. *The American Evangelical Story.* Grand Rapids: Baker Academic, 2005.

Tizon, Al. *Transformation after Lausanne: Radical Evangelical Mission in Global-Local Perspective.* Eugene, OR: Wipf & Stock, 2008.

Troeltsch, Ernst. *The Social Teaching of the Christian Churches.* Chicago: University of Chicago Press, 1960.

Wallis, Jim. *Agenda for Biblical People: A New Focus for Developing a Life-Style of Discipleship.* New York: Harper & Row, 1976.

———. *The Call to Conversion: Recovering the Gospel for These Times.* New York: Harper & Row, 1981.

———. *Faith Works: How Faith-Based Organizations Are Changing Lives, Neighborhoods, and America.* Berkeley: PageMill, 2000.

———. *God's Politics: Why the Right Gets It Wrong and the Left Doesn't Get It.* New York: HarperCollins, 2005.

———. *The Great Awakening: Reviving Faith and Politics in a Post-Religious Right America.* New York: HarperOne, 2008.

———. *Rediscovering Values: On Wall Street, Main Street, and Your Street.* New York: Howard Books, 2010.

———. *Revive Us Again: A Sojourner's Story.* Nashville: Abingdon, 1983.

———. *The Soul of Politics: A Practical and Prophetic Vision for Change.* New York: New Press, 1994.

———. *Who Speaks for God? An Alternative to the Religious Right—A New Politics of Compassion, Community, and Civility.* New York: Delacorte, 1996.

Ward, W. R. "Evangelical Identity in the Eighteenth Century." In *Christianity Reborn: The Global Expansion of Evangelicalism in the Twentieth Century,* edited by Donald Lewis, 11–30. Grand Rapids: Eerdmans, 2004.

Warner, R. Stephen. "Coming to America." *Christian Century,* February 10, 2004.

Wilkerson, Isabel. *The Warmth of Other Suns*. New York: Vintage, 2010.

Wolterstorff, Nicholas. *Justice: Rights and Wrongs*. Princeton: Princeton University Press, 2008.

Woodbridge, John, Mark A. Noll, and Nathan O. Hatch. *The Gospel in America: Themes in the Story of America's Evangelicals*. Grand Rapids: Zondervan, 1979.

Worthen, Molly. *Apostles of Reason*. New York: Oxford University Press, 2014.

Wuthnow, Robert. *The Restructuring of American Religion*. Princeton: Princeton University Press, 1988.

Yates, T. E. *Christian Mission in the Twentieth Century*. New York: Cambridge University Press, 1994.

Archives and Collections

Billy Graham Center Archives. Wheaton College, Wheaton, IL.

Sojourners. Records (SC-23). Wheaton College Archives and Special Collections, Wheaton, IL.

Wallis, Jim. Papers (SC-109). Wheaton College Archives and Special Collections, Wheaton, IL.

World Vision. Papers. World Vision International Archives, Monrovia, CA.

Notes

Introduction

1. Jim Martin, *The Just Church* (Carol Stream, IL: Tyndale, 2012), xvii. For further information and background on this paragraph see Vic Roberts, "50 Largest U.S. Charities," *Christian Science Monitor*, November 22, 2004; Kevin D. Miller, "De-Seipling World Vision," *Christianity Today*, June 15, 1998; Jonathan Bonk, "Mission and Mammon," *International Bulletin of Missionary Research* 31, no. 4 (October 2007): 1; Alan Wolfe, "A Purpose-Driven Nation? Rick Warren Goes to Rwanda," *Wall Street Journal*, August 26, 2005.

2. Mark Noll, *The Scandal of the Evangelical Mind* (Grand Rapids: Eerdmans, 1994), 8.

3. This paragraph summarizes Bebbington's view in *Evangelicalism in Modern Britain: A History from the 1730s to the 1980s* (Boston: Unwin Hyman, 1989), 2–17.

4. Charles E. Van Engen, "A Broadening Vision: Forty Years of Evangelical Theology of Mission," in *Earthen Vessels: American Evangelicals and Foreign Missions, 1880–1980*, ed. Joel A. Carpenter and Wilbert R. Shenk (Grand Rapids: Eerdmans, 1990), 210.

5. George Marsden, *Fundamentalism and American Culture* (New York: Oxford University Press, 2006), 92.

6. Marsden, *Fundamentalism and American Culture*, 93.

7. Robert Wuthnow, *The Restructuring of American Religion* (Princeton: Princeton University Press, 1988), 174.

8. Joel Carpenter, *Revive Us Again: The Reawakening of American Fundamentalism* (New York: Oxford University Press, 1997), 159.

9. Carpenter, *Revive Us Again*, 160.

10. George Marsden, *Reforming Fundamentalism: Fuller Seminary and the New Evangelicalism* (Grand Rapids: Eerdmans, 1987), 24.

11. Carpenter, *Revive Us Again*, 241.

Chapter 1: The Power of Personal Story

1. Portions of this section are taken from Soong-Chan Rah, *Prophetic Lament* (Downers Grove, IL: InterVarsity, 2015), 35–43, 86–88; and Soong-Chan Rah, "The Sin of Racism," in *The Image of God in an Image Driven Age: Explorations in Theological Anthropology*, edited by Beth Felker Jones and Jeffrey W. Barbeau. Copyright © 2016 by Beth Felker Jones and Jeffrey W. Barbeau. Used by permission of InterVarsity Press, P.O. Box 1400, Downers Grove, IL 60515, USA. www.ivpress.com

2. Historian Winthrop Hudson summarizes the expectation of the colonists for the American continent: "They were executing a flank attack upon the forces of unrighteousness everywhere. Their role, John Winthrop had reminded them, was to be 'a city set on a hill' to demonstrate before 'the eyes of the world' what the result would be when a whole people was brought into open covenant with God. . . . This was God's country with a mission to perform." *Religion in America*, 3rd ed. (New York: Scribner, 1981), 20–21.

3. William Clebsch notes that early Americans saw "the new world as locus for a new city. . . . The new world prompted Christians from the sixteenth century through the nineteenth to think of America as the last and best of human societies following the westward course of empire." *From Sacred to Profane America* (New York: Harper & Row, 1968), 39.

4. Harvie Conn notes that the colonial Puritans hoped "New England would one day become the New Jerusalem." *The American City and the Evangelical Church* (Grand Rapids: Baker, 1994), 28.

5. Robert Orsi, *Gods of the City* (Bloomington: Indiana University Press, 1999), 6.

6. Randall Balmer, *The Making of Evangelicalism* (Waco: Baylor University Press, 2010), 33.

7. Amanda I. Seligman notes that "in the years after World War II, a modern form of suburb, fostered by new tools, opened up around the country. Innovative financing techniques, subsidized by the federal government, enabled millions of white Americans to purchase property beyond city limits." *Block by Block: Neighborhoods and Public Policy on Chicago's West Side* (Chicago: University of Chicago Press, 2005), 210–11.

8. Isabel Wilkerson writes that "after World War II, Chicago, Detroit, Cleveland, and other northern and western cities would witness a fitful migration of whites out of their urban strongholds. The far-out precincts and the inner ring suburbs became sanctuaries for battle-weary whites seeking, with government incentives, to replicate the havens they once had in the cities." *The Warmth of Other Suns* (New York: Vintage, 2010), 378.

9. Harvey Cox, *The Secular City: Secularization and Urbanization in Theological Perspective* (New York: Macmillan, 1966); Edward Banfield, *The Unheavenly City: The Nature and Future of Our Future Crisis* (Boston: Little Brown, 1970); Mitchell Gordon, *Sick Cities* (New York: Macmillan, 1963); Martin E. Marty, *Babylon by Choice: New Environment for Mission* (New York: Friendship, 1965); George D. Younger, *From New Creation to Urban Crisis: A History of Action Training Ministries, 1962–1975* (Chicago: Center for the Scientific Study of Religion, 1987); Useni Eugene Perkins, *Home Is a Dirty Street: The Social Oppression of Black Children* (Chicago: Third World, 1975); Jacques Ellul, *The Meaning of the City* (Grand Rapids: Eerdmans, 1970); Donald W. Shriver Jr. and Karl A. Ostrom, *Is There Hope for the City?* (Philadelphia: Westminster, 1977).

10. Winthrop Hudson notes that while $26 million was spent on new church buildings in 1945, that number steadily increased to over $1 billion by 1960. *Religion in America*, 384n45. Harvie Conn asserts that these numbers reflect the expansion of churches in the suburbs requiring new buildings. *American City*, 97.

11. While church attendance increased in the suburbs, Herbert Gans's research on a quintessential suburban town revealed that families who moved from the city to suburbia entailed no change in church or synagogue attendance. *The Levittowners: Ways of Life and Politics in a New Suburban Community* (New York: Columbia University Press, 1967), 264.

12. Conn, *American City*, 98. See Dennison Nash and Peter Berger, "The Child, the Family, and the 'Religious Revival' in Suburbia," *Journal for the Scientific Study of Religion* 2, no. 1 (Fall 1962): 85–93; see also Dennison Nash, "And a Little Child Shall Lead Them: A Test of an Hypothesis That Children Were the Source of the American 'Religious Revival,'" *Journal for the Scientific Study of Religion* 7, no. 2 (Fall 1968): 238–40.

13. Craig W. Ellison, ed., *The Urban Mission* (Grand Rapids: Eerdmans, 1974); Larry L. Rose and C. Kirk Hadaway, eds., *The Urban Challenge* (Nashville: Broadman, 1982); Ronald D. Pasquariello, *Redeeming the City: Theology, Politics, and Urban Policy* (New York: Pilgrim, 1982); Jack Dennison, *City Reaching: On the Road to Community Transformation* (Pasadena, CA: William Carey Library, 1999); Harvie M. Conn et al., *The Urban Face of Mission: Ministering the Gospel in a Diverse and Changing World*, ed. Manuel Ortiz and Susan S. Baker (Phillipsburg, NJ: P&R, 2002).

14. James C. Hefley and Marti Hefley, *The Church That Takes on Trouble: The Story of Chicago's LaSalle Street Church* (Elgin, IL: David C. Cook, 1976); Keith W. Phillips, *They Dare to Love the Ghetto* (Los Angeles: World Impact, 1976); Roger S. Greenway, *Apostles to the City: Biblical Strategies for Urban Missions* (Grand Rapids: Baker, 1978); Lyle E. Schaller, *The Change Agent* (Nashville: Abingdon, 1972); John Dawson, *Taking Our Cities for God: How to Break Spiritual Strongholds* (Lake Mary, FL: Creation House, 1989).

15. Ron Sider, foreword to *Mobilizing for the Common Good: The Lived Theology of John M. Perkins*, ed. Peter Slade, Charles Marsh, and Peter Goodwin Heltzel (Jackson: University Press of Mississippi, 2013), xi.

16. A. G. Miller, "The Black Apostle to White Evangelicals," in Slade, Marsh, and Heltzel, *Mobilizing for the Common Good*, 7.

17. Miller, "Black Apostle to White Evangelicals," in Slade, Marsh, and Heltzel, *Mobilizing for the Common Good*, 9.

18. See Christine Heyrman, *Southern Cross: The Beginnings of the Bible Belt* (Chapel Hill: University of North Carolina Press, 1997).

19. John Perkins, *A Quiet Revolution* (Pasadena, CA: Urban Family, 1976), 18.

20. Perkins, *Quiet Revolution*, 19.

21. John Perkins, *Let Justice Roll Down* (Ventura, CA: Regal Books, 1976), 72.

22. Perkins, *Let Justice Roll Down*, 67.

23. Perkins, *Quiet Revolution*, 20.

24. Perkins, *Let Justice Roll Down*, 93.

25. Perkins, *Let Justice Roll Down*, 103 (emphasis original).

26. Perkins, *Let Justice Roll Down*, 118.

27. Perkins, *Let Justice Roll Down*, 154–62.

28. Perkins, *Let Justice Roll Down*, 204–5.

29. "About," CCDA, http://www.ccda.org/about.

30. "About," CCDA, http://www.ccda.org/about.

31. See Wayne LeRoy Gordon's biography online, "Interview with Wayne LeRoy Gordon," Collection 398, Billy Graham Center Archives, Wheaton, IL, http://www2 .wheaton.edu/bgc/archives/GUIDES/398.htm#3; and on the Lawndale Community Church website, http://lawndalechurch.org/bio.html.

32. The following explication of the core values of the CCDA comes from the "Relocation" page on the CCDA website, http://www.ccda.org/about/ccd-philosophy /relocation; the "Reconciliation" page, http://www.ccda.org/about/ccd-philosophy /reconciliation; and the "Redistribution" page, http://www.ccda.org/about/ccd -philosophy/redistribution.

33. Peter Slade, "A Quiet Revolution and the Culture Wars," in Slade, Marsh, and Heltzel, *Mobilizing for the Common Good*, 60.

34. This section is adapted from Soong-Chan Rah, "Moving toward the Next Evangelicalism," in Slade, Marsh, and Heltzel, *Mobilizing for the Common Good*.

Chapter 2: The Power of a Personal Connection

1. *Youth for Christ Magazine*, April 1949, 67.

2. Lori L. Silverman, *Wake Me Up When the Data Is Over: How Organizations Use Stories to Drive Results* (San Francisco: Jossey-Bass, 2006), 127.

3. Joel A. Carpenter and Wilbert R. Shenk, eds., *Earthen Vessels: American Evangelicals and Foreign Missions, 1880–1980* (Grand Rapids: Eerdmans, 1990), 170; Joel Carpenter, *Revive Us Again: The Reawakening of American Fundamentalism* (New York: Oxford University Press, 1997), 180.

4. Carpenter and Shenk, *Earthen Vessels*, 164; *New China Challenge* (film) advertisement, October/November 1957, *World Vision Magazine*, 9.

5. According to the NAE (National Association of Evangelicals) 1961 Annual Report, World Relief's income rose from $52,000 in 1955 to $114,000 (not including Gifts in Kind) in 1960. Collection 165, Box 4, Folder 26, Billy Graham Center Archives, Wheaton College, Wheaton, IL.

6. In 1959, six million pounds of food worth $346,000 and clothing worth $142,000 was shipped to Korea and Germany; in Korea, 177 feeding stations served 30,000 people. NAE, 1961 Annual Report, Collection 165, Box 5, Folder 5, Billy Graham Center Archives.

7. "I have compassion on the multitude. I will not send them away hungry" (Matt. 15:32) was often cited by Swanson and appeared on early organizational letterhead and other documents.

8. For more detail on Compassion's presentation of its early history, see *Compassion at Work*, Spring 2002; *Compassion Magazine*, September/October 1992; and Wesley Stafford, *One: Celebrating 50 Years of Compassion* (Colorado Springs: Compassion International, 2002).

9. The campus of that school, Pasadena College, later became Ralph Winter's US Center for World Mission, now Frontier Ventures.

10. Despite this denominational affiliation, Pierce claimed that his formative spirituality was Wesleyan: "My spiritual roots lie in the old Methodist Holiness traditions

of camp meetings and brush arbors." Bob Pierce, "Lausanne in Retrospect: A Personal View," *World Vision Magazine*, December 1974, 11.

11. *World Vision Magazine*, August/September 1957, 8. Ted Engstrom, World Vision's longtime vice president and later president, also served as Youth for Christ's executive director. Pierce attracted other frontline Evangelical figures into key leadership roles: Larry Ward, *Christianity Today*'s first managing editor, became World Vision's most influential voice in media and communications and later founded Food for the Hungry; Richard Halverson, who would later become chaplain of the US Senate, was World Vision's first vice president; and Carl F. H. Henry, editor of *Christianity Today* and writer of *Uneasy Conscience*, served as a theological consultant and speaker at World Vision's conferences for pastors in Asia.

12. Pierce was invited by the Oriental Missionary Society to lead the rallies.

13. This was the same year that a famed YFC colleague, Billy Graham, founded the Billy Graham Evangelistic Association.

14. Bob Pierce, World Vision appeal letter, September 5, 1960, World Vision International Archives, Monrovia, CA.

15. Bob Pierce, World Vision appeal letter, June 5, 1961, World Vision International Archives.

16. This statement was reproduced in many places, including *World Vision Magazine*, June 1957, 2.

17. See, e.g., *World Vision Magazine*, April 1959.

18. Reproduced in *World Vision Magazine*, August 1958, 38 (as well as in many other issues).

19. Bob Pierce, World Vision appeal letter, November 28, 1960, World Vision International Archives.

20. *Youth for Christ Magazine*, April 1949, 69.

21. Richard Gehman, *Let My Heart Be Broken with the Things That Break the Heart of God* (New York: McGraw-Hill, 1960), 112.

22. World Vision, *Other Sheep* (pictorial), 1955, 3, World Vision International Archives. See also Lillian Dickson, interview by Bob Pierce, available at http://vimeo.com/8359045.

23. Alyward's life was memorialized in the Ingrid Bergman film *Inn of the Sixth Happiness*.

24. Collection 415, Box 1, Folder 2, Billy Graham Center Archives.

25. "Bob Pierce: Missionary Ambassador," *Youth for Christ Magazine*, April 1951, 10.

26. Dana Lee Robert, *American Women in Mission: A Social History of Their Thought and Practice* (Macon, GA: Mercer University Press, 1996), 411–12.

27. Ironically, Pierce's tireless advocacy for the poor inspired by these female missionaries caused him to neglect his own wife and daughters. The painful impact of Pierce's constant travels on his family is respectfully but honestly chronicled in his daughter's memoir: Marilee Pierce Dunker, *Days of Glory, Seasons of Night* (Grand Rapids: Zondervan, 1984).

28. Bob Pierce, "How to Emphasize Missions in the Sunday School" (brochure), 1958, World Vision International Archives; reproduced in "Missionary Education in the Sunday School," *World Vision Magazine*, November 1958, 6.

29. See Bob Pierce, excerpt from *The Least Ones*, from the film produced in 1965, available at http://www.youtube.com/watch?v=hodEDMGDs-4.

30. Although Pierce founded his sponsorship scheme the year before Everett Swanson did, child sponsorship had its roots in the nineteenth-century women's missions movement. Pierce, however, spoke as if the inspiration came directly from his experience with White Jade.

31. *World Vision Magazine*, September 1960, 4–5. See also Norman Rohrer, *Open Arms* (Carol Stream, IL: Tyndale, 1987), 229.

32. See Nicholas Wolterstorff, *Justice: Rights and Wrongs* (Princeton: Princeton University Press, 2008), chap. 2.

33. W. R. Ward, "Evangelical Identity in the Eighteenth Century," in *Christianity Reborn: The Global Expansion of Evangelicalism in the Twentieth Century*, ed. Donald Lewis (Grand Rapids: Eerdmans, 2004), 12–13.

34. Ken Anderson, "Her Community Is Called Death," *Youth for Christ Magazine*, April 1949, 18.

35. Bob Pierce, World Vision appeal letter, February 23, 1959, World Vision International Archives.

36. When it came time for Pierce to add commentary to the footage of his films, he often had a hard time following a written script and was most effective when he spoke extemporaneously, from the heart. See John Robert Hamilton, "An Historical Study of Bob Pierce and World Vision's Development of the Evangelical Social Action Film" (PhD diss., University of Southern California, 1990), 112.

37. George Burnham, "News Stories Tell How Your Gifts Were Used," *World Vision Magazine*, October/November 1957, 9.

38. This emphasis on the individual was all the more striking since emerging development thought remained steadfastly focused on macro-level issues. Mainline mission to the poor also emphasized large-scale efforts; for example, in 1958 the WCC (World Council of Churches) launched a major effort advocating for Western governments to give 1 percent of their incomes to economic development programs. See Colette Chabbott, "Development INGOs," in *Constructing World Culture: International Nongovernmental Organizations since 1875*, ed. John Boli and George M. Thomas (Stanford, CA: Stanford University Press, 1999), 233.

39. Rohrer, *Open Arms*, 119.

40. *The Least Ones*, 16mm (World Vision Films, 1965), World Vision US Film Archive, Federal Way, WA.

41. Franklin Graham and Jeannette Lockerbie, *Bob Pierce: This One Thing I Do* (Waco: Word Books, 1983), 56.

42. *The Least Ones*, 16mm (World Vision Films, 1965), World Vision US Film Archive.

43. This motif was employed also by Everett Swanson of Compassion. When Swanson's wife Miriam accompanied him to Korea, she "would take special delight that thousands of Korean children called her 'Mommie.'" See "Remembering the 'Heart of Compassion': Miriam Swanson Westerberg, 1915–1994," *Compassion Magazine*, March/April 1994, 9.

44. World Vision, advertisement, January 1958, *Christian Herald*, 47.

45. Frank Phillips, World Vision appeal letter, May 1957, World Vision International Archives.

46. World Vision, *Other Sheep* (pictorial), 1955, 3, World Vision International Archives.

47. World Vision, brochure, June 27, 1958, World Vision International Archives.

48. World Vision, brochure, June 27, 1958, World Vision International Archives.

49. Bob Pierce, World Vision appeal letter, June 5, 1961, World Vision International Archives.

50. Bob Pierce, *New China Challenge*, 16mm (World Vision Films, 1952), World Vision US Film Archive.

51. For example, see "It Is Important for You to See *Cry in the Night*," Flyer, Program for World Vision's Festival of Missions, Winona Lake, IN, July 21, 1964, World Vision International Archives.

52. *World Vision Magazine*, January 1962, 5.

53. World Vision, *Going with God* (pictorial), n.d., 81, World Vision International Archives.

54. Bob Pierce, World Vision appeal letter, June 1965, World Vision International Archives.

55. Bob Pierce, World Vision appeal letter, December 25, 1956, World Vision International Archives.

56. *World Vision Magazine*, January 1959, 7.

57. Graeme Irvine, *Best Things in the Worst Times: An Insider's View of World Vision* (Wilsonville, OR: BookPartners, 1996): 23–24.

58. Graham and Lockerbie, *Bob Pierce*, 53 (emphasis original).

59. Ironically, the grant was sent through World Vision. Bob Pierce, *Samaritan's Diary* (pamphlet), 1973, vol. 1, p. 42, in Collection 593, Box 1, Folder 4, Records of Lillian Dickson, Billy Graham Center Archives; Graham and Lockerbie, *Bob Pierce*, 84.

60. Franklin Graham, *Rebel with a Cause* (Nashville: Nelson, 1995), 39, 78.

61. Pat Jordan, "Prodigal Son," *Gentlemen's Quarterly*, April 1993, available at http://www.maryellenmark.com/text/magazines/gq/906S-000-003.html.

62. Jordan, "Prodigal Son."

63. Graham, *Rebel with a Cause*, 173–78.

64. Graham, *Rebel with a Cause*, 183.

65. Graham, *Rebel with a Cause*, 220.

66. Graham, *Rebel with a Cause*, 224. "Putting out a fleece" refers to the practice of seeking God's will by imitating the example of Gideon, as told in Judges 6 in the Hebrew Bible.

67. Graham, *Rebel with a Cause*, 181.

68. Jonathan Bonk, "Mission and Mammon," *International Bulletin of Missionary Research* 31, no. 4 (October 2007): 170.

69. According to his mother, Ruth Graham, Franklin received his undergraduate degree not with honors but "with relief." Graham, *Rebel with a Cause*, 118.

70. Samaritan's Purse, 2001–2005 Annual Reports. Resource in author's possession.

71. Franklin Graham, interview by Greta Van Susteren, Fox News, May 5, 2010, available at https://www.youtube.com/watch?v=04rpb0iVFmU. Graham frequently made inflammatory remarks against the entire religion of Islam. For example, "I see what Islam has done. I see what it's doing today to Christians. I see what it's doing around the world, the persecution, the slaughter." Peter S. Canellos and Kevin Baron, "A US boost to Graham's Quest for Converts," *Boston Globe*, October 8, 2006, http://www.boston.com/news/nation/articles/2006/10/08/a_us_boost_to_grahams_quest_for_converts/.

72. Andrew Blake, "Franklin Graham: 'We should stop all immigration of Muslims to the U.S.,'" *Washington Times*, July 20, 2015, http://www.washingtontimes.com /news/2015/jul/20/franklin-graham-we-should-stop-all-immigration-mus/.

73. "Twenty Years of Joy," Samaritan's Purse, September 4, 2013, http://www .samaritanspurse.org/article/twenty-years-of-joy/.

74. Franklin Graham, Estelle Condra, and Dilleen Marsh, *Miracle in a Shoebox: A Christmas Gift of Wonder* (Nashville: Nelson, 1995), 8–20.

75. Samaritan's Purse advertisement in *Christianity Today*, June 14, 1999.

76. Christian Smith, "The Limits of Personal Influence Strategy," in *American Evangelicalism: Embattled and Thriving* (Chicago: University of Chicago Press, 1998), 187–203.

77. Charles Van Engen, "A Broadening Vision," in Carpenter and Shenk, *Earthen Vessels*, 211.

78. Recent critiques from an Evangelical perspective include Steve Corbett and Brian Fikkert, *When Helping Hurts: How to Alleviate Poverty without Hurting the Poor . . . and Yourself* (Chicago: Moody, 2014); and Robert D. Lupton, *Toxic Charity: How Churches and Charities Hurt Those They Help, and How to Reverse It* (New York: HarperOne, 2012).

Chapter 3: World Vision and the Work of Prophetic Advocacy

1. The following is a summary of Robert Linthicum's account in "Doing Community Organizing in the Urban Slums of India," *Social Policy* 32, no. 2 (Winter 2001): 34.

2. By 1975, Korea itself had become a "major donor" country. Linthicum, "Doing Community Organizing," 247.

3. Graeme Irvine, *Best Things in the Worst Times: An Insider's View of World Vision* (Wilsonville, OR: BookPartners, 1996), 47.

4. Irvine, *Best Things in the Worst Times*, 47. More than one hundred World Vision workers were also killed in the turmoil.

5. Irvine, *Best Things in the Worst Times*, 86.

6. Irvine, *Best Things in the Worst Times*, 266, 268; World Vision, 2003 Annual Report, 21. World Vision claimed to be serving one hundred million people in 2003.

7. World Vision, 1980 Annual Report, World Vision International Archives, Monrovia, CA.

8. Jonathan Bonk, "Mission and Mammon," *International Bulletin of Missionary Research* 31, no. 4 (October 2007): 169.

9. Kevin D. Miller, "De-Seipling World Vision," *Christianity Today*, June 15, 1998.

10. For more on the Lausanne Congress, see chap. 6 in this book.

11. Ron Sider and Tony Campolo taught at Eastern Seminary and Eastern College in Pennsylvania, respectively.

12. Nina Shapiro, "The AIDS Evangelists," *Seattle Weekly*, November 15, 2005, http://www.seattleweekly.com/2006-11-15/news/the-aids-evangelists/.

13. Norman Rohrer, *Open Arms* (Carol Stream, IL: Tyndale, 1987), 152.

14. The IRR (Institute of Rural Reconstruction) was founded by James Yen of China, who was an internationally renowned pioneer in rural development and adult education in the middle of the twentieth century. Although the IRR was nonsectarian,

Yen attended a China Inland Mission school in his youth and claimed to be a follower of Jesus during his adult life.

15. Rohrer, *Open Arms*, 153.

16. Rohrer, *Open Arms*, 152.

17. AERDO is now called Accord Network.

18. Gary VanderPol, "World Vision," in *Religious Leadership: A Reference Handbook*, ed. Sharon Henderson Callahan (Thousand Oaks, CA: SAGE Publications, 2013), 493.

19. Stanley Mooneyham, World Vision appeal letter, November 1969, World Vision International Archives.

20. Ted Engstrom, quoted in 1976 Annual Report of World Vision, World Vision International Archives.

21. *World Vision Magazine*, March 1978, 11.

22. *World Vision Magazine*, February 1977, 19. World Vision's commitment to agricultural technology was substantial but not unqualified. According to Stanley Mooneyham, "At World Vision we use every enhancing tool that God has made available through science. But we try not to forget that gadgets are second rate evangelists." *Christianity Today*, September 18, 1981, 19.

23. Stanley Mooneyham, World Vision appeal letter, February 1974, World Vision International Archives.

24. World Vision, 1976 Annual Report, World Vision International Archives.

25. "Vision Statement," *World Vision Magazine*, Spring 2005, 2.

26. Richard Stearns, "Tragedy in the Spotlight," *World Vision Magazine*, Summer 2005, 5.

27. Bryant Myers, *Walking with the Poor* (Maryknoll, NY: Orbis, 1999), 96–97.

28. Myers, *Walking with the Poor*, 141–43. In another article, Bryant Myers suggests that such techniques need to be supplemented with questions concerning the religious worldview and the perceived "spiritual geography" of a village. See Myers, "What Makes Development Christian? Recovering from the Impact of Modernity," *Missiology* 26, no. 2 (1998).

29. To multiply examples, every photograph in the 1999 World Vision Christmas gift catalog, entitled "International Gifts of Joy and Hope," includes a person smiling broadly. Aside from the text, its visual tone is difficult to distinguish from a fashion catalog. Resource in author's possession.

30. *World Vision Magazine*, Winter 2003.

31. Generally speaking, this change in the way the poor were represented occurred up to a decade earlier among most secular organizations and mainline Protestants working among the poor.

32. Kari Costanza, "Dollars and Sense," *World Vision Magazine*, Autumn 2002, 8.

33. James Addis, "Wonder Trees," *World Vision Today*, Spring 2003, 10.

34. Robert Seiple, *One Life at a Time* (Dallas: Word, 1990), xviii.

35. Seiple, *One Life at a Time*, xviii (emphasis original).

36. "Vision Statement," *World Vision Today*, Spring 2005, 2.

37. W. Stanley Mooneyham, *Come Walk the World: Personal Experiences of Hurt and Hope* (Waco: Word Books, 1978), 36.

38. W. Stanley Mooneyham, *What Do You Say to a Hungry World?* (Waco: Word Books, 1975), 117.

39. Mooneyham, *What Do You Say*, 128.

40. Mooneyham, *What Do You Say*, 50.

41. World Vision, press release, 1975, World Vision International Archives.

42. Mooneyham, *Come Walk the World*, 118.

43. See the account of Bob Pierce and White Jade in chapter 2 of this book.

44. W. Stanley Mooneyham, "Journeying Together toward Social Justice," *One in Christ* 28, no. 2 (1992): 169.

45. Irvine, *Best Things in the Worst Times*, 53.

46. World Vision, press release, 1975, World Vision International Archives.

47. World Vision, press release, 1975, World Vision International Archives.

48. Mooneyham, *What Do You Say*, 22.

49. Stanley C. Baldwin, "A Case against Waste and Other Excesses," *Christianity Today*, July 16, 1976, 13.

50. World Vision, "Let It Growl," curriculum for planned famine youth group event, n.d., 53, World Vision International Archives.

51. World Vision, "Let It Growl," 54.

52. Irvine, *Best Things in the Worst Times*, 147.

53. For example, on October 10, 2001, World Vision's government relations manager and Africa policy specialist Rory E. Anderson presented testimony entitled "Conflict Diamonds: Funding Conflict, Fueling Change" before the Trade Subcommittee of the Committee on Ways and Means, US House of Representatives, http://waysand means.house.gov/Legacy/trade/107cong/10-10-01/10-10ande.htm.

54. Irvine, *Best Things in the Worst Times*, 152.

55. See *World Vision*, Spring 2005, 32, for photographs of the billboard. The campaign took place in partnership with the US Department of Immigration and Customs Enforcement.

56. World Vision, "Survey Reveals U.S. Apathy toward International AIDS Crisis" (press release), May 21, 2001, https://www.worldvision.org/worldvision/pr.nsf/stable /pr_us_apathy.

57. Rich Stearns, "Bono, the Good Samaritan" (radio spot), World Vision, http:// www.worldvision.org/worldvision/pr.nsf/stable/worldview_index_2002_August.

58. Polls show evangelical attitudes about AIDS changing significantly by 2007. See Richard Stearns, *The Hole in Our Gospel* (Nashville: Nelson, 2009), 195–96.

59. See Shapiro, "The AIDS Evangelists"; Tim Stafford, "The Colossus of Care," *Christianity Today*, March 2005, http://www.christianitytoday.com/ct/2005/march /18.50.html.

60. For a critique of the popular media's role in causing compassion fatigue in the late twentieth century, see Susan D. Moeller, *Compassion Fatigue: How the Media Sell Disease, Famine, War, and Death* (New York: Routledge, 1999). World Vision began to explicitly combat "compassion fatigue" as early as 1961, but at that time the prescription was "commitment" and "confrontation." See *World Vision Magazine*, September 1961, 4.

61. *World Vision Magazine*, Spring 2005, insert.

62. World Vision, advertisement, *Christianity Today*, October 1992.

63. World Vision, advertisement, *Christianity Today*, June 2002, insert.

64. Katherine Kam and Jane Sutton, "Buying Back Childhood," *Childlife* (Spring 1994): 4.

65. The preceding two paragraphs were adapted from Gary VanderPol, "World Vision," in *Religious Leadership: A Reference Handbook*, ed. Sharon Henderson Callahan (Thousand Oaks, CA: SAGE Publications, 2013), 494.

66. Donald Miller, letter, June 19, 1981, Wheaton '83 Conference Records, Collection 598, Box 11, Folder 27, Billy Graham Center Archives; see also Donald Miller, letter to Tom Sine, October 16, 1981, regarding the Wheaton '83 missions conference: "Most of Compassion's work is to enable children, one way or another, to receive a formal education."

67. *Compassion at Work*, Spring 2002, 4; Compassion International, 2004 Annual Report. Resource in author's possession.

68. Compassion International, 2004 Annual Report.

69. Don Miller, "What Compassion Believes," *Compassion Update*, January/ February 1991, 5.

70. "Your Investment in Child Development," *Compassion Magazine*, Fall/Winter 1995, 5.

71. Miller, "What Compassion Believes," 3.

72. "One Tough Question," *Compassion Magazine*, September/October 1992, 7.

73. Wesley Stafford, "25 Years with Compassion," *Compassion at Work*, Fall 2002, 2.

74. Miller, "What Compassion Believes," 6.

75. Wesley Stafford, "Making Children Matter in the Great Commission Strategy," *Compassion Magazine*, Fall 1994, 3.

76. Kamon Sampson, "A Compassionate Milestone," *Colorado Springs Gazette*, June 28, 2003.

77. Stories of sponsored children succeeded so well for Evangelical relief and development organizations (RDOs) partly because of the deep, historically grounded importance of testimonies and "bearing witness" within the tradition.

78. Wallace Erickson, "Reclaiming Women's Dignity," *Compassion Update*, March/ April 1991, 3.

79. Janet Root, "Reclaiming the Daughters of the Poor," *Compassion at Work*, Winter 2001, 7.

80. Erickson, "Reclaiming Women's Dignity," 3.

81. Root, "Reclaiming the Daughters," 4.

82. Root, "Reclaiming the Daughters," 9.

83. For some instructive examples, see Gary VanderPol, "The Least of These: American Evangelical Parachurch Missions to the Poor, 1947–2005" (ThD diss., Boston University, 2010), 269–70, available at https://open.bu.edu/handle/2144/1337.

84. Mark Labberton, *The Dangerous Act of Loving Your Neighbor: Seeing Others through the Eyes of Jesus* (Downers Grove, IL: InterVarsity, 2010), 96.

Chapter 4: Sojourners as a Prophetic Voice for Those on the Margins

1. Tim Egan, "State of the Union: The Evangelical Vote," *BBC News*, November 9, 2004, http://news.bbc.co.uk/2/hi/programmes/3992067.stm.

2. See also Donald W. Dayton and Robert K. Johnston, eds., *The Variety of American Evangelicalism* (Downers Grove, IL: InterVarsity, 1991); Donald W. Dayton with Douglas M. Strong, *Rediscovering an Evangelical Heritage*, 2nd ed. (Grand Rapids: Baker Academic, 2014).

3. See Soong-Chan Rah, "The Necessity of Lament for Ministry in the Urban Context," *Ex Auditu* 29 (2013): 54–69.

4. See H. Richard Niebuhr, *Christ and Culture* (New York: Harper & Row, 1951). See also Craig Carter, *Rethinking Christ and Culture: A Post-Christendom Perspective* (Grand Rapids: Brazos, 2006).

5. Robert Putnam and David Campbell, *American Grace: How Religion Divides and Unites Us* (New York: Simon & Schuster, 2010), 91–133.

6. Seth Dowland, *Family Values and the Rise of the Religious Right* (Philadelphia: University of Pennsylvania Press, 2015).

7. See Joel Carpenter, *Revive Us Again: The Reawakening of American Fundamentalism* (New York: Oxford University Press, 1997), xii, 3–12, 245.

8. See Molly Worthen, *Apostles of Reason* (New York: Oxford University Press, 2014), 27–30, 216–19, 259–65.

9. Frank Schaeffer, *Crazy for God: How I Grew Up as One of the Elect, Helped Found the Religious Right, and Lived to Take All (or Almost All) of It Back* (Cambridge, MA: DeCapo, 2007), 242–64.

10. Randall Balmer, *Thy Kingdom Come* (New York: Basic Books, 2006), 11–17.

11. Richard Quebedeaux, *The Young Evangelicals* (New York: Harper & Row, 1974), 37–41, 81–86.

12. For a fuller description, see Dayton and Johnston, *Variety of American Evangelicalism.*

13. John D'Elia, *A Place at the Table* (New York: Oxford University Press, 2008), xi–xxvi.

14. George Marsden, *Reforming Evangelicalism: Fuller Seminary and the New Evangelicalism* (Grand Rapids: Eerdmans, 1987), 4–11.

15. See David R. Swartz, *Moral Minority: The Evangelical Left in an Age of Conservatism* (Philadelphia: University of Pennsylvania Press, 2012), 170–78.

16. See Jim Wallis, *Revive Us Again: A Sojourner's Story* (Nashville: Abingdon, 1983), 19–34; see also Wallis, *Faith Works: How Faith-Based Organizations Are Changing Lives, Neighborhoods, and America* (Berkeley: PageMill, 2000), 16–23.

17. Wallis, *Revive Us Again*, 71.

18. Wallis, *Revive Us Again*, 18.

19. Jim Wallis, *God's Politics: Why the Right Gets It Wrong and the Left Doesn't Get It* (New York: HarperCollins, 2005), 19.

20. As George Marsden describes: "'The Great Reversal' took place from about 1900 to about 1930, when all progressive social concern, whether political or private, became suspect among revivalist evangelicals and was relegated to a very minor role." George Marsden, *Fundamentalism and American Culture* (New York: Oxford University Press, 2006), 86.

21. See Carpenter, *Revive Us Again*, xii, 211–32; see also Matthew Sutton, *Aimee Semple McPherson and the Resurrection of Christian America* (Cambridge, MA: Harvard University Press, 2007), 3, 69–77.

22. In the foreword to *The Soul of Politics*, Garry Wills wryly notes that "if Richard Nixon could have chosen a school to send his children to, Trinity would have looked like the ideal choice—rural, old fashioned, patriotic, respectful of authority." Wills, foreword to Jim Wallis, *The Soul of Politics* (New York: New Press, 1994), ix.

23. "Our History," Sojourners, https://sojo.net/about-us/our-history.

24. Wallis, *Revive Us Again*, 16.

25. "Jim Wallis at Trinity," Series 5, Box 12, Folder 6, Jim Wallis Papers, 1971–1988, Wheaton College Archives and Special Collections, Wheaton, IL.

26. Garry Wills states that "alumni tried to expel Wallis when he organized protests, prayer vigils for peace, and appeals to forgotten texts of the Bible." Wallis, *Soul of Politics*, ix. "Trinity's administration and alumni . . . frequently confronted him concerning his activism and the negative publicity it attracted to the college. Once, to assuage doubts, he received a summons before the board of trustees to affirm his testimony of faith in Jesus Christ." "Historical Note," Jim Wallis Papers, Wheaton College Archives and Special Collections, http://archon.wheaton.edu/index.php?p=creators/creator&id=184.

27. David Swartz notes: "Not only was this the first explicitly evangelical organization in twentieth-century American politics launched to elect a President, it was endorsing a liberal Democratic candidate." David Swartz, "Left Behind: The Evangelical Left and the Limits of Evangelical Politics, 1965–1988" (PhD diss., University of Notre Dame, 2008), 389.

28. Swartz, "Left Behind," 61.

29. Brantley Gasaway, *Progressive Evangelicals and the Pursuit of Social Justice* (Chapel Hill: University of North Carolina Press, 2014), 10. See also Ronald Sider, ed., *The Chicago Declaration* (Carol Stream, IL: Creation House, 1974).

30. In his withdrawal letter to TEDS, Wallis claims that "the work of the *Post-American* is my first priority," and he acknowledges that his seminary work suffered accordingly. "My experience at Trinity has been valuable to me and the sound theological basis I have gained will be with me through my life and ministry." "Jim Wallis at Trinity," Series 5, Box 12, Folder 6, Jim Wallis Papers, Wheaton College Archives and Special Collections.

31. Wes Michaelson, "Crucible of Community," *Sojourners*, January 1977, 17.

32. See Randall Balmer, *The Making of Evangelicalism* (Waco: Baylor University Press, 2010); Dowland, *Family Values*; Charles Marsh, *Wayward Christian Soldiers* (New York: Oxford University Press, 2007); William Martin, *With God on Our Side* (New York: Broadway, 1996); and Frank Schaeffer, *Crazy for God*, for fuller treatments of the rise of the religious right.

33. Kenneth Woodward, John Barnes, and Laurie Lisle, "Born Again!," *Newsweek*, October 25, 1976, 78.

34. Swartz, "Left Behind," 5.

35. "Readership Survey, 1979," Series 4, Box 59, Folder 9, Sojourners Collection, Wheaton College Archives and Special Collections, Wheaton, IL. The same survey revealed that Catholic readership hovered around 21 percent, while liberal readership pushed 25 percent.

36. "Editorial Response," *Sojourners*, November 1977, 39.

37. Wes Michaelson and Jim Wallis, "The Plan to Save America: A Disclosure of an Alarming Political Initiative by the Evangelical Far Right," *Sojourners*, April 1976, 4.

38. Wallis, *Revive Us Again*, 135.

39. By 1975, the fragile coalition that had formed around the Chicago Declaration had fragmented. Identity politics and theological differences resulted in a weakened coalition and a splintering of the movement. David Swartz, "Identity Politics and

the Fragmenting of the 1970s Evangelical Left," *Religion and American Culture* 21, no. 1 (Winter 2011): 81–120.

40. Jim Wallis, "Word and Deed," *Sojourners*, February/March 1994, 50.

41. Jim Wallis, "Beyond the Christian Right," *Sojourners*, September/October 1994, 4.

42. "Our History," Sojourners, https://sojo.net/about-us/our-history.

43. Jim Wallis, *Who Speaks for God?* (New York: Delacorte, 1996), 13.

44. See the March/April 1995 issue of *Sojourners*.

45. Wallis, *Revive Us Again*, 92–108. See also Michaelson, "Crucible of Community."

46. Wallis, *Revive Us Again*, 94.

47. Michaelson, "Crucible of Community," 17.

48. Wallis, *Revive Us Again*, 99.

49. "Our History," Sojourners, https://sojo.net/about-us/our-history.

50. Michaelson, "Crucible of Community," 24.

51. A January 1987 Sojourners community budget demonstrates that the community continued to pool its resources and shared expenses. Wallis's living expenses of $677 placed him approximately in the middle of the community's twenty-four units. Financial reports, 1987, Series 6, Box 72, Folder 11, Sojourners Collection, Wheaton College Archives and Special Collections.

52. Jim Wallis, *The Call to Conversion* (New York: Harper & Row, 1981), ix.

53. Wallis, *Revive Us Again*, 111.

54. Letters, Series 6, Box 78, Folders 2 and 4, Sojourners Collection, Wheaton College Archives and Special Collections. This collection holds a large number of letters from around the country inquiring about issues related to intentional community.

55. See Wallis, *God's Politics*, xvii–xxvi.

56. *Sojourners*, February 2004, insert.

57. Jim Wallis, "The Religious Right Era Is Over," *Sojourners*, October 2004, 4.

58. The term "emerging church" refers to the specific movement of former evangelicals engaging with postmodern thought. Brian McLaren's writing and speaking is representative of this movement. McLaren served as the chair of the Sojourners board for several years.

59. Jim Wallis, *The Great Awakening* (New York: HarperOne, 2008), 13.

60. Sojourners, national organizer advertisement, *Sojourners*, May/June 1995, 26.

61. "Our History," Sojourners, https://sojo.net/about-us/our-history.

62. Jim Wallis, "The One Constant Is Change," *Sojourners*, July/August 1998, 9.

63. Wallis, "One Constant Is Change," 9.

64. Wallis, "One Constant Is Change," 9–10.

Chapter 5: African-American Evangelicals and the Challenge of True Racial Reconciliation

1. Edward Gilbreath, "A Prophet out of Harlem," *Christianity Today*, September 16, 1996, http://www.christianitytoday.com/ct/1996/september16/6ta036.html; Carl Ellis, interview by Soong-Chan Rah, June 27, 2010.

2. William Pannell, interview by Soong-Chan Rah, April 27, 2010.

3. Donald W. Dayton with Douglas M. Strong, *Rediscovering an Evangelical Heritage*, 2nd ed. (Grand Rapids: Baker Academic, 2014), 41–43, 182. See also Donald W.

Dayton and Robert K. Johnston, eds., *The Variety of American Evangelicalism* (Downers Grove, IL: InterVarsity, 1991), 1–4, 245–51.

4. Douglas A. Sweeney, *The American Evangelical Story* (Grand Rapids: Baker Academic, 2005), 22.

5. John Woodbridge, Mark A. Noll, and Nathan O. Hatch, *The Gospel in America: Themes in the Story of America's Evangelicals* (Grand Rapids: Zondervan, 1979), 43.

6. Woodbridge, Noll, and Hatch, *Gospel in America*, 276, 282.

7. Edward Gilbreath, *Reconciliation Blues* (Downers Grove, IL: InterVarsity, 2006), 40–41.

8. A. G. Miller, "The Rise of African-American Evangelicalism in American Culture," in *Perspectives on American Religion and Culture*, ed. Peter W. Williams (Malden, MA: Blackwell, 1999), 261.

9. With permission, this section uses material previously published in Soong-Chan Rah, "Prophetic Voices and Evangelical Seminary Education," *Common Ground Journal* 8, no. 1 (Fall 2010): 32–48.

10. William Pannell, "The Religious Heritage of Blacks," in *The Evangelicals: What They Believe, Who They Are, Where They Are Changing*, ed. David F. Wells and John D. Woodbridge (New York: Abingdon, 1975), 99.

11. Sweeney, *American Evangelical Story*, 127.

12. The history of the NBEA is best documented in two works that help form this section: Miller, "Rise of African-American Evangelicalism," in Williams, *Perspectives on American Religion*, 259–69; and the self-published history of the NBEA by William Bentley, *The National Black Evangelical Association: Reflections on the Evolution of a Concept of Ministry* (Chicago: self-published, 1979).

13. Whitfield Nottage, Talbot Nottage, and Berlin Martin (B. M.) Nottage (1889–1966). B. M. Nottage was the most prolific and well-known of the Nottage brothers. See Miller, "Rise of African-American Evangelicalism," in Williams, *Perspectives on American Religion*, 262.

14. B. M. Nottage (in a privately published sermon cited by Miller) asserts that "the 'all welcome' sign of the doors of most evangelical churches does not include the Negro. . . . Usually he isn't welcome and is not allowed to enjoy such fellowship." See Miller, "Rise of African-American Evangelicalism," in Williams, *Perspectives on American Religion*, 264.

15. Included in this thread is the contribution of John Davis Bell of the Christian and Missionary Alliance.

16. Miller, "Rise of African-American Evangelicalism," in Williams, *Perspectives on American Religion*, 261.

17. Miller, "Rise of African-American Evangelicalism," in Williams, *Perspectives on American Religion*, 263.

18. Soong-Chan Rah, "The Sin of Racism," in *The Image of God in an Image Driven Age*, ed. Beth Felker Jones and Jeffrey W. Barbeau (Downers Grove, IL: InterVarsity, 2016). Quoting Miller, "Rise of African-American Evangelicalism," in Williams, *Perspectives on American Religion*, 265.

19. Bentley, *National Black Evangelical Association*, 19–20.

20. Bentley, *National Black Evangelical Association*, 20.

21. Bentley, *National Black Evangelical Association*, 18.

22. Tom Skinner, interview with Robert Shuster, transcript by Wayne D. Weber, February 1999, Collection 430, Billy Graham Center Archives, Wheaton College, Wheaton, IL, http://www.wheaton.edu/bgc/archives/trans/430t01.htm.

23. Gilbreath, "Prophet out of Harlem."

24. Tom Skinner, *Black and Free* (Grand Rapids: Zondervan, 1968), 29.

25. Skinner, interview.

26. Skinner, *Black and Free*, 29.

27. Skinner, *Black and Free*, 56.

28. Gilbreath, "Prophet out of Harlem."

29. Tom Skinner, "The U.S. Racial Crisis and World Evangelism," sermon presented at Urbana Student Missions Conference, Urbana, IL, December 1970, https://urbana.org/transcript/us-racial-crisis-and-world-evangelism-1970.

30. Skinner, "U.S. Racial Crisis and World Evangelism."

31. Pannell, interview.

32. Pannell, interview.

33. Gilbreath, "Prophet out of Harlem."

34. Gilbreath, "Prophet out of Harlem."

35. David R. Mains, *Full Circle: The Creative Church for Today's Society* (Waco: Word Books, 1971), 24, 26.

36. Mains, *Full Circle*, 9.

37. Mains, *Full Circle*, 18–19.

38. Manuel Ortiz, "Circle Church: A Case Study in Contextualization," *Urban Mission* 8, no. 3 (January 1991): 7.

39. Russ Knight, interview by Soong-Chan Rah, March 23 and April 20, 2010.

40. The written description of the David Mains Collection at the Wheaton College Archives focuses on his work in creative worship: "The David Mains Collection is composed of manuscript and media material. Manuscripts include the guide for the 'Planning Creative Sunday Morning Services' while media material represents approximately . . . 20+ audio cassettes on the same topic." David Mains Papers, 1970–1980, http://archon.wheaton.edu/index.php?p=collections/controlcard&id=137.

41. Mains, *Full Circle*, 27.

42. One of Mains's early teachings at the church emphasized the values of ministering to the poor and the oppressed. Mains also taught on the kingdom of God, which reflected his social justice emphasis.

43. "The New Ministry: Bringing God Back to Life," *Time*, December 26, 1969, http://content.time.com/time/magazine/article/0,9171,219330,00.html.

44. Ortiz, "Circle Church," 9.

45. According to former church members Russ Knight and Peter Sjoblom, the African-American population at Circle Church never exceeded 15 percent.

46. Ortiz, "Circle Church," 9.

47. Mains, "Full Circle," 40.

48. Ortiz, "Circle Church," 8.

49. Ortiz, "Circle Church," 8.

50. Knight, interview.

51. Ortiz, "Circle Church," 10.

52. Mains, "Full Circle," 41.

53. Knight, interview; Peter Sjoblom, interview by Soong-Chan Rah, March 23 and April 20, 2010; Circle Church board meeting minutes, October 20, 1975, asking the staff "to deal with the concept of Senior Pastor"; Letter from Clarence Hilliard and the Black Fellowship, "Statement of Response and Appeal of Pastor Hilliard and the Black Members of Circle to the Elders' Request for Pastor Hilliard's Resignation," December 20, 1975, questioning the decision to establish David Mains's authority over all of the worship services. All Circle Church documents from an unpublished, private collection.

54. Mains, "Full Circle," 43.

55. Russ Knight asserts that Mains preferred classical music over soul music. In addition, Mains's desire to launch "Step Two" meant that he wanted more strict control over the Sunday service.

56. Ortiz, "Circle Church," 8.

57. Ortiz, "Circle Church," 11. The quote comes from a response letter written by David Mains after reading the rough draft of Manuel Ortiz's article on the Circle Church crisis (which was eventually published in *Urban Mission* 8, no. 3 [January 1991]).

58. The never-preached sermon became popularly known as "Down with the Honky Jesus and Up with the Funky Gospel."

59. Clarence Hilliard, "The Funky Gospel" (undelivered sermon manuscript), 4.

60. Hilliard, "Funky Gospel," 4.

61. Hilliard, "Funky Gospel," 6.

62. Hilliard, "Funky Gospel," 9.

63. Drawn from Circle Church board meeting minutes, "Chronological Events through the Crisis."

64. Elders of Circle Church, letter to the members of Circle Church, November 15, 1975.

65. Knight, interview.

66. Mains, "Letter to Circle Elders," November 20, 1975.

67. Circle Church elders meeting minutes, December 9, 1975, 2.

68. Circle Church elders meeting minutes, December 9, 1975, 2.

69. Circle Church elders meeting minutes, December 15, 1975, 4.

70. Circle Church elders meeting minutes, December 15, 1975, 4–5.

71. Circle Church elders meeting minutes, December 15, 1975, 4.

72. Circle Church elders, "Letter to Clarence Hilliard," December 17, 1975.

73. Clarence Hilliard and the Black Fellowship, "Statement of Response and Appeal of Pastor Hilliard and the Black Members of Circle to the Elders' Request for Pastor Hilliard's Resignation," December 20, 1975.

74. Elder board letter to Clarence Hilliard, January 5, 1976.

75. The Hilliard and Black Fellowship letter states, among other things, concern over favoritism shown to Mains by the elders, Mains's practice of forcing authority over the Sunday morning services, the prohibition of preaching "The Funky Gospel," unfair treatment toward the black children of the church, superior attitude of whites toward blacks, the lack of black elders, and complete disregard of the concerns of blacks at Circle Church.

76. The Black Fellowship, "Letter to Elders," January 9, 1976.

77. Sjoblom, interview; Knight, interview.

78. Sweeney, *American Evangelical Story*, 127 (emphasis original).
79. Edith Blumhofer, "Houses of Worship: The New Evangelicals," *The Wall Street Journal*, February 18, 2005, Easter edition.
80. David Van Biema et al., "The 25 Most Influential Evangelicals in America," *Time*, February 7, 2005.
81. As noted in Soong-Chan Rah's *The Next Evangelicalism*, the percentage of nonwhite student enrollment in evangelical seminaries increased from approximately 15 percent in 1997 to 31 percent in 2005. However, the number of faculty of color in 2005 stood at 12 percent, which is disproportionally and significantly lower than the 31 percent minority student enrollment. Furthermore, the last available study on the percentage of minority faculty at Evangelical Christian colleges and universities (1998) shows that minority faculty made up only 3.6 percent of Christian college faculty, which was actually a drop from the percentage of minority faculty in 1995. A random sampling of twenty different Christian colleges and evangelical seminaries provided by the Chronicle of Higher Education in 2007 reveals that ethnic minorities comprise less than 7 percent of the faculty at those twenty schools. Soong-Chan Rah, *The Next Evangelicalism* (Downers Grove, IL: InterVarsity, 2009), 19–20.

Chapter 6: The Fraternidad Teológica Latinoamericana and the Sharing of Power in a Globalized Christianity

1. C. René Padilla, ed., *The New Face of Evangelicalism* (Downers Grove, IL: InterVarsity, 1976), 9.
2. Space does not allow us to cover many important events and key leaders. Perhaps the most regrettable omission is Puerto Rican-American theologian Orlando Costas. For the most comprehensive account of the FTL's rise and influence, see David Salinas, *Latin American Evangelical Theology in the 1970s: The Golden Decade* (Leiden, Netherlands: Brill, 2009).
3. Donald A. McGavran, *Understanding Church Growth* (Grand Rapids: Eerdmans, 1980), 163.
4. For more detail see McGavran, *Understanding Church Growth*, especially chap. 1.
5. Carl F. H. Henry and W. Stanley Mooneyham, eds., *One Race, One Gospel, One Task*, vol. 1 (Minneapolis: World Wide, 1967), 28.
6. Cited in Joel A. Carpenter and Wilbert R. Shenk, eds., *Earthen Vessels: American Evangelicals and Foreign Missions, 1880–1980* (Grand Rapids: Eerdmans, 1990), 220.
7. Clyde W. Taylor to Billy Graham, July 1, 1968, Collection 324, Box 2, Folder 3, Billy Graham Center Archives, Wheaton College, Wheaton, IL, cited in Salinas, *Latin American Evangelical Theology*, 70.
8. C. René Padilla, cited in Salinas, *Latin American Evangelical Theology*, 76.
9. From a translated and edited version of Escobar's address, "The Social Impact of the Gospel," in *Is Revolution Change?*, ed. Brian Griffiths (Downers Grove, IL: InterVarsity, 1972), 84, 87.
10. Escobar, "Social Impact of the Gospel," in Griffiths, *Is Revolution Change?*, 90.
11. Escobar, "Social Impact of the Gospel," in Griffiths, *Is Revolution Change?*, 85.
12. Escobar, "Social Impact of the Gospel," in Griffiths, *Is Revolution Change?*, 96.

13. Samuel Escobar, "Heredero de la Reforma Radical," in *Hacia Una Teología Evangélica Latinoamericana. Ensayos en Honor de Pedro Savage*, ed. C. René Padilla (Miami: Caribe, 1984), 64.

14. Escobar, "Heredero de la Reforma Radical," in Padilla, *Hacia Una Teología Evangélica Latinoamericana*, 64.

15. Escobar, "Social Impact of the Gospel," in Griffiths, *Is Revolution Change?*, 89.

16. Salinas, *Latin American Evangelical Theology*, 97.

17. Orlando Costas of the Seminario Bíblico Latinoamericano in Costa Rica was the most prominent omission.

18. "High Theology in the Andes," *Christianity Today*, January 15, 1971, 28–29.

19. Samuel Escobar, "My Pilgrimage in Mission," *International Bulletin of Missionary Research* 36, no. 4 (October 2012): 206–11.

20. Brian Stanley, *The Global Diffusion of Evangelicalism: The Age of Billy Graham and John Stott* (Downers Grove, IL: IVP Academic, 2013), 156.

21. Salinas, *Latin American Evangelical Theology*, 123.

22. Salinas, *Latin American Evangelical Theology*, 126.

23. C. René Padilla, "Evangelism and the World," in *Let the Earth Hear His Voice: International Congress on World Evangelization, Lausanne, Switzerland*, ed. J. D. Douglas (Minneapolis: World Wide, 1975), 141.

24. Padilla, "Evangelism and the World," in Douglas, *Let the Earth Hear*, 122, 128.

25. Padilla, "Evangelism and the World," in Douglas, *Let the Earth Hear*, 144.

26. Padilla, "Evangelism and the World," in Douglas, *Let the Earth Hear*, 131.

27. Padilla, "Evangelism and the World," in Douglas, *Let the Earth Hear*, 130.

28. Padilla, "Evangelism and the World," in Douglas, *Let the Earth Hear*, 138.

29. Padilla, "Evangelism and the World," in Douglas, *Let the Earth Hear*, 125.

30. Padilla, "Evangelism and the World," in Douglas, *Let the Earth Hear*, 126.

31. Padilla, "Evangelism and the World," in Douglas, *Let the Earth Hear*, 131.

32. Salinas, *Latin American Evangelical Theology*, 132.

33. Samuel Escobar, "Evangelism and Man's Search for Freedom, Justice and Fulfillment," in Douglas, *Let the Earth Hear*, 303–4.

34. Escobar, "Evangelism and Man's Search," in Douglas, *Let the Earth Hear*, 316.

35. Escobar, "Evangelism and Man's Search," in Douglas, *Let the Earth Hear*, 326.

36. "Theology Implications of Radical Discipleship," in Douglas, *Let the Earth Hear*, 1296.

37. "Lausanne Covenant," Lausanne Movement, http://www.lausanne.org/content/covenant/lausanne-covenant.

38. T. E. Yates, *Christian Mission in the Twentieth Century* (New York: Cambridge University Press, 1994), 207.

39. C. René Padilla, *Mission between the Times: Essays on the Kingdom* (Carlisle, UK: Langham Monographs, 2010), 73.

40. Padilla, *Mission between the Times*, 81.

41. Padilla, *Mission between the Times*, 71.

42. Padilla, *Mission between the Times*, 76.

43. Padilla, *Mission between the Times*, 161, 162 (emphasis original).

44. Padilla, *Mission between the Times*, 182–83.

45. "Lausanne Covenant," Lausanne Movement, http://www.lausanne.org/content/covenant/lausanne-covenant.

46. Padilla, *Mission between the Times*, 198.

47. Padilla, *Mission between the Times*, 198.

48. For more information on the Micah Network, see http://www.micahnetwork.org/.

49. Tim Chester, ed., *Justice, Mercy and Humility: Integral Mission and the Poor* (Carlisle, UK: Paternoster, 2002), 2.

50. See Diana Eck, *A New Religious America: How a "Christian Country" Has Become the World's Most Religiously Diverse Nation* (San Francisco: HarperSanFrancisco, 2001).

51. R. Stephen Warner, "Coming to America," *Christian Century*, February 10, 2004, 20.

52. For more background on how Emmanuel Gospel Center became aware of the Quiet Revival in Boston, see "EGC's Research Uncovers the Quiet Revival," *Inside EGC* 20, no. 4 (November 2013), available at http://egc.org/qr-discovery.

53. Dana L. Robert, "Shifting Southward: Global Christianity since 1945," *International Bulletin of Missionary Research* 24, no. 2 (April 2000): 53, 56.

54. Jenny Hwang Yang, "Immigrants in the USA: A Missional Opportunity," in *Global Diasporas and Mission*, ed. Chandler H. Im and Amos Yong (Oxford: Regnum Books, 2014), 148.

55. Soong-Chan Rah, *The Next Evangelicalism* (Downers Grove, IL: InterVarsity, 2009), 210.

56. Peggy Levitt, "Transnational Ties and Incorporation: The Cases of Dominicans in the United States," in *The Columbia History of Latinos in the United States since 1960*, ed. David Gutierrez (New York: Columbia University Press, 2003), 241.

57. For a fascinating study of religious transnationalism in Houston, Texas, see Helen Rose Ebaugh and Janet Saltzman Chafetz, eds., *Religion across Borders: Transnational Immigrant Networks* (Walnut Creek, CA: AltaMira, 2002).

58. For a constructive critique of these attitudes toward short-term missions, see David Livermore, *Serving with Eyes Wide Open* (Grand Rapids: Baker Books, 2013), chap. 7.

59. Andrew Walls, "Missions and Migration: The Diaspora Factor in Christian History," in Im and Yong, *Global Diasporas*, 36.

Index

Broken BREAD

1st Collection

Reinhard Bonnke

Broken Bread · 1st Collection
English

Copyright © Full Flame GmbH 2005
ISBN 3-937180-17-6

1. Edition, 1. Print
11,000 copies

Cover Design: Isabelle Brasche
Backcover photo: Rob Birkbeck
Frontcover photo & Typeset: Roland Senkel

Publisher:

Full Flame GmbH
Postfach 60 05 95
60335 Frankfurt am Main
Germany

info@fullflame.com
www.fullflame.com

Printed in Germany

Table of Contents

They say the great Greek writer Homer wandered from town to town begging his bread and telling his stories of the siege of Troy. In his day, storytellers made a living that way. There were no theatres, dramas, books or television and everybody loves a good story.

Scripture uses that method to teach us. It is not a book of academic theology. But with a Divine author there is all the subtle character drawing that creates faith in God. We will look first at some gospel incidents.

Commitment to Christ

There was the royal official mentioned in John 4:46-54. He showed faith in Christ's powers by coming all the way from Capernaum to Cana (a day's journey) to ask Christ to go to his house and heal his son who was dying. Jesus said a strange thing to the poor man. *"Unless you people see miraculous signs and wonders you will never believe."* It was strange because he had believed enough to come to see Christ. But Jesus had another kind of

> He had believed that Jesus could heal his son if he came, and it would involve a journey to do it. But now he had to believe Jesus was bigger than that.

faith in mind. The man was not put off by this apparent cold reception. He still believed and said, *"Sir, come down, before my son dies!"*

Jesus did not do what the official wanted. He did not go down to Capernaum. Whatever John's gospel records Jesus as doing it is never because he is asked. He simply said to the man, *"You may go. Your son will live."* This meant extra faith. He had believed that Jesus could heal his son if he came, and it would involve a journey to do it. But now he had to believe Jesus was bigger than that.

> It was not the miracle they believed. They believed in the way John always talks about believing: commitment to Christ.

The official departed and we read, *"The man believed the word that Jesus had spoken to him."* It was the next day before he arrived. All that way, all that the man had was this brief word of Jesus, every step and every minute. But when he discovered a miracle had taken place, then John records that real faith came. *"He and all his household believed."* It was not the miracle they believed. That was there to see, not just to be believed. They believed in the way John always talks about believing: commitment to Christ.

How Faith develops

Another telling incident is in John 9. Without so much as saying, "Excuse me," Jesus healed a blind man. He plastered mud across his eyes and sent him to wash in the famous pool of Siloam. The man came back with good sight. On his return, he learned that it was Jesus who had performed this miracle. When asked he said, *"The man they call Jesus"* did it. The people seemed unfamiliar with Christ's identity and asked, *"Where is this man?"* Then when a group of Pharisees questioned him they said, *"This man is not from God."* That is where it stood: Jesus a man.

> *"This man is not from God."* That is where it stood: Jesus a man. Who was Jesus? They asked the man who was healed, and he said, *"He is a prophet. If this man were not from God, he could do nothing."*

However, faith began to arise. First, some of the Pharisees said, *"How can a sinner do such miraculous signs?"* Then the question developed about him – Who was Jesus? They asked the man who was healed, and he said, *"He is a prophet."* But the leading jews had agreed to excommunicate from the temple anybody who said Jesus was the Christ; so faced with such a fact as a man born blind but now seeing, they questioned further and prompted the man to say Jesus was a sinner. But he would not and declared, *"God ... listens to the godly man who does his will ... If this man were not from God, he could do nothing."* His faith was developing, and he believed Christ was not a sinner, but from God. For this he suffered persecution and was blamed as a disciple of Jesus.

Jesus then found the man. The authorities had thrown him out of the temple, typical of a world that rejects those who testify to the goodness of God. He had one important question to ask the man. It wasn't whether he felt grateful or if he had started to work. He asked, *"Do you believe in the Son of man?"* The man did not know what Jesus meant. *"Who is he, Sir? Tell me so that I may believe in him."*

> The man looked at Christ, and his faith exploded – he had no problem accepting Christ's declaration. Faith was complete.

He had enough faith in Jesus to feel his way to the pool of Siloam when blind because Jesus told him to go. That brought him physical sight. But another kind of faith could bring him far greater illumination. His faith had not reached that point. Then Jesus said, *"You have now seen him; in fact he is the one speaking with you."* The man looked at Christ, and his faith exploded – he had no problem accepting Christ's declaration. He said, *"Lord, I believe."* Then, *"He worshipped him"*. Faith was complete.

Sinners can take a Leap of Faith

The account of the woman of Samaria in the gospel of John, chapter 4, is another powerful lesson from history on faith. It is an illustration of the fact that a sinner can take a profound leap of faith into the heights of the supernatural. A nameless woman came to draw water from a well at the time when Jesus was resting there from a hot and long walk. He asked her for a drink of water and astonished her. She thought he was an odd sort of Jew to be so free, breaking all the rules by speaking to a Samaritan. And even more so, when he said he could give her a drink of water that would be *"living water, a spring of water welling up to eternal life."*

At that point she decided to humour him, thinking him slightly irrational. So she just said, *"You just give me a drink like that so I won't get thirsty and keep coming back to this well!"* She certainly expected nothing of the kind. Jesus simply said, *"Go and bring your husband."* She put on an air of innocence and said she had no husband. Jesus then shattered her with a recitation of her sullied life and her Hollywood-like record of husbands. The woman stared at him shocked, and said, *"I can see you are a prophet."* She had advanced in perception and faith.

Jesus next shook her ideas about worship. She made a retort, which represented 400 years of argument about where to worship. Christ's reply was totally new. Worship had nothing to do with place or time. Worship was anywhere, everywhere and always. The people God wanted were those whose worship was not confined to a local spot or fixed schedule. She felt lost now in such a theological depth, so she tried to edge around it. She said such matters would be settled when the Messiah came.

> Worship has nothing to do with place or time. Worship can be anywhere, everywhere and always. The people God wants are those whose worship is not confined to a local spot or fixed schedule.

The woman was getting closer, and then Jesus said, *"I who speak to you am he."* Her faith soared. She looked at this man who saw her past like a filmed record and swept her out of her depth with his profound teaching. Excited, she rushed into the town telling everybody about Jesus and asking, *"Could this be the Messiah?"* Many men then went back to the well to see who this man was that had so affected

> Being a mere believer in God has a long way to go, but it is a gap that can be leaped, as fast as light – one minute far from God and the next minute bound to him eternally through faith – one with Christ.

her. They too fell under his divine spell and invited him to stay in the town. For two days he was among them with the result that they said, *"This man really is the Saviour of the world."* The woman had believed, sinful as she was.

In each of these incidents, the development of faith is swift and always ends by a commitment, a relationship, and a taking hold of Jesus personally. Being a mere believer in God has a long way to go, but it is a gap that can be leaped, as fast as light – one minute far from God and the next minute bound to him eternally through faith – one with Christ. We become in a moment as he said about the disciples to the Father, *"They are yours ... and yours are mine, and I am glorified in them ... and none of them is lost"* (John 17:9-12).

Faith's Embrace

Faith in Christ is different to any other kind of faith. It is not found in the Old Testament. In the New Testament, the word used means believing "into" Christ (Greek "eis"). That word suggests movement. The ordinary Greek word for "in" (Greek "en") describes a set position, but the Greek expression used for faith **in** Christ means moving close to him in trustful love. It is an embrace.

This kind of loving embrace between man and his Maker comes only through Christ. Nobody in the Old Testament days could think of such a thing. God was spirit, another kind of Being, holy, and too awesome to be approached except with fear and trembling. Yet one inspired book in the Old Testament Scriptures touches the heart of a new experience – the Song of Songs, a lyric of love that gathers up all its word of supreme love in one phrase, *"I am my beloved's and my beloved is mine"* (Song of Songs 6:3). This was an attitude towards God that nobody understood, until Christ came.

The Song of Songs fulfilled

When Jesus came, the Song of Songs was fulfilled. He is the great beloved. A woman emptied a flask of priceless ointment upon the head of Christ in holy adoration. A street-girl washed his feet with the water of her eyes and towelled them with her hair. A hard-hearted tax collector (Zacchaeus) went wild with joy and wanted to give his money away. Jerusalem had never seen anything like that. They had seen fanatical fury burning murderously in men's eyes, but not this adoring wonder.

But then, he began it himself, for we read, *"Having loved his own who were in the world, he loved them unto the end ... [and] knowing ... that he had come from God and was going to God rose from supper and began to wash the disciples' feet"* (John 13:1-5). That was the Lord God whom everyone could fling his or her arms around. His mother Mary did and so did Mary Magdalene.

Faith the golden Gift

However, there is an amazing thing. Faith is suddenly there. Perhaps undramatically, we step over a border, and we believe. We just know who Jesus is. It doesn't always come framed in all the right words, or it may not conform to a classic conversion experience, but within our souls there is intuition. We see it; we know he is the one that should come if this world has any meaning. He is the key, the answer to the riddle of existence, the focus. Jesus Christ crystallizes people's ideas about God.

In the Old Testament, revelation came to people about God, but it seemed to be only to rare individuals, such as Abraham, Jacob, and the prophets. The mass of people moved very slowly – and often moved backwards. God used various circumstances and methods to help them to have faith. But the coming of Jesus has swept the world. Somehow, Calvary does what the awesome manifestations of Sinai couldn't do. Jesus is the great faith-creator. Looking back over the long cheerless world history of uncertainty and doubt, we can see when it changed. It came with the gospel. It awakened sleeping trust. The dawn had come.

> When Jesus came, the Song of Songs was fulfilled.
> He is the great beloved. That was the Lord God whom everyone could fling his or her arms around.

Jesus said, *"No one comes to the Father except through me"* (John 14:6). It was a pragmatic simple fact. Nobody ever had found God and nobody ever has to this day except through Christ. There are religions enough, pointing a thousand different ways, but Christ **is** the way. He doesn't point to a way. He is the door and flings heaven wide open. *"Come unto me ... and I will give you rest"* (Matthew 11:28). *"Fear not"* (Luke 12:32).

> Jesus is the one that should come if this world has any meaning. He is the key, the answer to the riddle of existence, the focus.

Who among us shall dwell with the devouring fire?
Who among us shall dwell with everlasting burnings?

Isaiah 33:14

God on Fire

The Bible contains over 500 references to fire, linking it with God 90 times. God in action is like a blazing fire, we are told. *"The people shall be like the burnings of lime; like thorns cut up they shall be burned in the fire"* (Isaiah 33:12). Lime burns slowly and thorns quickly. The fire of God has the same effect on all it touches. Fire is his essential characteristic: *"The Lord your God is a consuming fire"* (Deuteronomy 4:24).

Ezekiel, for example, often uses the language of fire to talk about God, e.g. *"I will pour out my wrath on them and consume them with my fiery anger, bringing down on their own heads all they have done, declares the Sovereign Lord"* (Ezekiel 22:31, NIV).

Is your God like that? A God of fire is the only one there is. Our God is like a forest fire not an iceberg. He is never likened to the moon with its cool light, but rather to the sun, radiating warmth. His

> God is never likened to the moon with its cool light, but rather to the sun, radiating warmth. His dwelling is the light of rising suns.

> God is never halfhearted, but a God of tireless vigour and total commitment. He is an enthusiast! What he does, he does with fervour.

dwelling is the light of rising suns. What he does he carries out with intense desire and blazing purposes. He cannot abide in anything tepid. There is nothing pastel pink in his presence, pale or anaemic, neither one thing nor another.

That is God. Can you take it? Isaiah asks, *"Who among us shall dwell with the devouring fire? Who among us shall dwell with everlasting burnings?"* (Isaiah 53:14). Who indeed?

Elijah presents us with a real challenge: *"The God who answers by fire, he is God"* (1 Kings 18:24). Well, if you want to be another Elijah you have to have the God who answers by fire. Can you get along with that sort of religion – incandescent Christianity, hot gospel, the fire in your bones type of faith? Or do you want a casual, easygoing God? The God of Elijah and of Isaiah is never halfhearted, but a God of tireless vigour and total commitment. He is an enthusiast! What he does, he does with fervour: *"The zeal of the Lord of hosts will do this"* (2 Kings 19:31).

Isaiah 33 speaks of God's consuming anger against wickedness, God being a devouring fire to Israel's enemies. Then comes the crunch: the fire will have widespread effect. *"The sinners in Zion are afraid; fearfulness has surprised the hypocrites. Who among us shall dwell with the devouring fire? Who among us shall dwell with everlasting burnings?"* (Isaiah 33:14). Either in or out of Zion he is a devouring fire.

Fire – Promise, not Threat!

God is the same God to everybody, both in the church and in the world. The God who is angry with sinners every day is the God we deal with. He does not change. True partnership with the Lord means being on fire; the God of fire has no fellowship with icicles. He does not get on well with mild, cool, flabby folk who are undisciplined and haphazard and who work in fits and starts, blowing neither hot nor cold. No matter who we are, God does not adapt to please us; we always have to adapt to him. Is God too much for you? Too zealous, too unremitting in his activity?

Church leaders and pastors represent God, the God of fire. Our ministry is to bring that God into people's lives, putting fire into their hearts.

Jesus baptizes with fire (Matthew 3:11-12, Luke 3:16-17). John the Baptist said, *"I indeed baptize you with water unto repentance, but he who is coming after me is mightier than I, whose shoes I am not worthy to carry. He will baptise you with the Holy Spirit and fire. His winnowing fan is in his hand, and he will thoroughly clean out his threshing floor, and gather his wheat into the barn; but he will burn up the chaff with unquenchable fire."*

When John spoke of a baptism of the Spirit and fire, it was a promise, not a threat. Throughout Scripture the fire of God comes both to purge and to bless.

Scholars question whether John the Baptist ever said such

> The fire of God is not given to make us cosy, but holy, and to stir us up.

words, and if he did what he meant. Some say that his words about Jesus baptising in the Holy Spirit and fire refer to cleansing Israel and judgment. I am sure they are wrong. When John spoke of a baptism of the Spirit and fire, it was a promise, not a threat, although it was also a kind of forewarning of things to come. Throughout Scripture the fire of God comes both to purge and to bless.

The fire of God is not given to make us cosy, but holy, and to stir us up. When Moses saw the burning bush God first warned him that he was standing on holy ground, and then told him of the great thing he was about to do, to release Israel from the captivity of Pharaoh (Exodus 3). When Isaiah was in the temple and it filled with smoke of

> People are not finding their way to Jesus because of pollution. Nobody can see God through a polluting cloud of doubt and sin. But he is still there, shining forever.

the burning holiness of God, his awareness of being unclean preceded God's equipping him to be his messenger.

If the God of fire takes over, it will not be a comfortable experience for those who sit at ease in Zion. The idea of being filled with the Spirit is not to give us nice emotions and lovely church meetings, but to set us going for God. In giving power, Jesus makes his purpose clear: *"You shall be witnesses to me"* (Acts 1:8). It is glorious to be anointed, but it is for service, not just for nice services.

Life without Fire

Can we live without fire? Not on this earth. The universe is full of fire. The sun is a great globe of incandescence, every star shines by its own fires, and even the centre of our planet is fire – a molten iron core. Every volcano is a dynamic illustration of God's character. He is a Vesuvius of goodness, life and energy.

Some think God is extinct and have published books, which claim to demonstrate just that. What happened to God? They may as well ask what happened to the stars! If they are not visible it is because of modern pollution in the atmosphere. That is the price we pay in our great cities – lots of lamps but no stars. These days the Magi would be hard put to find a star to guide them to Bethlehem. But this is a modern-day parable. People are not finding their way to Jesus because of pollution. We are too clever by half. Nobody can see God through a polluting cloud of doubt and sin. But he is still there, shining forever.

On the day of Pentecost there was not only fire but also wind. Wind disperses fog and mist. It clears the atmosphere just as surely as fire warms it. The disciples had doubts galore even after Jesus had risen from the dead and spoken to them. We read that Jesus appeared to the eleven as they sat eating a meal together. Some had believed reports of his appearance but others had doubted; Jesus rebuked them for their hardness of heart. But when the winds of God tore the heavens open and swept into the upper room, no doubts were left. The tornado and the tongues of fire on every head were no hallucination. Jesus had reached the power centre of the universe, just as he had said. He had kept his promise.

The Scale of Pentecost

Jesus did all these things after he had gone from the earth. What a Jesus! Dead? Forgotten? How can a dead man set 120 living people aflame all at once – and first thing in the morning, too? However, he did not come back, stand among them and say, "Receive the Holy Spirit." You would have thought that for such a historic, vital occasion he might personally have supervised the event. In fact, he did not. The Holy Spirit had come in his place – the other comforter. He could be and do all Jesus was and did. In fact, all Jesus had ever done was by the Spirit.

> Jesus was born in Bethlehem, the coming of the comforter took place in Jerusalem, and the coming of the Holy Spirit occurs in each individual as a personal experience.

That is the scale of Pentecost. It is not an insignificant or minor event. Jesus was born in Bethlehem, the coming of the comforter took place in Jerusalem, and the coming of the Holy Spirit occurs in each individual as a personal experience. It is as if Jesus himself was back again and we are his disciples. The day of Pentecost was not something the disciples looked back upon with nostalgia and longing. That day extended throughout their lives. We read a little about their experience on the day of Pentecost, but it takes the whole book of Acts to tell the full story – and even then it is not over! The fires of God do not diminish as time goes by. Their fuel sources are eternal, inexhaustible.

At the time of Pentecost in Jerusalem magnificent aqueducts brought water from the hills to the city of Rome. Now all that remains of that remarkable piece of engineering are ruins. The arches are broken and the channels are dry. Is that also true of Pentecost? Does it belong to a long-ago age, 20 centuries before modern times? Is there no longer an upper room, no more wind and fire? Is an idealized, stiff representation in stained glass all that a church now has of what was once its vitality?

Notice what Jesus himself said: *"If a son asks for bread from any father among you, will he give him a stone? Or if he asks for a fish, will he give him a serpent instead of a fish? Or if he asks for an egg, will he offer him a scorpion? … How much more will your heavenly Father give the Holy Spirit to those who ask him?"* (Luke 11:11-13).

Notice how Jesus puts it. A son asks for bread, fish, and an egg – the basic necessities of life. Jesus did not talk about caviar, silk robes, rich wines, gold, diamonds, and other luxuries, but bread, fish, and eggs. The Holy Spirit is the same – he is a gift on a par with other life-giving necessities. God gives us bread, fish and eggs all the time and has done so for thousands of years. But he also gives us the Holy Spirit. I can live without fish, bread or eggs. But why should I? I would not like to try it! I could live without chocolate and many other things, but why should I? So why should I live without the Holy Spirit?

Missing the most important Happening!

Paul said that Jesus appeared to over 500 brethren at once (1 Corinthians 15:6). That was before Pentecost. Where were they all on the Day of Pentecost I wonder? They missed it. The Day of Pentecost was a feast at which all jews within 20 miles of Jerusalem were obliged to be present. So they could have been there. People do miss Pentecost – perhaps because they are too busy with other concerns. Some people do not like tongues any more than some like cod-liver-oil. I do not think that anyone has the right not to like a gift of the Holy Spirit. His gifts are disposed by his will, not our preference. Maybe those early brethren had a sneaking suspicion that the upper room was going to be a place of fiery tongues and chose to stay in the temple, with the gentler, easy ritual. Perhaps the God of fire does not suit everybody. But there isn't any other kind of God, whether people like it or not.

Why should I live without the Holy Spirit?

True fire is lit by the Lord, just as he lit the fires on Israel's altars. Leviticus 9:24 describes the original altar of Moses. The fire was not begun by wood drilling on wood, as was customary in those days. We read, *"Fire came out from before the Lord and consumed the burnt offering and the fat on the altar. When all the people saw it, they shouted and fell on their faces."* When, long afterwards, Solomon opened the first temple in Jerusalem, he prayed and the fire fell. *"When Solomon had finished praying, fire came down from heaven and consumed the burnt offering and the sacrifices; and the glory of the Lord filled the temple. And the priests could not enter into the house of the Lord, because the glory of the Lord had filled the Lord's house. When all the children of Israel saw how the fire came down, and the glory of the Lord on the temple, they bowed their faces to the ground on the pavement, and worshipped and praised the Lord"* (2 Chronicle 7:1-3).

Israel's religion had fire and glory. The priests had to keep that original fire going. Fire was at the heart of Temple worship. When Solomon prayed and the fire-glory of God fell, nobody objected. The gathered multitudes responded with a vast roar of wonder and praise to God. Nobody said, There's too much excitement in those meetings; I'd rather go where it's quiet. In that case the ideal spot for them would have been the cemetery.

In fact, a tireless faith would be a false faith. It would not be true to the nature of God. He is a consuming fire, and I could not contemplate a faith

> When you damp down the fire you damp down God, you quench the Spirit. He is an eternal fountain of passion. He is changeless, or if he had a passionate mood he would consume us.

without God as he actually is. I cannot visualize God at 0° C. He is always a midday sun, always at its zenith. If my religious attitude has no feelings, no passion, no inward burning, and no driving energy then it spells the damp darkness of the tomb. The thought gives me the shivers! When you damp down the fire you damp down God, you quench the Spirit. Some say God has compassion but no passion. I disagree. He is an eternal fountain of passion. True, he does not display passions as we do at times. He is changeless, or if he had a passionate mood he would consume us, as Malachi said.

False Fire

However, there is another side to it. *"Nadab and Abihu ... each took his censer and put fire in it, put incense on it, and offered profane fire before the Lord ... So fire went out from the Lord and devoured them, and they died before the Lord."* The Lord said, *"By those who come near me I must be regarded as holy; and before all the people I must be glorified"* (Leviticus 10:1).

Not only do we not want false fire, we do not need it. Nadab and Abihu could have taken God's fire easily enough from the altar, but they made their own. The fire of the Lord is special, not man-generated, excitement without passion. In the case of Nadab and Abihu, two of them came together, when priests were always to come singly. There is no safety in numbers when we stir up secular heat.

> All Christian work depends on the Spirit. What I am stressing here is that all the works of the Spirit have fire behind them.

Before you can receive the fire of the Spirit, you must want it. Perhaps that is why only 120 appeared in the Upper Room. *"Blessed are those who hunger and thirst for righteousness, for they shall be filled,"* Jesus said (Matthew 5:6). What a promise!

Facing Facts

Now let's get down to realities. Fire is a symbol of the Holy Spirit himself, not just one of his qualities. The Spirit is not just exuberance. There are other facets – the Holy Spirit is a dove, the water of heaven, the guide, the one sent in place of Jesus to walk alongside us; he is the wind of heaven and the oil of anointing. His work therefore has to be seen in its many varieties. Those varieties are expressed through our work as we are filled and moved by the Spirit. It goes without saying that all Christian work depends on the Spirit. What I am stressing here is that all the works of the Spirit have fire behind them.

If you want to save souls clinically, or nicely, without emotion, the Holy Spirit would find it difficult to cooperate with you. Some want Pentecost with dignity but Pentecost may find you charged with being drunk. The power of the Spirit can be too great for our fragile bodies. When the fire fell at the Temple they all fell flat on their faces.

What I mean is this – you cannot remain as cool as a cucumber when the fire falls on you. Indeed, you will never be the same again. When King Saul received a touch of the Spirit, he was like another man. If you do not want to be different, do not hope for the fire. If you have it in church, you will have it out of church. You will be different, a spotted bird among the sparrows. And that is what the world needs more than anything – people with a distinctiveness created by God, people who shine as lights *"in the midst of a crooked and perverse generation"* (Philippians 2:15).

> If you do not want to be different, do not hope for the fire. You should be different, a spotted bird among the sparrows.
> And that is what the world needs more than anything – people with a distinctiveness created by God, people who shine as lights

Moses noticed the bush burning and said, *"I will turn aside to see this strange sight"* (Exodus 3:3, NIV). Strange! God strange! How will we ever impress people by being the same as they are? I do not know. We need to be men whose hearts are aflame – which is not necessarily comfortable. Paul once shaved his head to show he had made a vow (Acts 18:18). People would notice that – a skinhead apostle!? But he was not ashamed to look like that, and it told everybody that here was a deeply devoted man who had sworn on oath to do something for God. Why should fire-baptized believers not do the same?

Being filled with the Spirit is often a public Event

The disciples emerged from the upper room different, and Peter invited everybody's attention, saying, *"We are all witnesses"* (Acts 2:32). In other words, "We are evidence that Jesus is alive – look at us." What do people look like when they emerge from our churches on a Sunday morning? Suppose the fire fell in

> The Holy Spirit is not given to make you cosy, but to drive you out of that nice little burrow and into the raw weather of the world.

Westminster Abbey and everybody came out drunk with the Spirit! Being filled with the Spirit is not something that you can keep to yourself; it is often a public event. Nor is it for personal reassurance or comfort. In fact, it may bring you considerable discomfort. The Holy Spirit is not given to make you cosy, but to drive you out of that nice little burrow and into the raw weather of the world. You will have a purpose in life – to fish for men in stormy waters.

> How will we ever impress people by being the same as they are? We need to be men whose hearts are aflame, men deeply devoted who had sworn on oath to do something for God.

It is not a feeling or a power you are dealing with, but the person of the Holy Spirit. He cannot be handed out by any preacher or evangelist – here, have some Holy Spirit – any more than you can hand out your wife or your son or daughter! That great Spirit is a person, the Holy One. He is not given to create astounding stage effects, like something in a magician's act. His true sphere is the preaching of Jesus. Take Jesus out, and the Holy Spirit goes too. When that happens you really are on your own.

Stand up, speak up and never shut up

We want a fire-baptized church. It is time for us to stand up, speak up and never shut up. Let our tongues be set on fire by the Holy Spirit. Early Christians were burned like candles to light the gardens of Nero. We must burn like candles of God in the pitch darkness of this God-ignorant world. A man on fire is not afraid of what man can do to him. We know him who is true; let us speak as if we do.

> The Holy Spirit is not given to create astounding stage effects, like something in a magician's act. His true sphere is the preaching of Jesus.

The fire can only do as much as we let it. The Holy Spirit will only bless where we go.

We must set nations ablaze if only with our contention. Yes, we will be controversial figures but we will also make godlessness controversial, showing it up for what it is, an object of scorn. Unbelief and the rejection of Christ bring every kind of wrong and wickedness in their train. The world is insane. It is insane to doubt God, the resurrection, and the word of God. People aglow and churches ablaze, create a national forest fire. Revival means fire, people who have real fire, burning publicly. Revival does not come if you

> Early Christians were burned like candles to light the gardens of Nero. We must burn like candles of God in the pitch darkness of this God-ignorant world.

stay comfortably indoors and pray for God to move. God will fire-baptize you and then send you out as Samson sent out the foxes with torches tied to their tails.

Jeremiah the prophet was the sort of man we want, millions of them. He was discouraged, but he could not keep quiet, for he said the word of God was like a fire shut up in his bones (Jeremiah 20:9). Our God is a consuming fire. Can you live with him, with the everlasting burnings?

> *Unto us a child is born.*
> *Unto us a son is given.*

Isaiah 9:6

The fact that Jesus would come was the world's worst kept secret. It was as if the Father in heaven could not keep it to himself, almost like someone wanting to open a gift marked, "Not to be opened until Christmas Day!" He whispered in the glades of that early Eden about the off-spring of the woman, and hints at it all the way through the long Scripture story. Peter said the prophets spoke about it but did not really know what it was all about.

For a thousand years godly men had cried, *"Rend the heavens, o Lord and come down!"* At last he came, though not the man of war they expected but the prince of peace. Now 2000 years have passed and again the anniversary of his birth puts half the world in festive mood. True, some celebrate only on Christmas Day but millions celebrate for Christmas Day, and *"worship God in the spirit and rejoice in Christ Jesus"* not one day but every day (Philippians 3:3).

Jesus was a family son like all sons. He shared domestic inti-macies in conditions that the poorest people today would consider utterly squalid and unacceptable. He worked as a carpenter-builder in times when physical work was despised and left mainly to slaves. Finally he stepped out into the street as the promised Son. In his hidden years of obscurity the Father had been watching him. On his first public appearance he owned him, declaring from the very heavens *"This is my beloved Son in whom I am well pleased."* For that matter we now respond, "Yes! And so are we well pleased!" The Son of God is the Son of Man, our most beloved Son, more loved than any son that ever graced this earth.

> The Bible begins with one man: Adam. And immediately becomes the story of the whole world and the flood. Then the story starts again with one man: Abraham. It ends with the tragedy of the nation of Israel as the Old Testament closes. But then another book is opened: the New Testament. Again with the account of one man: the man Christ Jesus.

It is interesting that the first 11 chapters of the Bible begin with one man: Adam. And immediately becomes the story of the whole world and the flood. Then the story starts again with one man: Abraham. Again the picture merges into the nations. It ends with the tragedy of the nation of Israel as the Old Testament closes. But then another book is opened, the New Testament. Again with the account of one man, this time the man of all men, the man Christ Jesus. The story also ends but with a beginning. The book of Revelation is a preview of a new creation, the entire cosmos vibrant with joy. We are now in process to that glorious consummation.

The living Word
behind the written Word

Turning to the gospels of Matthew and Luke we are given details of his advent. One special feature of Matthew is many quotations from the Old Testament. Scriptures it says are fulfilled in Christ. When we look up those texts we don't always find they were predictions of Christ, or originally had anything to do with his coming. How then were they a fulfilment?

For instance, we read Joseph and Mary escaped from the threat of king Herod and lived in Egypt. They returned when Herod died and Matthew 2:15 states, *"So was fulfilled what the Lord had said through the prophet: Out of Egypt I called my son."* The prophet was Hosea. But the verse quoted, 11:1, refers to Israel being brought out of Egypt led by Moses centuries before. It is not a prediction about Christ. So how was it fulfilled when the child Jesus came back home from Egypt?

The answer is wonderful. Everything in the Old Testament relates to Christ. He is the great representative of Israel. He was with Israel in the Exodus and it is reenacted in his own person, as in his exit from that land. The Old Testament has to be interpreted and understood through Jesus. He is the living word behind the written word. He casts true light on the whole volume of Scripture and makes every verse glow with higher meaning. Luke's gospel also brings that out. Luke 24:15-55 is the account of two disciples meeting Christ after his resurrection. Verse 27 says,

> Everything in
> the Old Testament
> relates to Christ.
> He is the living word
> behind the written word.

"Beginning with Moses and all the prophets, he explained to them what was said in all the Scriptures concerning himself." All the Scriptures – they all relate to him. No matter what it recounts, you can't leave him out.

Hints of him

It is quite normal to find Old Testament prophecies that were fulfilled in Christ. The scholars consulted by Herod said the birth of Christ would be in Bethlehem, quoting Micah 5:2, *"But you Bethlehem … out of you will come a ruler who will be the shepherd of my people Israel."* Jesus was born there. That was correct. From their Bible Israel's teachers built up a whole picture of the Messiah (Christ). But in his life Christ did not merely fulfil in some neat fashion precisely what the prophets said. He showed what their Messiah was really like. His life was an exposition of the prophetic promises of the Messiah. He revealed what they meant.

An example is Jeremiah 31:15 *"A voice is heard in Ramah, weeping and great mourning, Rachel weeping for her children … because they are no more."* He was talking about his own times when northern armies would sweep the land with destruction. But Matthew quotes this about babies slaughtered by Herod who wanted to kill Christ. He saw rising above Jeremiah's lament the great figure of Christ as it affected the slaughter of the innocents at the hand of a jealous Herod.

That is how he fulfilled all the Scriptures. Not only was the life of Jesus illuminated by the Old Testament Scriptures, but far more, he illuminated the Scriptures. His life showed their unsuspected depth and scope. He was the great archetype of all that was written.

This is the marvellous and important thing; Jesus was bigger than the picture of him the teachers had drawn from their Scriptures. The living word is greater than the written word.

> Jesus is our ark of the covenant and our mercy seat. He brings it into living reality. The sacrifices on the Temple altars, the festivals, the ups and downs of their history – you see him in it all.

The Bible has hints of him all the way through, beginning with Adam. Christ was the second Adam. Genesis does not say Noah's ark had anything to do with Jesus, but we speak commonly of him as our ark of refuge amid the judgments of God. Take a random character, Joseph for instance, and it echoes with a hundred suggestions of Jesus for those who know him. The book of Exodus tells the immortal story of Israel's deliverance from the yoke of Egyptian slavery, but it is eclipsed by the story of deliverance in Christ the Saviour. Exodus surprisingly includes five long chapters of fine details about making a box with a golden lid, calling it the ark of the covenant and the lid is called the mercy seat. Why? Because we are to read into it all that Jesus was. He is our ark of the covenant and our mercy seat. He brings it into living reality. The sacrifices on the Temple altars, the festivals, the ups and downs of their history – you see him in it all.

However, as I thought about Christ being the illumination of the story of the Old Testament, it struck me that he can illuminate and make the story of our own lives glow.

Christ changes life. He gives meaning to the dullest facts and situations. Nothing else can. What meaning has anything, or anybody without Christ?

In Christ, our great Son, born to us, these are not empty wishes but weighty with all the living reality of Christ. Remember us as we go to tell the nations about this wonderful Son. What a privilege is ours, all of us, who have any part to play and anything to do with him!

In the Old Testament New Years had religious importance, as also birthdays and people's ages. I had amusing
thoughts of Methuselah having 969 birthday parties and
who would be there! In contrast, the New Testament
indulges in no such sentiment about the passing seasons.
I wondered why.

Annual celebrations are absent from the New Testament
because pictures have given way to reality. Colossians 2:16-17
explains they were *"a shadow of the things that were to
come. The reality, however, is found in Christ"*. In Christ
we pass from the broken to the unbroken.

Here is something that is so misunderstood. Jesus did not
come to found a religious system. Rites, days, observances
or any other such acts or rules are "religion" but Christ
mentioned none. Some people like to have a ceremonial
type of worship, with special furnishings and garb but Jesus
never required them of us, and they do not save. They may
mean something to individuals but are meaningless to God.
Christ offers us a Kingdom. His work is all sufficient and
complete. The Jiate is opened and we enter in by faith.
Passover, for example, is not one day a year, for Christ is
our Passover – 1 Corinthians 5:7-8. *"Christ our Passover
lamb had been sacrificed. Therefore let us keep the festival
with the bread of sincerity and truth."* That festival is not
one day, but every day.

The Christian experience is not occasional and spasmodic.
The New Year adds nothing, nor the new millennium. Figures on the calendar are blotted out by the glory of Christ.
The flow of blessing and power and goodness is eternal
without reference to times and dates and ceremonies.

However, Jesus did ask us to take bread and wine in
memory of him. Why? Not because he exists only as
a historical figure to remember, but for love's sake. A
husband remembers his living wife on birthday or wedding
anniversary. Christ asks us to break bread and drink wine
as an act of worship and devotion. It is not a saving act, but
it recalls his all-sufficient saving act. He performed it; the
only saving act needed was when he gave himself and his
blood was poured out at the altar of Calvary. We remember
him, our great salvation, and immeasurably greater than
the deliverance from the Red Sea. Christianity is not a
religious system founded by Jesus. It **is** Jesus!

Jesus living forever

Tiberius was the Roman emperor for only 23 years. When
he died, events were dated according to the year of Caligu-
la's reign, the next emperor. He was assassinated after
4 years and Claudius followed, and events were reckoned
by his 13 years reign as in Acts 11:28, then Nero and so
on. But, importantly, it was always by the living emperor,
not any past emperor, not even Julius Caesar though he
had invented the calendar. We date events according to
Christ.He is the living and reigning Lord, never dies, has
no successor and no other Lord will ever take his place.

When he was born we are not sure, more probably 4 BC, but Jesus Christ is the same today as yesterday and will be the same tomorrow. Christ's advent gave meaning to all human existence. Unless the world relates to him it has relevance to nothing. Its significance rests on a relationship with him.

No unlucky Numbers

The second coming of Christ is undated and unknown. Some Christians recently were adamant that Christ would return at the end of the second millennium – by **our** calendars! But any old day could be the day. God has no sentimental regard for our special days or years.

With God every day and every year is special. For those who trust in God there are no unlucky days, no Fridays the 13th, no lucky or unlucky numbers. In fact it is not luck but the blessing of God, which is the one great overriding reality for God's people. The Psalmist said, *"Goodness and mercy shall follow me all the days of my life." "My times are in your hand"*, and not controlled by dead planets. With God there are no ordinary days because he makes

> God is faithful! Life for the believer is not haphazard, a matter of change, or chance, or fate. What God is, he does.

each day extraordinary. God is greater than the stars. We can laugh at the awful forces of the universe for he holds us safe in his hand.

God is faithful

One great change has taken place. Christ came. His coming instituted a changeless change. He declared, *"Repent, for the Kingdom of God is at hand."* The world lives by changes. The believer lives by the unchanging. The world lives by the transient, the believer lives by the immutable. There is foolish talk of the post-Christian age, but it is premature. The Christian age is eternal. It is the reality of the kingdom of God.

For the New Year we draw one tremendous fact from the Bible – God is faithful! Life for the believer is not haphazard, a matter of change, or chance, or fate. What God is, he does. What he is, he is to us, not affected by our fickle nature, or generated by our faithfulness, our constancy or our flawless spirituality. We may not be ideal Christians but the truth of Christianity is that nothing can separate us from the Lord God in Christ. We can lose a lot by our sin and foolishness, but we can't get away from the love of God any more than escape from air to breathe.

The great truth behind the universe for the year 2001 is that of the flowing river of God. The light and life of God floods us, on and on. The blessing of God, the presence of God, the Holy Spirit, the promise of God, his saving power, his compassions, are new every morning unconditionally, not by our whim and fancy, but by God's nature and determination. Even in wickedness, we read *"All day long have I held out my hands to a disobedient and obstinate people"*.

John Lennon, a member of the Beatles rock group told a London reporter, "Christianity will go, it will vanish and shrink. I needn't argue about that. I'm right and I will be proved right. We are more popular than Jesus now." Since then in Britain, his own country, the main BBC radio for young people refused to air Beatle songs as no longer popular, but Christianity has grown faster than any other movement. In 2000, I myself saw over 6 million people turn to Christ in one country alone. People write Christ's RIP epitaph on a gravestone but are tapped on the shoulder by Christ watching and smiling.

> God the Father proclaims himself the everlasting changeless and faithful Lord. Christ promises never to leave us, and that the Holy Spirit will abide with us forever.

God the Father proclaims himself the everlasting changeless and faithful Lord. Christ promises never to leave us, and that the Holy Spirit will abide with us forever. That's theology, and it is also our Christian experience.

Vision is Revelation

Like a tune you find yourself humming all the time, a line from Proverbs 29:18 (King James Version) followed me around for a while and blessed me:

"Where there is no Vision, the People perish."

Those words stuck with me. My first impression of this Scripture seems so negative, but then I suddenly saw its positive side. I saw that if people perish without vision, with vision they do not perish! To an evangelist that is something worth pondering. I also understood that "vision" is a great gift that is available to us all.

Firstly, **vision saves people**. If we have vision, we have a mission - and an effective one.

> If people perish **without** vision, **with** vision they do not perish!

Secondly, if vision is a gift (as we will see in a moment), it imparts zest, direction, and fulfilment. To me, this line from Proverbs is what leads to spiritual muscles for the flabby and feeble, boldness for the nervous and new strength for the ineffective. It could raise up an army for God from dead bones! (Ezekiel 37)

However, to grasp its meaning properly I went to the experts. As different scholars have struggled to convey the true meaning of the original word "vision", they have come up with a different choice of words. For example, the King James Version says, *"Where there is no vision,"*

> A vision saves people. It imparts zest, direction, and fulfilment.

while the New International Version reads, *"Where there is no revelation."* So, vision is revelation, and we know that the word of God is the fountain of all true revelation. This is the key to unlock the secret of this wonderful asset of vision. True vision is founded on the word of God. Hosea clearly tells us where vision comes from: *"I am the Lord your God … I spoke to the prophets, gave them many visions"* (Hosea 12:9-10 NIV). The word of God gives us many examples of visions but, at the end of the day, they are just parts of one vision, as I will point out. Vision is not a natural gift, nor is it to be confused with enthusiasm. It is not caught from the example of the great and the wise. It is from God. It certainly doesn't come from television! Joel prophesied that God would pour out his Spirit, and *"your old men shall dream dreams, your young men shall see visions"* (Joel 2:28). Vision shows us God, the truth, and ourselves. That is the promise and privilege for anyone who feels useless. The hand of God sets the compass of our lives towards a positive objective, and sets us going. We can be like an arrow with a target, *"the arrow of the Lord's deliverance"* (2 Kings 13:17). Think

> The hand of God sets the compass of our lives towards a positive objective, and sets us going.

what it means when we read *"As many as are led [aimed] by the Spirit of God, these are sons of God"* (Romans 8:14). We truly are children of the king, princes of heaven, the nobility of glory. We know what we want and where we are going.

The supreme Dream

What is the supreme vision and the supreme dream? It is nothing less than the same vision burning in God's own heart ever since it was revealed in Moses' flaming bush. His fire ignites our own dry lives. We are born to share his desire, share his will and be participants in his eternal enterprise. Vision is not blind! Trust in God is not founded on ignorance. We are not blinkered horses driven by explicit commands, unable to see more than a step ahead. We are guided, but by the shining light of our destination. Many a worthy objective may occupy us along the way to fulfil the vision. *"As they pass through the valley of Baca, they make it a spring,"* as the Psalmist puts it (Psalm 84:6), but as Paul, with all his many projects, said, *"one thing I do"* (Philippians 3:13); there is one thing that remains constant. It has to be said that followers of Christ are not the only people with vision. The world's own great ones have their visions – perhaps heroic, self-sacrificing, dedicated and undeviating – but they are looking no farther ahead than the present passing scene. Yet those filled with the vision of God stretching to eternity can show equal dedication and single-minded

> We are born to share his desire, share his will and be participants in his eternal enterprise.

> Vision is not blind! Trust in God is not founded on ignorance. We are not blinkered horses driven by explicit commands, unable to see more than a step ahead. We are guided, but by the shining light of our destination.

adherence to that vision, whatever our immediate tasks and duties. It is tragic when believers have no vision, and fill in their years without shape or direction, following their own fancy, wandering this way or that according to circumstances, leaving no more of a mark upon the world than a falling leaf. Let the word of God speak to their heart! Let the winds of the Spirit fill their sails! They leave their cosy anchorage in the bay, cast off the moorings that bind them to earthly interests, and sail off into the great waters, vessels of divine destiny.

Open your sealed Order!

Our verse from Proverbs goes on to say, *"Blessed is he who keeps the law"* (Proverbs 29:18 NIV). The terms "vision" and "keeping the law" are synonymous. We cannot expect to have vision from God is we do not obey the law – the word of God. The word of God is like having a bicycle; you have to get on the road and ride it before you really find out what it can do. Paul said, *"I was not disobedient to the heavenly vision"* (Acts 26:19). The word is a light to our path – but only on the path of obedience. Other roads are not illuminated.

> The word is a light to our path – but only on the path of obedience. Other roads are not illuminated.

Vision is active. It is not about knowing what is in the Bible, but about knowing and obeying it. Some talk about "moving in the Spirit." They wait for promptings, prophecies, impulses, but the aged apostle

John would not have been happy with that. He wrote, *"I have no greater joy than to hear that my children walk in truth"* (3 John 1:3). Our first obedience is to the word – it is our vision. Weigh anchor! The word is our sealed order to be opened on route. As you move forward, you, like Abraham, will be given a divine plan. No one else, no college, no theologian, can give us that kind of understanding. Divine vision is sight, insight, and long-sightedness.

> Our first obedience is to the word – it is our vision. Weigh anchor! The word is our sealed order to be opened on route.

Bible translators offer us some challenging versions of this verse from Proverbs. The NIV, for example, says that if they have no vision "people cast off restraint" which could be translated "people are made naked." This echoes what the Lord said to the church in Laodicea: *"You say, I am rich, have become wealthy, and have need of nothing, and do not know that you are wretched, miserable, poor, blind* [i.e. have no vision] *and naked"* (Revelation 3:17). People like these are like sheep shorn of their wool, going their own mindless way without restraint, and perishing. The Bible puts it so well: *"All we like sheep have gone astray; we have turned, every one, to his own way"* (Isaiah 53:6). Ultimately, this turns out to be the *"way of death"* (Proverbs 14:12, 16:25).

For two centuries criticism of the Bible has battered the Christian faith in Europe. Denying Christ's birth, miracles and resurrection and questioning the gospels. The very foundations of civilised life were undermined – forgetting the biblical warning: *"If the foundations are destroyed, what can the righteous do?"* (Psalm 11:3) The nations threw off restraint, to use the words of our verse. What followed were wars that created a century of unprecedented bloodshed and misery. What began in the cosy university lecture halls bore bitter fruit on the battlefields. The third millennium is now upon us, and many talk optimistically of a new and brighter world. But calendars can produce no magic. Time has no power to change human nature.

There is an old story about a new farmhand learning to plough, who was instructed to keep his eye on a point at the other end of the field as he drove the tractor. At the end of the day the field looked like a bombsite. He had kept his eye on a cow! We Christians have one steady point on which to fix our gaze – Jesus. Two thousand years ago heathen night darkened the skies of every nation. The apostle Paul had a vision of Christ, and set out to change the world, and he did, saying, *"I was not disobedient unto the heavenly vision"* (Acts 26:19). Paul, like all people with a vision, Abraham, Joseph, Moses, belonged to tomorrow and can therefore change the present.

All God's Commands are impossible!

Men with a vision are movers, not stick-in-the-muds. In tidal river estuaries great barges, unmoveable by man, lie bedded in the silt. A few hours later a child could move them because the tide has lifted them. When we read the word

> Men with a vision are movers, not stick-in-the-muds.

of God, the tide comes in. The tides of heaven are rising today. What could not be done a short while ago now becomes possible. *"I can do all things through Christ who strengthens me"* (Philippians 4:13). All God's commands are impossible, meaning that we quickly know the truth of his words, *"Without me you can do nothing"* (John 15:5). 2 Kings 7 tells of a scoffer who said that God could not provide food for Samaria overnight, but the next day he was trampled to death by the people rushing to get it! When the Israelites, said "it cannot be done" visionaries Joshua and Caleb possessed the land! Once we have that vision, we shall see the unseen, hear the inaudible, believe the incredible, love the unlovable, scale the unscalable. We shall have the resilience of steel, the eye of an eagle, the heart of a lion, the steadfastness of a rock, the courage of a conqueror. In Christ there are no pygmies – they have all become giants.

> Once we have that vision, we shall see the unseen, hear the inaudible, believe the incredible, love the unlovable, scale the unscalable.

The great Question: What is the Vision?

The vision is to see the people as Jesus saw them. He saw them with compassion, as sheep without a shepherd, but he came to save them. They need not perish. His whole purpose was that *"whoever believes in him should not perish but have eternal life"* (John 3:15).

> In Christ there are no pygmies – they have all become giants.

Humanitarian and social aims are a worthy purpose to have in life. Indeed, Jesus fed the hungry and healed the sick. But he also died for sinners. When we look from the cross, our aims expand so that we give, care, and serve with a new purpose and motivation, for we carry the message of salvation to a lost world.

> When we look from the cross, our aims expand so that we give, care, and serve with a new purpose and motivation, for we carry the message of salvation to a lost world.

Be a person of vision not only to keep your Christian life vibrant, but also to bring a message of salvation to those who are perishing.

Now he had to go through Samaria.

John 4,4

Let us look at this account of Jesus in Samaria. The situation is summed up in the above verse. The King James Version reads, *"He must needs go through Samaria,"* and the New King James Version reads, *"He needed to go through Samaria."* But the closest rendering of the Greek is probably found in The Amplified Bible: *"It was necessary for him to go through Samaria."*

The Greek uses an impersonal verb, "dei," which is used 105 times in the New Testament. Only once does it mean a physical necessity. In all other cases a moral or emotional necessity is implied. Each time the text indicates the Lord's sense of what he had to do, an obligation – the very purpose of his being on earth rather than a mere physical necessity. We read, for example: *"The Son of Man must suffer many things"* (Mark 8:31). *"I must preach the good news of the kingdom of God"* (Luke 4:43).

"I must work the works of him who sent me" (John 9:4). *"The Son of Man must be lifted up"* (John 12:34). *"He must rise again from the dead"* (John 20:9). For Jesus, the work of saving men and women was no more to be ignored than the fact that he was one with God. This work was his very being. Not only did he save; he was salvation. As fire is to heat, so Christ is to salvation. Evangelism was for him

the true categorical imperative. Jesus said that his food was
to do the will of God. He later said that he had sent his disciples to do the things he had done:

*"As you sent me into the world, I also have sent them into
the world"* (John 17:18). *"As the Father has sent me, I also
send you"* (John 20:21).

John does not set out the obligation of evangelism in quite
the same way as the synoptic gospels, but it is nonetheless
present throughout the book of John, both latent and
potent.

The Obligation of the Disciples

Disciples are sent into the world – a world that was, and
still is, hostile and unregenerate. The church today must
concern itself not merely with "church growth," which
can mean something akin to business growth by wooing
other people's customers. Somebody said that we are called
to be fishers of men, not keepers of aquariums, pinching
fish from other people's aquariums.

The church in America has a huge religious pool in which
to fish. In Europe there is no such religious pool and few
potential converts. Not only has Europe become extremely
secularized, but part of the tradition of those countries is
to be completely free from any religious claim. To win one
soul, churches have had to be extremely resourceful and
enterprising. Leaders work extremely hard, going all out,
and most of the seed seems to fall on infertile ground.

I was told that America is a society composed of two main groups, the religious and the nonreligious, and it is very hard for the religious group to make a real invasion of the other group. Perhaps I am misinformed. I certainly hope so. However, some people consider it a waste of time to reach out to the world of the godless. Yet when I look at the stories emerging from America, I don't think it is impossible. Even now, God is raising spiritual Lazaruses from the dead.

However hard it may or may not be, to reach out to the godless is our task. If American churches are merely family churches, continuing their existence from parents to children and getting by on membership switching, then we had better declare a state of emergency. There has to be a council of war – full-scale war. Desperately needed is a call back to our primary purpose of evangelizing the lost. We are sent into the world, not just the Christian realm. We are fishers of men, not just feeders of sheep. We are here to save the nation, not half the nation.

> Some people consider it a waste of time to reach out to the world of the godless. However, to reach out to the godless is our task.

The outside world is a dangerous place, a place of confessors and martyrs. The opposition is not just intellectual but is sometimes armed with guns, knives and stones, as I have seen. The question is, will that world of slaughter overcome the world of the love of Jesus? And are we prepared to let it?

Disappointment can be overcome

Disappointments will come, but they must not be allowed to stop us. Let's go back to John 2:23-25 and read on into 3:2, ignoring the chapter break. The text reads like this:

"In Jerusalem … many people saw the miraculous signs he was doing and believed in his name. But Jesus would not entrust himself to them, for he knew all men. He did not need man's testimony about man, for he knew what was in a man. Now there was a man of the Pharisees named Nico- demus, a member of the Jewish ruling council. He came to Jesus at night."

> Disappointments must not be allowed to stop us!

Some people are shallow, superficial and unreliable, but not everybody. In fact, chapter one of John ends with Jesus describing Nathaniel as an Israelite without any guile. Nicodemus proved himself and was the one man among the ruling leaders in Jerusalem to be true to Jesus and identify with him after he was crucified (see John 19:39-40). Some seeds are sown without bearing fruit. Some bear a little, some bear more and some are very successful. The same seed, the same sower, but different ground. It all depends to whom you are preaching. Jesus had no success at all in one Samaritan town; in fact, the locals wouldn't allow him even to spend the night there. Yet in Sychar it was different.

More than once in Africa, we have lost a great deal of money invested in a campaign that was canceled at the last minute by the government. We have seen riots like Paul saw in Ephesus (see Acts 19:23-34), but what does it matter? In the end, we shall overcome (see 1 John 4:4). Jesus promised it.

Paul often spoke of patience and perseverance; they are necessary virtues for any evangelist. But God alone gives them. Jesus exemplified them. And he says, *"Follow me"* (Matthew 4:19). Well, he has gone ahead. So somebody must follow him, and we want to be included!

Some time ago I celebrated my birthday with family and friends at home in Frankfurt. I feel a little bit like that grand old man of faith in the Bible of whom is written in *"When Joshua was old and well advanced in years, the LORD said to him, You are very old, and there are still very large areas of land to be taken over."* (Joshua 13,1).

People talk about the evangelistic gift and debate what it really means. Simply put, the evangelistic gift is an infectious faith. To enthuse others we must be enthused ourselves. Voltaire said he didn't believe Christians were redeemed because they didn't look redeemed. Christian messengers are not just audio-tapes – words only. They're more like videos – words with visuals. When Philip went to Samaria, the Bible tells us

> The evangelistic gift is an infectious faith.

"there was great joy in that city" (Acts 8:8). The kind of faith on display in the life and preaching of Philip made people jubilant.

Faith in John's Gospel

The word "faith" is conspicuously missing from the gospel of John. John seems to avoid it. Even in his three epistles the word occurs only once. This is surprising because the word "faith" (Greek: pistis) is found 244 times in the New Testament. Instead of the noun "faith", John chooses to use the verb "to believe" (Greek: pisteuo) – exactly 100 times in

> "Faith" is an abstract concept. "Believe" describes an action. Faith is static, but believing is dynamic.

fact. Oddly, the other three gospels don't use "believe" or "believing" much at all – only 11 times in Matthew, 15 times in Mark, 9 times in Luke.

"Faith" is an abstract concept. "Believe" describes an action. Faith can be static, but believing is dynamic. "Believing" is one word in John's gospel that is important for any understanding of evangelism, but there is another word that must go along with it: "witnessing".

> The 2 words "believing" and "witnessing" represent something ongoing, active, and not static. They are connected – while we are believing, we are also witnessing.

You might expect to find the word "gospel" or "evangelism" in John, but there is no mention of either word. Again, John chooses a different, more dynamic term: the verb "to witness" (Greek: martureo), sometimes translated as "testify". That particular Greek verb is used 33 times by John. Now these two words "believing" and "witnessing" represent something ongoing, active, and not static. They are connected – while we are believing, we are also witnessing.

John never treats the gospel as just a doctrine, a definition of truth in words. He always refers to something happening. He knows the gospel is truth. In 2 John 9, he says, *"Anyone who runs ahead and does not continue in the teaching of Christ does not have God; whoever continues in the teaching has both the Father and the Son."* The gospel of John is written to show that the gospel is a dynamic, ongoing happening. It is both truth and light. His readers see exactly where they are and exactly where they will go if they opt to believe in Jesus Christ.

John uses action words wherever possible. He speaks, for example, of the truth as something shining on and on, constantly lighting the world, not just a light that once shone. The NIV offers the closest rendering of the original text of John 1:9: *"The true light that gives light to every man was coming into the world."* Again, John never speaks about "knowledge" of the gospel or "knowledge" of God; instead he talks about "knowing" – something you are in the process of doing. Christ is not someone you heard about or know about, but someone you are knowing, experiencing, in the here and now. He is with you.

To John, faith is alive. It is not a creed – something you accept, but something you do. As Smith Wigglesworth used to say, "Faith is an act."

A living Faith

John's objective was to show that the Christian faith is a living thing, not a static religion. Christ is life; believing is life; knowing him is life. The characteristics of life are reproduction and adaptation. The Bible itself is a fine example: it is the living Word. It reproduces itself in human experience. *"The word of God grew and multiplied"* (Acts 12:24). It speaks and is a force in the world. Some think of the word of God as nothing more than ancient documents that the church has preserved

> The Christian faith is a living thing, not a static religion. Christ is life; believing is life; knowing him is life. The Bible is the living Word.

> We are saved,
> but we are not preserved.
> We have eternal life!

– a kind of museum piece. It is nothing of the kind. It lives! Its activity is ongoing.

The Scriptures are with us today by virtue of being the *"very words of God"* (Romans 3:2), and not because the church preserved them. The Bible preserved the church! There are many societies for preserving things – the environment, ancient buildings, peace, the species, traditions and so on, but, thank God, there is no need of a society for the preservation of the ancient scriptures. Living things don't need to be preserved; only dead things are placed in preserving fluids.

In the New Testament, the word "preserve" is found only in the King James translation of 2 Timothy 4:18: *"And the Lord shall deliver me from every evil work, and will preserve me unto his heavenly kingdom"*, but the original Greek word literally means "saved." We are saved, but we are not preserved. We have eternal life! We won't go to heaven as mummies or deep-frozen personalities. The palpitating life of eternity flows in our souls.

Our Role is clearly defined

The gospel must be preached to make it the gospel. The word "gospel", as you probably know, comes from the Greek for good news, evangelion. If you keep news to yourself, it isn't news at all. News is information broadcast on an extensive scale. If you put news in a book on the shelf, it is then history. The gospel is not history, although it is historical truth. The gospel happens! It becomes good news when it is preached. You may call it anything you like – theology, the word, the truth – but if it is not articulated, it is not good news and the word "gospel" doesn't fit. Faith is not a truth that can be enclosed within the covers of a theological dissertation, put on the shelf and called "the gospel". The truth of the gospel can, of course, be written down, but the gospel is you and me telling the story of Christ, whatever the chosen means of transmission.

We are stewards of the gospel, not its prison wardens. The steward has to disburse what he controls, not lock up treasures of truth protectively out of harm's way. Exposing

> The gospel is you and me telling the story of Christ, whatever the chosen means of transmission.

the gospel to its enemies defends the Christian faith best; it is fully capable of dealing with them. We are stewards assigned to dispense the good news with the liberality of God to all. The church is not a strong room built to keep the truth intact, but "a philanthropic institution", a distribution centre. Elisha gave a woman the never-failing jar of oil but God has given us an oil field, a gusher that will never dry out.

When faith and witness combine, it produces something like an explosion. Paul said the gospel is *"the power of God"* (Romans 1:16). Proclaiming the gospel releases the power of God. Many people pray for power, but power is hidden within the gospel itself. Preach the Word and power is unleashed.

> Elisha gave a woman the never-failing jar of oil but God has given us an oil field, a gusher that will never dry out.

There is said to be enough oxygen locked up in the rocks of Mars to restore its atmosphere. Well, there is enough "spiritual oxygen" stored in the gospel to restore this whole world! Preach it and the proclamation of Christ acts as a catalyst causing interaction between the power of the Holy Spirit and those who hear the message. The Holy Spirit will act when Jesus is preached, for example, convicting people of sin. But it all begins with our believing, doing what we are supposed to do. Put your faith to work, preach the word and God goes into action! That is the dynamic of the gospel.

What is true Faith?

> The proclamation of Christ acts as a catalyst causing interaction between the power of the Holy Spirit and those who hear the message. Put your faith to work, preach the word and God goes into action! That is the dynamic of the gospel.

There are characters we could describe as "unbelieving believers". They are sound in doctrine but have no trust. They preach what they call the gospel, but it is lifeless, just a statement of their orthodoxy. When a man describes the beauty of a lovely girl, he can do so quite clinically. But if he is in love with her, then he makes her sound like a very alive person, worthy of drawing him into a relationship.

Preaching must in itself be a believing act, fully reliant on God. The truth of Christ is the seed we must sow. But without faith it is seed that has never been fertilized. The gospel won't germinate, spring up, blossom or produce fruit unless it is preached with faith. To have faith in the faith once delivered to the saints (see Jude 3) is very important, but it is not sufficient. Faith should be fruitful, life generating *"by believing you may have life in his name"* (John 20:31). It is a vibrant, living process. You are believing, you are receiving, you are knowing, you are seeing, you are abiding in him. The gospel is not truth on ice, but truth on fire.

Jesus did not say, "I am the way and the truth;" He said, *"I am the way and the truth **and the life**"* (John 14:6, emphasis mine). The outcome of believing is income from God: ongoing faith enjoys incoming life.

The David and Goliath episode (see 1 Samuel 17) is a perfect example of the difference between active and passive faith. Israel had a faith. They declared that Jehovah was God. It was a tremendous truth for them. But they may just as well have said and believed that the moon was made of green cheese. Their statement of faith in Jehovah God may just as well not have been true, because it did nothing in their lives.

Here they were, a whole army with the king himself, a namby-pamby half-wit, as their field leader. They shouted the name of the Lord and made a fearful racket with their weapons. They believed they were the people of God, that he was on their side. But that's as far as it went. It didn't inspire one soldier to move out of the ranks to go one-on-one with Goliath. Of course, to do that required real faith, as nobody in Israel could hope to match Goliath physically, not even King Saul.

> Evangelism calls for active believing. It is testifying, witnessing, seeing, knowing and doing.

The shepherd boy David was an outsider. But he walked into the valley, was outraged by the giant's blasphemy and declared he would take Goliath's head off. And he did. *"Faith without works is dead,"* exactly as the Bible tells us (James 2:26).

Evangelism calls for that kind of active believing. It is testifying, witnessing, seeing, knowing and doing. But we need some grounds for that kind of bold trust. Believing God has nothing to do with being naive, credulous or ignorant. If you want faith, put God's word into action. The assurance of faith is like the assurance of swimming – you must act!

Co-Workers together with him

Yes, we are acting by *"going into all the world to preach the gospel to all creatures"*. By his grace we see today that even a small offering brings great eternal fruit, simply because the people in Africa are pushing through the narrow gate into the Kingdom of God. Who would have ever thought that one campaign could yield one million registered decisions for Jesus Christ? But this is a fact.

A new Word

The resurrection of Jesus Christ is not only the central truth of our faith, but all history and creation turns on it.

The word "resurrection" exists in European languages only to express Christian

> Jesus makes people sit up – even the dead!

teaching. Other religions have no Easter day. Hebrews and Greeks had no experience or thought of it and therefore had no term for it, just as we had no word for "television" a century ago. When Christ rose, Bible writers had to use ordinary expressions like getting up, sitting up, standing up, and rousing from the heaviness of sleep.

Jesus told the dead young man at Nain "Sit up!" Jesus makes people sit up – even the dead! To Jairus' 12-year-old daughter Jesus said *"Talitha cumi. Little girl, arise!"* The word "cumi" or "qum", means "to arise".

Now Jairus' child was dead but Jesus said she was asleep. This was a new way of referring to death. It was more than a euphemism, it was unique. He said it to express a new truth, because by his resurrection, death became a mere sleep, a limited rest until he comes. That is what Christ's resurrection did to language but it is typical of the vast effects of that mighty event. It transforms everything. I want to look at that in Scripture – it is exciting.

What really took place?

We read *"God chose the things which are not to nullify things that are!"* One of those nothings is the emptiness of Christ's tomb. *"He is not here. He is risen"*. God trumpeted joy to the whole universe by the silent emptiness of Christ's tomb.

One Friday, Jesus was slain. His bloodless corpse was left in a little cave chiselled into the cliff face. On the Sunday, all they found of him were the wrappings that had been around his body, stiffened with gum and spices, left behind like a hollow shell. He had vanished out of them and out of the solid rock of the sepulchre, as through thin air. He did not break the Roman seal. This pathetic item was a crude effort to confine the Lord of life. It simply fell off when angels pushed aside the stone block of the doorway and opened the place to display, vacated by its occupant. The fact of the empty tomb nobody ever questioned. All Jerusalem, the Romans, the Jewish authorities, everybody knew it was empty. It was there, a few minutes walk away.

But how did the broken body of a victim of crucifixion leave? Tomb robbers? What! With Roman seal and Temple guard? Enemies? Then why didn't they produce the corpse to disprove the disciples' claim that he was alive? There was no other way except by his disciples. But they were the most unlikely characters, cringing in fear, not master criminals plotting to organise the world's most monstrous fraud. They always stuck to their story even when it meant torture and death because they could not deny what they had seen.

But do we need that kind evidence? When I return from a campaign in Africa nobody needs an academic degree to ascertain I left there. Anyone can meet me, personally, even in the street. Nor do we believe Christ left the tomb because historic research suggests it – that's only circumstantial information or opinion. *"By wisdom the world knew not God"*. Christ is to be known by meeting him. Daily experience confirms Jesus left the tomb. The Holy Spirit and the word of God bring him to us. This is the testimony of millions upon millions, about which I want to say more presently.

Christ is to be known by meeting him. Daily experience confirms Jesus left the tomb. The Holy Spirit and the word of God bring him to us.

New Meaning to Death

The tomb was like a cocoon. Christ emerged immortal with glorious life. He was emancipated from the limitations of earthly humanity but still *"the man Christ Jesus"*. He became a spiritual body, a second Adam, human but with heavenly capacities.

Christ's resurrection appearances were not as a mere spirit or ghost. He was not a hologram, nor an hallucination of grieving people for sometimes they did not recognise him immediately. John saw him in indescribable glory.

He could also be present instantly wherever he chose. *"After that I am risen I will go before you into Galilee"*.

Nobody has made a promise either before or since to arrange to meet people posthumously. Time and circumstances no longer tied him down. He walked, talked, ate, as a human being, but also had immediate access to heaven. He belonged to us and God, being free in earth and heaven.

> The tomb was like a cocoon. Christ emerged immortal with glorious life. He was emancipated from the limitations of earthly humanity but with heavenly capacities.

What he is, is a promise of what we shall be. We will participate in the same transformation.

Let the Holy Spirit highlight this cluster of wonderful assurances:

We are *"predestined to be conformed to the image of his Son that he might be the firstborn among many brethren"* Romans 8:29.

"The firstborn of the dead" Revelation 1:5.

"He is the image of the invisible God, first born of all creation" Colossians 1:15.

"As we bore the image of the earthy man we shall bear the image of the heavenly man"(Greek literal) 1 Corinthians 15:49.

"We shall all be changed, in a moment, in the twinkling of an eye" 1 Corinthians 15:51.

Jesus was the prototype of mankind: *"We eagerly await a saviour from heaven, who will transform our lowly bodies so that they will be like his glorious body"* Philippians 3:19.

"When he shall appear, we shall be like him" 1 John 3:2.

That is our future, but his resurrection also has promise for the present, as we next see.

The Resurrection gives new Meaning to Life

The resurrection demonstrated that *"the kingdom of God is at hand"*, that the realm of spiritual things is close. Existence has a dimension that had never been suspected. We are not flat-earthers but children of the kingdom. Our citizenship is of heaven.

Everything takes on a larger than life reality. Jesus showed us this in the Lord's table. He took bread, broke it, and then gave it transcendent meaning *"This* [bread] *is my body broken for you"*. At the communion table we partake of more than bread, it is a spiritual reality, satisfaction of soul and mind, the bread of God.

Even that most earthy thing, money, the essence of the secular, takes on a new dimension by Christ's resurrection. He has opened a new order in which cash can be transferred as "treasure in heaven" as we seek the kingdom and God's righteousness. Cash does not procure redemption but what is invested to the praise of God takes on an eternal value. Earthly currency receives heavenly validity.

Our work too takes on resurrection quality. What seems a labour, a grind, is sublimated now that Jesus is alive. We serve the Lord Jesus Christ, doing all things in his name. Slaves have the status of the bond slaves of Jesus. The Christian work ethic is spiritual, a divine vocation and calling. Earthly effort has heavenly consequences.

> The Christian work ethic is spiritual, a divine vocation and calling. Earthly effort has heavenly consequences.

It is symbolised by the work of temple priests. Anointed with sacred and perfumed oil to perform their holy tasks, priests were chosen to rake out the ashes from the altar fires and chop the wood for burning! Any service is invested with a spiritual dimension and reward, even a cup of cold water, caring for the hungry, the naked, the sick and lonely. Christ links earth with heaven in himself. What we do to the needy is done to him. His resurrection established solidarity with us all.

He brings new meaning to family life, music, singing, beauty, so nothing done is lost. The irreligious like to speak of the spiritual experience of music, but without Christ that kind of spirituality dies the moment the concert ends. But making his praise glorious echoes across the vault of heaven forever, even making melody in our hearts to the Lord. Perhaps we only echo on earth the music of heaven and eternity.

Creation itself, the skies and all its mystery are the garments of the risen Christ. The silent stars speak of him and declare his glory. Without him it is a frightening universe of terrifying and menacing forces. But he overcame their threat, and conquered even death. Could such a Lord of life do justice to himself with less than an infinite creation? To signify his greatness it needs every galaxy our science ever discovers. It provokes our worship and adoration of the lamb that was slain and lives again.

The Resurrection shows us what God is

Modern times began with Roman times. The resurrection is part of the history of Roman times in a famous city full of people. When Christ rose it was not a rumour, a report of some mythical situation, but it crashed across everyday affairs with all the notoriety of headlined news. It showed what God thought of us. It was for us, toward us, for real, to do for us what it would. God revealed himself in the midst of every day life, the greatest of God's self-disclosures. It established hope, comfort, threw light upon the unknown for all who carry the incommunicable ache of bereavement, or the fear of death. It became a source of strength in the agony of life's misfortunes, disappointments, betrayals, deprivations and injustices. Jesus being alive casts a glow of joy, and no trouble matters quite the same.

The resurrection brings God into our very world and our lives. God is not merely transcendent, untouchable, but God is Jesus, the Son of Man, who loved us, hugged the children, wept with the broken, and ate with sinners, lived with all the intimacies of a peasant family. He came and went through death to be with us, to be our Jesus, our loved and adored Lord, our understanding and caring friend. John said, *"The word became flesh and dwelt among us"*, claiming *"we beheld his glory"*, but by his resurrection his presence is still here, and becomes the environment of those who love him. He assures us *"I will never leave you"* and speaks of making his home with us if we love him. He can, because he rose with an unrestricted physical-spiritual form, after demolishing the powers of death.

The resurrection is the consummation of the Creator's intentions. He did not plan a world shadowed by dread death. Death came by sin. When God created space and time, it was an act of love and perfect goodness. It also held the secret of resurrection. The Holy Spirit awaited his moment. The unseen event in a tomb at Jerusalem began a work, which will ultimately fill heaven and earth with divine life. Those who die in Christ will reign in life with him.

The resurrection released the powers of life for mankind. Previously we knew the power of death and dissolution. But we are *"begotten again unto a living hope by the resurrection of Jesus Christ from the dead"*. The resurrection made the power of God in all its physical reality and possibility known to us. What God shows us about himself only he can show us, because it passes carnal observation. But what he shows us is not to satisfy our curiosity but for our experience. Because he lives, we can live in his life. From the tomb a river of life, of resource, of healing, of strength and holiness flowed, waters to swim in, not an overflowing cup just for me as David knew it, but an overflowing flood across the whole prospect of our lives. Paul spoke of the might of God, which worked in him mightily. That is what Christ's resurrection offers to all mankind.

That is why I dare go and preach to millions in Africa and across the globe. It is a resurrection message of life, renewal, miracle, of lifting and rising, of wonder and hope. What a gospel! Hallelujah! May you throw your whole being into the wonder stream of his love and power.

The Bible – a Medicine Chest

*The ordinances of the Lord
are sure and altogether righteous.*
Psalm 19:9

*Great and marvellous are your deeds,
just and true are your ways, king of the ages.*
Revelation 15:4

I've been noticing how positive the Bible is. It is full of terms of assurance. "We know" is a phrase repeated again and again. In contrast, in Roger's Thesaurus the long lists of terms for uncertainty astonished me. Obviously they were needed because of the variety of life's unresolved questions.

The mood of the age is post-modern, it is confused, neither denying anything, believing nothing, neither reason nor science.

> People want reality, but God is the only sure reality.

For anybody afflicted by negative infections, the Bible is a medicine chest. A man, who knows God, knows, even if he knows nothing else. The most ignorant man on earth can be sure of what he knows. A child could know that an animal lifted a heavy log with his eight foot long nose. No ridicule could persuade a child he was wrong if he has seen an elephant.

Faith in God doesn't need a mighty intellect. You know what you know. People want reality, but God is the only sure reality. A weather expert said the mist obscuring a mighty mountain is no more than the vapour of a pint of water. A little doubt can blot out the reality of all truth and Christian testimony.

> Unbelievers may think Christians are too cocksure.
>
> Is it cocksure to say two and two make four? So why question what history books tell what Jesus did at that same time?

Millions have confidence in God. It is a steady drum beat in the hubbub of argument. Unbelievers may think Christians are too cocksure. We are sure, but why cocksure? Is it cocksure to say two and two make four? It isn't a dogma, but a matter of common knowledge. History books tell us what the Romans did in Israel at the time of Jesus, and nobody questions it, so why question what history books tell what Jesus did at that same time?

Communicating the Incommunicable

The Bible is not dreams and visions, but a factual account right across 3,000 years. Christians are not Bible thumpers with a dogmatic doctrine. They state a fact - that Jesus saves. This is a stubborn fact that won't go away. Jesus does save, all the time, clearly, dramatically, and indisputably. That is what the Bible is all about. With all the toleration of other religions, does anybody but Jesus even claim to save, either here or hereafter?

Some think God who holds the heavens in the hollow of his hand is too great for us to know him. But surely because he is so great he can get through to us and make himself known. If God could not, he would be a very little God. God is light and reveals himself, brilliantly. The incarnation of Christ needed a great God. *"The Word was made flesh and dwelt among us and we beheld his glory"*. The invisible became visible. He communicated the incommunicable.

He came. He is not a cloud on a far horizon, a shadow in a cloister, or a sort of a something somewhere. Biblical scholarship left one preacher with nothing but tatters of the Scriptures and he said he thought of God as "a kind of oblong blur." The living God burns in splendour in Scripture, like the fire in the bush of Moses.

The Secret of the Lord

Some say, Christians made God in their own image, reasoned him out, but it is a mindless parrot-cry. The God of the Bible is in total contrast to human nature, with our shabby selfishness, pride and self-importance. If we made a God to suit ourselves he would be rather less challenging and more accommodating to our sinful ways! Read in Scripture what he really is and we soon realize we can't treat him like plastic and shape him to our fancy. Jesus Christ is not a cardboard cutout to be coloured to match our lifestyle.

> If we made a God to suit ourselves he would be rather less challenging and more accommodating to our sinful ways!

The great Bible statement is *"The secret of the Lord is with them that fear him"*. I saw that it says "The secret of the Lord", not secrets but **the** secret, the secret of himself the greatest wonder of all. They that fear and love him understand him. *"God in all his love made known."* Only those who love us really know us. A simple man knows his own wife better than can all the world's philosophers! Those who love God know him.

Our God is the rock, decisive, unequivocal, and never ambiguous with 50 fleeting interpretations. Firmness marks all he does. *"Firm as his throne his promise stands, and he can well secure what I've committed to his hands till the decisive hour"*. His word is more than words. It is his works. Psalm 19 begins *"The heavens declare the glory of God, day after day pour forth speech"*. It first sets the stars above as indicators of truth, and then next his word, saying, *"The law of the Lord is perfect."*

The Lord does not need to compromise

My notice was jolted reading the Exodus episodes. Again and again Moses asked the Pharaoh king to let enslaved Israel take a 3-day journey to worship the Lord (Exodus 3:8, 5:3, 8:27, 10:26). Under the pressure of worsening calamities Pharaoh finally said, *"Go, worship the Lord, only leave your flocks and herds behind"*. Moses said no, not a hoof should be left behind. He had learned the Lord does not need to compromise.

Then Moses led that famous escape, but within hours Israel was trapped at the impassable Egyptian boundary of the Red Sea. Pharaoh had needed only to wait. To get clean away Israel had to put that stretch of water between themselves and their

> The Exodus was not a close shave, furtive, dodging pursuers by good luck. God did it with flair, a majestic, historic drama.

pursuers. Impossible? That is precisely what they did, or what God did for them. The Exodus was not a close shave, furtive, the tribes escaping by the skin of their teeth, dodging pursuers by good luck. God did it with flair, a majestic, historic drama. They went to the sea, passed through the waters, passed out of their past into a new day. That is the fact that caught my notice.

Years later Moses told the story of their Bedouin wanderings in the wilderness. He used the usual expressions, but running through his account is the theme of passing across, leaving behind what used to be, and standing on new ground. He used one special Hebrew word meaning "to pass over", or "crossing" 17 times in Deuteronomy chapters 2 and 3. Each time they moved on, it was not aimless or casual, but a firm directed step. When Israel wanted to use the highway through Edom country (Numbers 20:17-21) again the same word describes it. Earlier Jacob had fled from Laban and crossed the river (Euphrates) and the same term occurs. Genesis 31:21.

God's leading is always an event

God's leading is always an event, never incidental, a casual stroll, but purposeful. Day by day. By ourselves we just jog along hopefully, the best we can. Jeremiah 10:23 says, *"I know, o Lord, it is not for man to direct his steps"*. Jesus said, *"Follow me!"* Keeping an eye on life's changing interests, fashions or ambitions, is as bad and as mad. God does guide, point to point, always positively, through all our days, and in all we do, our whole way of life. *"Let us fix our eye on Jesus, the author and perfector of our faith"*. He guides only via Calvary the fountain of life and cleansing.

> God does guide,
> point to point,
> always positively,
> through all our days,
> and in all we do,
> our whole way of life.
> He guides only via
> Calvary the fountain of
> life and cleansing.

Looking again at that Old Testament word I found it in Micah 7:18, like the KJV translates it *"Who is a God like unto you, that pardoned iniquity and passed by the transgression of the remnant of his heritage. He retained not his anger for ever because he delights in mercy"*. Israel crossed over from Egypt, left the Egyptian gods behind, and moved on following the pillar of cloud and fire. They left their paganism and God forgave it and they entered a new future.

This tremendous drama always comes back to me when I read about John the Baptist preaching in the wilderness and baptizing in Jordan. It is as if his work was a recapitulation of the Exodus and of Israel crossing Jordan with Joshua.

John was baptising all Israel if possible, passing them through the waters as at the beginning, and calling them to repent because the kingdom of God was at hand. One of the jewish leaders, a noted rabbi, Nicodemus, affected by this

> The waters of baptism, that is the water of repentance, are not enough. There must be a work of the Holy Spirit.

hope of a new Israel kingdom sought out Jesus. Jesus knew his mind, and came straight to the point. Jesus said *"I tell you the truth, no one can enter the kingdom of God unless he is born of water and the spirit"*. The waters of baptism, that is the water of repentance, are not enough. There must be a work of the Holy Spirit.

That is how God does things, no compromise, no half way, turning over a new leaf and hiding all the previous blotted pages, but God does a new thing. To be a Christian is a real crossing over into a new world of the Spirit. That glorious truth bursts into flower everywhere in the New Testament. *"He that believes has life; he who does not believe has not life"*. *"The Father ... delivered us out of the authority of darkness and translated us into the kingdom of the Son of his love"*. Colossians 1:13 (Literal translation).

Repeating the Exodus

New! *"Behold I make all things new"*. A new kingdom, a new birth, a new life, a new covenant, new tongues, new wine, and a new song.

Our salvation is new and firm. We are chosen in him, called and separated. Many believe strongly in the teaching that God foreordains who shall be saved, but they don't know whether God has included them. If he has, they will be saved, they are sure, but they are not sure about themselves. They try to prove to themselves that doing good works saves them, because good works are a sign of salvation. If God has predestined them, they don't know how to read the mind of God. But they should know, for New Testament people certainly knew. *"We have the mind of Christ"*.

However, right through the New Testament runs this wonderful certainty. John could say to his followers *"We know that we have eternal life"*. Paul's letters flow with certainty: *"Nothing can separate us from the love of God in Christ Jesus"*. The Lord wants nobody to be in doubt, but to rejoice in his or her salvation.

One sure word is given us by Jesus in John 6:36. *"All that the Father gives to me will come to me and whoever comes to me I will not drive away. My Father's will is that everyone who looks to the Son and believes in him shall have eternal life, and I will raise him up at the last day"*.

This is so positive and clear. Those who do look to him are the elect. They who do come to him come because God has given them to him. All comers come that way. Just come, and we know God has given us to him, for we come only by his grace and calling. Whoever we are, sinful, bad as we may be, we need not wonder. If we look to him we are the predestined. The fact that we come reveals the mind of God. He must have drawn us or we would never have come at all. It is final proof and evidence. Therefore *"Whosoever will may come"*. If we will, he says, "I will". *"To all who received him, to those who believed in his name, he gave the right to become children of God … born of God"* John 1:12.

For the greatest minds, or the simplest people, all and sundry, the flotsam and jetsam thrown upon as wreckage upon sea shores of life, the door is wide open, "Welcome!" Step over that threshold and you repeat the Exodus in your own life, from death to life, from bonds to freedom.

Hallelujah 'tis done,
I believe in the Son,
I am saved by the blood
of the crucified One.

Please visit our Internet-Shop: